PENGUIN CANADA

GREENIOLOGY

TANYA HA is an author, environmentalist and green commentator in the Australian media. She is also campaign development manager for Planet Ark, a non-political, non-confrontational, unashamedly populist environment group that defines itself by what it's for, not what it's against. A science graduate and former model, she is a passionate advocate for the ways that ordinary people can help save the planet. Tanya lives in Melbourne, Australia, with her husband and two children.

How to live well, be green and make a difference

GREENIOLOGY
TANYA HA

PENGUIN
CANADA

PENGUIN CANADA

Published by the Penguin Group

Penguin Group (Canada), 10 Alcorn Avenue, Toronto, Ontario, Canada M4V 3B2
    (a division of Pearson Penguin Canada Inc.)

Penguin Group (USA) Inc., 375 Hudson Street, New York, New York 10014, U.S.A.
Penguin Books Ltd, 80 Strand, London WC2R 0RL, England
Penguin Ireland, 25 St Stephen's Green, Dublin 2, Ireland (a division of Penguin Books Ltd)
Penguin Group (Australia), 250 Camberwell Road, Camberwell, Victoria 3124, Australia
    (a division of Pearson Australia Group Pty Ltd)
Penguin Books India Pvt Ltd, 11 Community Centre, Panchsheel Park, New Delhi – 110 017, India
Penguin Group (NZ), cnr Airborne and Rosedale Roads, Albany, Auckland 1310, New Zealand
    (a division of Pearson New Zealand Ltd)
Penguin Books (South Africa) (Pty) Ltd, 24 Sturdee Avenue, Rosebank, Johannesburg 2196, South Africa

Penguin Books Ltd, Registered Offices: 80 Strand, London WC2R 0RL, England

First published in Canada by Penguin Group (Canada), a division of Pearson Penguin Canada Inc., 2005.
Originally published in Australia in 2003 by Allen & Unwin Pty Ltd, 83 Alexander Street,
    Crows Nest NSW 2065.

(WEB) 10 9 8 7 6 5 4 3 2 1

Text copyright © Tanya Ha, 2005
Foreword copyright © Severn Cullis-Suzuki, 2005
Illustrations copyright © Andrew Treloar and Nick Mau, 2003

All rights reserved. Without limiting the rights under copyright reserved above, no part of this
publication may be reproduced, stored in or introduced into a retrieval system, or transmitted in
any form or by any means (electronic, mechanical, photocopying, recording or otherwise), without
the prior written permission of both the copyright owner and the above publisher of this book.

Cover and text design by MAU Design

 Printed on 100% recycled paper

Manufactured in Canada.

LIBRARY AND ARCHIVES CANADA CATALOGUING IN PUBLICATION

Ha, Tanya, 1972–
    Greeniology : how to live well, be green and make a difference / Tanya Ha.

Includes bibliographical references and index.
ISBN 0-14-301733-0

1. Household ecology. 2. Environmental protection—Citizen participation. I. Title.

TD171.7.H3 2005   363.7'0525   C2005-905386-8

National Library of Australia Cataloguing in Publication data available.

Visit the Penguin Group (Canada) website at **www.penguin.ca**

To my two green teachers,
Mum and Jon Dee,
and my two green babies,
Jasmin and Archer

Contents

Welcome to the green house

Lifestyle   2

Hot topics   3

Foreword

by Severn Cullis-Suzuki

When Canadians say, "I can't change the world," I say, "You already *are* changing it." In terms of ecological footprint (the amount of land required to produce the resources we consume), if resources were distributed equally and sustainably around the world, each person would have 1.9 hectares of land. At the moment, Canadians consume 8.8 hectares, while in a country like India they consume 0.8 hectares.* As global resources decline, Canadians are playing a large part in changing the face of our planet.

Personally, I'm tired of feeling guilty. I know it's not my fault that I was born into the wealthy fraction of the world, yet I also know that I am part of the imbalance of world wealth and consumption. While one might not necessarily be a bleeding heart altruist, I believe the average Canadian doesn't want to do *harm*. For me, Greeniology is not about being altruistic, it's about living without the guilt.

This book goes beyond recycling. It's about exercising responsible choice, about taking a stand. It's about breaking free of the destructive habits we've been brainwashed into. It's about changing both the standards and the market for household products. But it's also simply about doing the little things that just make sense. For example, on the subject of rain barrels Tanya Ha asks, "Why do we fail to make the connection between the water we pay for and the free stuff that falls from the sky?"—a dose of practical sense from a shopping- and media-savvy lady. These actions have been called "light green," but if advocates of deep ecology don't act on these tips, how will they change The Way Things Are?

Leading by example is the most powerful way each of us influences the world every day. We do it whether we're aware of it or not. For me, it's more powerful than protesting in the streets or talking someone's ear off about why they should care. It's real action, real evidence that it *is* possible to walk the talk, it *is* possible to live in a way that doesn't cause harm. We *are* changing the world, like it or not. Let's change it in a way that makes us proud.

* Note: Ecological footprint stats from Redefining Progress, http://www.earthday.net/goals/footprintnations.stm.

A new shade of green

Have you ever seen a news story about thousands of hectares of rainforest being felled each year to provide grazing land for hamburger cattle? Have you heard that we're seeing the extinction of species at the fastest rate ever, and that the air is filling with greenhouse gases and turning the earth into a toaster oven, and that we're playing Russian Roulette with nuclear energy? You probably found yourself caring, but couldn't imagine how you could stop any of it happening. You couldn't see yourself going on a hunger strike or being chained to a bulldozer in protest.

You're not alone. While there are a few hard-core greenies at the frontline of the environmental movement who are not afraid to further the green cause through extreme and very public acts, this approach is not for everyone.

Public protest was (and still is) necessary. Someone had to bring the plight of the environment to the attention of the average person. It took the very public activities of Greenpeace, a hole in the ozone layer, an inevitable backlash against eighties consumerism and a rather gorgeous-looking rock star named Sting to make us understand that human activities haven't been the best thing for all creatures great and small.

The truth is that birds are dying because they're covered with oil, ships carrying nuclear waste are probably trying to dock at your local port, and the Pacific Islands may well be flooded by rising ocean levels. It's not pretty and it's all our fault!

But I've got good news for the armchair spectator of green sports – protesting isn't the only way to help save the planet. Coming up behind the frontline there's a new wave in the environmental movement, defining itself by what it's for rather than what it's against. The new environmentalist knows that it's not just the fault of governments and big businesses, and that we all share the blame for damaging the planet. After all, we purchased the products that harmed the earth through their manufacture or disposal. We bought and used the hairsprays that contained ozone-destroying CFCs. Perhaps we even wore fur and ate shark's fin soup.

Our generation has made many environmental mistakes innocently. The way to move forward is to take back responsibility for looking after the planet – to stop complaining – and to start concentrating on being part of the solution, rather than just feeling guilty.

So who is part of this new wave of environmentalism? It's hard to tell because they look like ordinary people. They *are* ordinary people. They have jobs, friends, families and busy lives. They like fashion, they go out, they want to enjoy the best lifestyle possible. They're also determined to help save the planet but don't want to waste time just sitting around and talking about it.

They would rather get up and do something, by changing their everyday lives, by not using the products that cause harm and by supporting those that are greener. They draw the line at excessive consumption. They wash their latest purchase with a greener detergent in an energy- and water-efficient washing machine, powered by green electricity from EcoLogo-certified sources.

They're not heroes, ready to scale tall buildings. They're not selfless saints, making sacrifices for their cause. Far from that, they're actually sensible and slightly selfish people, who happen to be very far-sighted and want to preserve this beautiful planet and enjoy it for years to come. They want enough resources for their children and grandchildren.

Greeniology gives you everything you need to know about how to change your life to make it greener, and helps you to understand why those changes matter. It's the science and art of living a greener life. There are so many little things that we can all do to preserve the planet: saving energy and water in our homes, recycling, buying wisely and using less paper at work. They may seem like small things, but if we all do them, they'll achieve a huge result.

I'd love your feedback on the book and to know how the advice, tips and information have made your life greener. E-mail me at greeniology@planetark.org.

Start today! Then each week, try to change one habit in your life to a greener alternative. It's easy, and the world will reap the benefits of your efforts.

—*Tanya Ha*

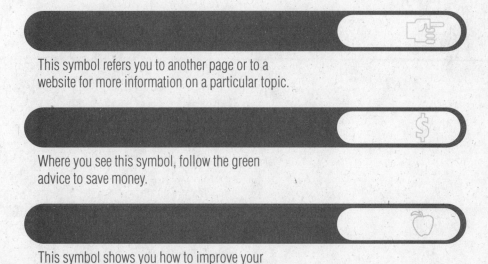

This symbol refers you to another page or to a website for more information on a particular topic.

Where you see this symbol, follow the green advice to save money.

This symbol shows you how to improve your health while caring for the environment.

1

 welcome to the >>
green house

Greeniology begins at home. The things we do that use energy – keeping clean and warm, eating and preparing food, the way we relax and entertain ourselves – all revolve around where we live. This tour of the average home gives you ideas for a green makeover, room by room. There are literally thousands of things we can do at home to lessen our impact on the planet. Some changes will take time, but you can start applying lots of the eco-tips and practical advice right now – without making major sacrifices to your lifestyle.

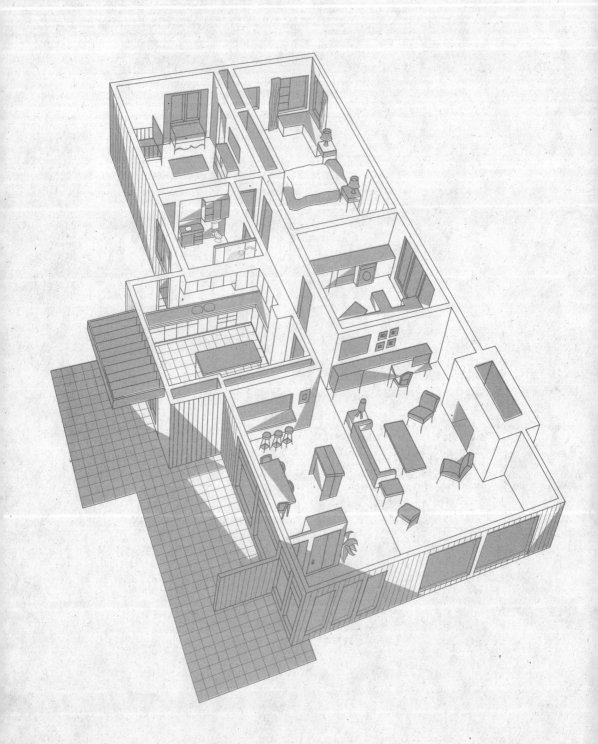

>> **Keys to a greener house**

Before you make your way around the green house, there are some fundamental eco-principles to do with energy and water use in the home that you'll need to be familiar with.

We use water and energy so much we tend to take them for granted, yet these two precious resources and the way we use them have a huge impact on the health of the planet. Energy and water are used in some form in every room in our homes, and it is in their use that individuals can make a real difference, good or bad, to the environment.

Here's what you need to know.

Energy

Energy is one of the greatest global green issues. First, consider different **energy sources**. We know that there is a limited amount of fossil fuels in the earth's crust. Greenhouse and pollution issues aside, fossil fuels are not renewable, and therefore alternatives need to be investigated. The extraction and refinement of oil, coal and natural gas take a toll on the surrounding environment, causing local pollution and harming natural habitats. Politically, the distribution of fossil fuels among the nations is uneven, making some nations dependent on others for their energy security. Wars have been fought over oil. However, some of the alternatives to fossil fuels also have drawbacks. For example, large-scale hydroelectric projects can disturb aquatic ecosystems, stop the migration of fish, and flood land areas upstream of dams. These environmental costs need to be considered when comparing energy sources. The good news is that these costs can be minimized by making the energy we use go further – in other words, by doing more with less energy, regardless of its source.

Second, consider the different effects on the health of the planet from our **energy use**, and in particular the use of fossil fuels. It is well known that the burning of fossil fuels to produce electricity or to power vehicles is producing an excess of greenhouse gas emissions. It is also widely accepted that this is contributing to global warming and climate change, as well as local pollution.

To understand why your choice and use of energy can make such a big difference, you need to know a bit about **greenhouse gases**.

A layer of greenhouse gases in the atmosphere insulates the earth. This layer allows sunlight in, which warms the earth. When fossil fuels are burned, they produce carbon dioxide and other greenhouse gases. Rotting waste and plant matter also produce greenhouse gases. These gases build up in the atmosphere and act like a big blanket, stopping the reflected heat from the sun from escaping into space, in much the same way as a garden greenhouse traps heat. This **global warming** could lead to changes in our climate, such as more frequent and severe droughts or flooding, weird weather and rising sea levels. The **greenhouse effect** is necessary to make life on earth possible, but the big environmental problem is that our increased reliance on energy-using products means we're seeing an *enhanced* greenhouse effect taking place.

In Canada we each contribute an average of slightly over 5 tonnes of greenhouse gas emissions each year to the greenhouse effect through our energy use. Just the amount of gasoline we use produces copious amounts of greenhouse gases – around half of the average Canadian's emissions.

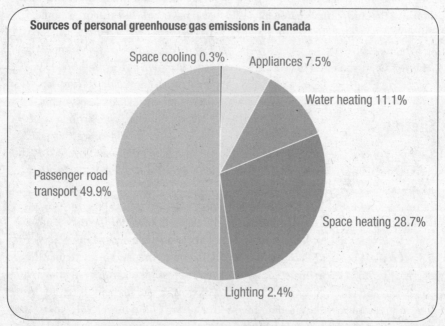

Sources of personal greenhouse gas emissions in Canada

Space cooling 0.3%

Appliances 7.5%

Water heating 11.1%

Passenger road transport 49.9%

Space heating 28.7%

Lighting 2.4%

Source: Reproduced with permission of the Minister of Public Works and Government Services, 2004.

The One-Tonne Challenge

The Government of Canada has set a target for each Canadian individual to reduce his or her annual greenhouse gas emissions by one tonne. The One-Tonne Challenge website has an interactive calculator so that you can estimate your current greenhouse gas emissions as a benchmark and later re-estimate them, once you've made some changes to the way you live and use energy. Take the One-Tonne Challenge today at www.climatechange.gc.ca/onetonne.

Some of this greenhouse gas is produced in the home – for example, the carbon dioxide from an open fire. However, much of it is produced away from the home, at the power stations that provide our electricity. Personal greenhouse gas contribution as pictured in the graph refers to the average amount of greenhouse gases produced directly by a person's energy use. However, if you also take into account the gas emissions outside homes – for example, those produced by industry or agriculture – then Canada's total greenhouse gas emissions per capita are much higher – over 16.8 tonnes per person of just the greenhouse gas carbon dioxide.

The key to greener household energy lies in being careful with both the energy we choose and the amount of energy we use. Household energy largely comes from electricity, natural gas, and oil.

How green is my electricity?

Most Canadian homes get their energy in the form of electricity supplied through the provincial electricity grid – a network of power lines that draws electricity from where it is produced and distributes it to the users.

Electricity from both polluting sources and from greener, renewable sources supplies local areas, with the remainder fed into the grid system. Once fed into the grid, electricity from green sources is indistinguishable from that produced by more harmful methods.

How "green" your electricity is depends on where you live. For example, the bulk of electricity generated in Nova Scotia, Alberta and Saskatchewan comes from greenhouse-intensive coal. Electricity from all fossil fuels also causes air pollution and acid rain. Conversely, most of the electricity produced in British Colombia, Manitoba and Quebec comes from low-emission hydroelectric schemes. That doesn't let residents of these provinces off the energy-saving hook – they should still conserve electricity so that the excess electricity produced with lower emissions can be sold to other markets, ideally replacing some of the electricity generated from high-emission-producing fossil fuels.

Canada is a world leader in hydroelectric power generation. Although hydroelectricity is low in greenhouse gas emissions, large-scale hydro projects are generally not considered to be green power sources. Large-scale projects create dams and reservoirs, disrupting the natural flow of rivers and waterways. This has significant effects on aquatic ecosystems, including fish habitats. These changes to natural river flows affect estuaries, river deltas, silt movement, the flow of nutrients to the ocean and even the temperature of water downstream from reservoirs. Dams also block the migration of fish. In fact, hydroelectricity is a major concern for Canada's fisheries. Small-scale hydro power (sometimes called "run of the river" hydro) is a greener way to produce electricity from the flow of water. Small-scale hydro projects minimize environmental impacts because they don't use dams or create reservoirs.

Green power sources

Alternative electricity generation needs to be considered to ensure a secure, long-term electricity supply. The people who lived through the major power blackout that hit Ontario in 2003 will vouch for the importance of dependable power.

Renewable energy brings an exciting range of energy alternatives. The sun doesn't stop shining, providing solar energy and moving air, which in turn provides wind energy. Hydro power is theoretically an option as long as there's flowing water. Alternative energy gives nations the opportunity to lessen their dependence on oil and other fossil fuels.

It's important to remember that renewable energy sources, while better than fossil fuels for the health of the planet, are not without their own environmental impact. Alternative energy sources need to be chosen wisely and developed carefully so that the solution to our energy question doesn't itself become a problem. Some countries are better suited to particular energy sources because of their natural environment. For example, areas with moderately high but stable wind patterns are ideal places to put wind turbines.

The table on pages 8–9 shows the main sources of renewable energy and how they compare.

Buying green electricity

Many Canadian households and businesses can now choose to buy their electricity from greener, renewable sources through "green electricity" or "green power" programs. This is particularly the case in Ontario and Alberta, where electricity deregulation allows people to choose the source of their power.

In green electricity programs, customers agree to pay a small premium for the electricity they use. In return, the electricity provider ensures that the equivalent amount of electricity is sourced from greener sources, such as wind, biomass or small-scale hydro, instead of power from fossil or nuclear fuels. Green electricity costs more because it is still a developing field. In real terms, it's only around the cost of a cappuccino or two a week, and it is money that is being invested in energy companies that are working toward a sustainable future. Any increase in your electricity bill from choosing to buy green power can be more than offset by improving your home's energy efficiency using the tips in this book.

Whether you're buying electricity for your home or for your business, purchasing green power energy makes the greatest difference in areas where it will displace the use of oil or coal. The following table is a general guide showing for each province the marginal energy sources that will be displaced by the use of green electricity.

See page 280 in Further Information for a list of some of the green electricity products and suppliers on offer.

PROVINCE	MARGINAL SOURCE DISPLACED BY GREEN ENERGY USE
Alberta	Coal
British Columbia	Large-scale hydro/natural gas
Manitoba	Large-scale hydro
New Brunswick	Oil
Newfoundland	Large-scale hydro
Nova Scotia	Coal/Oil
Prince Edward Island	Oil
Quebec	Large-scale hydro
Ontario	Coal
Saskatchewan	Coal

Comparison of the main sources of renewable energy

TYPE	PROS	CONS
Solar >>	• Limitless. • Available all around the world (the polar regions get their supplies in bulk). • Useful for remote areas. • Produces no greenhouse gases. • Once the initial cost of equipment is covered, ongoing power is free. • Passive solar energy can be used to heat homes, without the cost of photovoltaic (PV) cells.	• Active solar systems using solar panels and photovoltaic (PV) cells are expensive to produce and set up. • Cloudy and overcast days can impair their performance. • Solar generators require a lot of space, which can sometimes be a problem.
Wind >>	• Once the initial cost of equipment is covered, ongoing power is free. • Wind, like sunshine, won't run out. • Useful for remote areas. • Produces no greenhouse gases. • The land used for wind farms can be used for other purposes as well.	• Wind speed can frequently change, and on some days there is no wind at all. • Windy areas tend to be on coastlines, where land value is often high. • Wind farms can be noisy. • It's believed that wind turbines can harm wildlife (particularly birds) and so can't be built near particular bird habitats. • Some people think that they're an eyesore, so they may be opposed by local tourism operators.
Biomass (energy from plant fuels) >>	• Because fuel crops can be harvested and replenished, it is renewable. • Plant alcohols can be made from the waste parts of some crops and so make better use of our resources.	• Still polluting, though less so than fossil fuels. • Land used for growing fuel crops may one day be needed for producing food for our planet's growing population.

TYPE	PROS	CONS
Hydro >>	• Once the initial cost of the hydro-electric power station is covered, ongoing power is relatively inexpensive. • Water can be stored, so it can be a more reliable power source. • Produces no greenhouse gases or waste products. • Small-scale projects can be used instead of large-scale projects to reduce the environmental impacts.	• Large dams take up a lot of land and flood previously "dry" areas, requiring fish, animals and sometimes people to relocate. • Hydroelectric schemes can greatly upset and disturb aquatic ecosystems. In particular, they can stop the migration of fish. • Stations reduce the flows in these river systems, causing environmental problems downstream.
Landfill gas (the gas from rotting garbage) >>	• Can be considered renewable (we haven't yet stopped producing waste). • Captures and uses the greenhouse gases produced by landfills, which would otherwise contribute to the greenhouse effect. • Collection and use of the gas reduces the odours in the area of the landfill.	• Stations are very expensive to build. • Landfill volumes will change as we change our waste-producing habits. • Much larger amounts of landfill gases are needed to produce electricity (compared with fossil fuels).
Geothermal >>	• Once the initial cost of equipment and installation is covered, ongoing power is free. • Renewable (the molten core of the earth isn't going to cool down in the near future). • Doesn't require a lot of land.	• Geothermal energy is restricted to areas with geothermal activity. • There is a limit to how much steam or water can be drawn from one geothermal site.
Hydrogen >>	• Gives non-polluting carbon-free energy. The only by-product is water. • One of the most common elements in the universe.	• Difficult to concentrate and store.

Gas versus electricity

Many homes use natural gas (and sometimes propane) for cooking, space heating and water heating. One of the benefits of natural gas and propane as fuels is that they are burned to provide heat energy for immediate use in the home. Whenever energy is converted from one type to another (e.g., from energy stored in fuel, to heat energy at a power station, to kinetic energy driving a turbine, to electricity), a certain amount is lost, dissipated as heat. The more conversions an energy source goes through, the less useful energy you get for the amount of fuel and pollution produced. For this reason, gas is more efficient than electricity, resulting in around one-third of the greenhouse emissions produced by coal-fuelled electricity. Using gas instead of electricity for heating and cooking will mean a lower greenhouse gas contribution. However, natural gas and propane can contribute to poor indoor air quality, and they are fossil fuels and therefore not renewable. In short, they are a good interim energy source while we develop renewable energy sources.

The EnerGuide energy efficiency product-labelling system

If you've been shopping for appliances lately, you may have noticed a label or sticker like those pictured. This is the EnerGuide label. EnerGuide is an initiative of Natural Resources Canada that gives the public information about how much energy appliances and heating or cooling systems consume. This scheme helps people who are shopping for these products to make an informed choice. The program measures how much energy individual products typically use by testing them in line with Canadian Standards Association procedures. It then compares them with the least and most efficient equivalent products available.

There are different types of EnerGuide label. The **EnerGuide label for appliances,** which covers a broad range of appliances, including fridges, freezers, ranges, dishwashers, washers and dryers, shows a gradually darkening horizontal bar scale. The lighter left edge of this scale represents the appliance in a given product size and category with the lowest energy consumption (the highest energy efficiency); the darker right edge represents the appliance with the highest energy consumption. An arrow along the line shows the specific typical energy consumption of an individual product. A product with an arrow toward the left of the EnerGuide scale is more efficient and cheaper to run and will save you money in the long term. Compare the rating when comparing two appliances of similar size.

The EnerGuide label for appliances also shows a number. This number is the EnerGuide rating – the amount of energy in kilowatt hours (kWh) the appliance uses under average use in a year. The smaller this number is, the better for both the environment and your energy bills. You can use this number to estimate the running costs of a given appliance. For example, a fridge that uses 620 kWh/year running on electricity costing the national average of $0.0814 per kWh will cost around $50.47 in electricity to run for a year. Over a lifespan of 17 years, that's over $850. This amount is often referred to as the "second price tag" – the cost of running an appliance over its life after the initial outlay of the purchase price or the first price tag. Consider the second price tag when you compare appliances, and remember that when it comes to energy-efficient products, saving money parallels saving the environment.

The **EnerGuide label for room air conditioners,** which generally appears

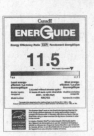

on the back of product literature instead of directly displayed on the product itself, is slightly different from that for appliances. With room air conditioners, the EnerGuide rating scale indicates energy efficiency instead of energy consumption. Consequently, greener, more efficient products have arrows toward the right of the scale. The EnerGuide program for room air conditioners covers a range of heating and cooling equipment, including

residential gas furnaces, central air conditioners and air-to-air heat pumps.

For more information about EnerGuide, go to http://oee.nrcan. gc.ca/equipment/.

The ENERGY STAR® symbol

ENERGY STAR is an international symbol for energy-efficient electrical goods. Rather than rating products along a scale, the ENERGY STAR initiative sets a single standard and awards the ENERGY STAR symbol to products that meet specific technical criteria and are typically 10 to 50% more efficient than the legislated minimum performance level. The ENERGY STAR initiative covers a huge range of products. ENERGY STAR product categories include:
• home appliances such as clothes washers or dehumidifiers,
• heating, cooling, and ventilation,
• lighting,
• consumer electronics such as televisions and VCRs,
• office equipment such as printers and computers,
• windows and sliding glass doors, and
• commercial and industrial products.

By improving the energy efficiency of a product, ENERGY STAR also saves money on your energy bills. Look for the ENERGY STAR symbol on products or packaging when you are buying products or equipment in the categories listed.

For more information see energystar.gc.ca.

ENERGY STAR

did you
know...

By reducing the power consumed
by a product, ENERGY STAR saves
money on your electricity bills.
Look for this symbol when buying
electronic products.

ENERGY STAR
HIGH EFFICIENCY
HAUTE EFFICACITÉ

Water

Water is an integral part of Canada's identity. It is an inseparable element of both our natural environment and our culture.

There are around 1385 million cubic kilometres (1 cubic kilometre equals 1 billion litres) of water in the world, covering nearly three-quarters of the earth's surface. This sounds like a lot of water, so you may well be wondering why there's so much fuss about conserving it and keeping it clean.

We think of ourselves as a water-rich country, with abundant supplies of fresh water. This is reflected by our water use. Canadians are the second highest users of water per capita in the world, largely because we take fresh water for granted. Very few people realize the colossal effort and investment that goes into making sure our tap water is drinkable and in good supply, our wastewater is safely treated and disposed of, and the run-off from our roofs and streets is appropriately managed.

The trouble with water is that even though most of the planet is covered with the stuff, over 97% is undrinkable salt water. A further 2% is fresh water trapped in icecaps and glaciers. More fresh water is locked too deep below the earth's surface to be extracted. What remains is a tiny 0.003% of all the earth's water as available fresh water in the forms of surface water (in lakes, reservoirs and dams, for example), groundwater, soil moisture, water vapour, clouds and rain.

How much water we use

did you
know...

Canada's water use averages out to 1600 cubic metres of water per
capita each year. This is double the amount used in France per
person, nearly four times the water use of the average Swede
and more than eight times that of the average Dane.

There are concerns that our ongoing supply of renewable fresh water won't meet our growing demands if our consumption trends continue. To ensure that we always have enough water for both the human population and the rest of the environment, everyone should continually aim to conserve water at home and watch what they put down the drain.

How green you are with water comes down to two things. In the simplest terms these factors and their solutions are:

1. How much water do you use?   **Use water wisely.**

2. What do you put down the drain with your wastewater?   **Avoid water pollution.**

Water use in the home

Each Canadian uses on average 343 litres of water each day. This can vary greatly, depending on the size of the yard, the use of rainwater, the family itself and the climate in the area where they live. The diagram below shows where this water is generally being used. Water use in the bathroom represents over half the total water use in the home.

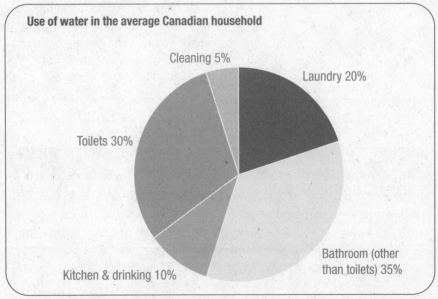

Use of water in the average Canadian household

Cleaning 5%

Laundry 20%

Toilets 30%

Bathroom (other than toilets) 35%

Kitchen & drinking 10%

Source: Environment Canada's Freshwater Website (www.ec.gc.ca/water), 2004. Reproduced with the permission of the Minister of Public Works and Government Services, 2005.

Water is a precious resource that we have to conserve. Alternative water supplies for the home are being looked at in drier countries overseas. For example, in Australia a growing number of yards are watered with rainwater collected in storage tanks fitted to downspouts. Progress is being made in the development of home plumbing systems that recycle grey water – the wastewater from baths and showers or the washing machine, for example.

There are many things that you can do to save water and avoid pollution without installing new plumbing systems or adding to existing systems. The bonus is that saving water will save you money, especially if you reduce your use of hot water and therefore the use of the energy needed to heat it.

Saving water

Why save water? The obvious reason is because we don't have an endless supply of it. But there is more to it than that. Have you ever stopped to think about where it comes from and how it gets to suburban taps?

Water is transported through tunnels and pipes from reserves, via regional storage tanks to homes. It is moved by pump, sometimes with the help of gravity. Along the way it is generally filtered, disinfected and put through a series of tests. The flow and water pressure are maintained by pressure control valves on the mains. It takes resources and money to make sure that the water that flows through our taps is fit for human consumption. In effect, we use drinking water to wash our bodies, houses and clothes, water the garden and flush the toilet.

When we reduce our consumption of tap water, we reduce the demand on the complicated system that works to transport and purify reserves of water for the good of our health.

The three Rs of saving water

There are three basic ways to cut down your use of water from urban water mains.
Reduce your water consumption by changing your water use habits. For example, don't leave the tap running while brushing your teeth, and don't overwater the garden. Try the many water-saving tips included in this book.
Repair any leaking taps or faulty plumbing devices. A small drip can waste 75 litres a day.
Retrofit your home with more efficient water-using fixtures, such as dual-flush toilets.

When it comes to saving water, do the easiest things first. Efficiency – using less water by using it wisely – is the first step. It's also the most cost-effective. When you have an opportunity to buy or replace a water-using appliance or device, such as a washing machine or tap fitting, choose products that use less water.

Water-saving product features are covered later, in the Bathroom, Laundry and Garden chapters.

In the near future it will become easier to identify water-efficient products. Already Australia has an extensive product-labelling program that promotes water efficiency ratings. The US Environmental Protection Agency (EPA) has begun establishing a water efficiency labelling program for fixtures, appliances and irrigation (garden-watering) equipment based on the ENERGY STAR initiative for energy-efficient products. The Government of Canada and the Canadian Water and Wastewater Association are looking at opportunities to partner with the EPA on a North American program. In the future, look out for this program, which will most likely be promoted as Water Star. For more information visit the EPA website at www.epa.gov/water/water_efficiency.html and the Canadian Water and Wastewater Association's website at www.cwwa.ca.

Summer soaking
In the summer months, household water use can increase by 50% or more. Much of this is used in the yard.

>>

Find out more

Throughout this book you'll find key environmental issues mentioned such as acid rain, genetically modified organisms, Kyoto or water pollution. In Part 3: Hot Topics on pages 245-68, you'll find brief explanations of these issues with enough information to help you understand why your actions can make a big difference to the state of our planet.

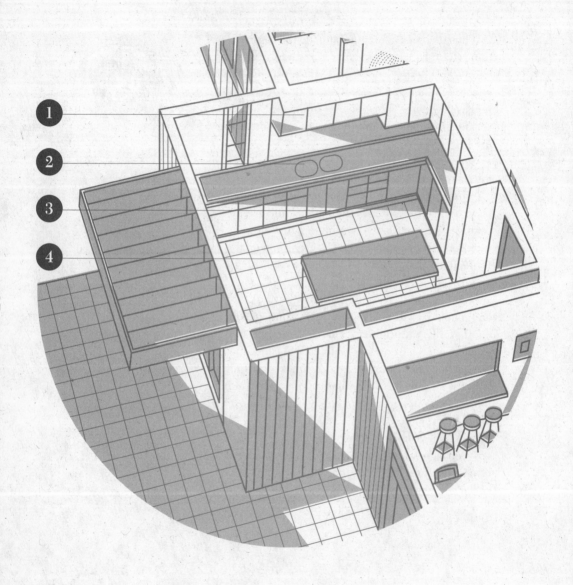

1 Cupboards with green groceries
2 Water-wise sink
3 Recycling bin under sink
4 Green-cleaned floor

>> The green kitchen

The unfortunate thing about environmental advice relating to the kitchen, bathroom and laundry is that it's really about housework, and housework takes time.

Reality check: you don't have to apply all the advice in this book, chapter and verse, immediately upon reading it. For one thing, lifestyle changes don't happen overnight. For another, we don't all have the time to devote ourselves to being perfect homemakers.

When we talk about the kitchen, we're really talking about food – the kinds of food we choose, how it is made and packaged, how we prepare and cook it and how we clean up afterward. First, there's the food itself and how it is (or isn't) packaged. As far as the environment goes, not all foods are created equal. For example, a kid's meal from a fast-food chain represents a far greater toll on the environment than a cheese and lettuce sandwich made from local produce. Second, there's the energy that is used in the kitchen, both for cooking and to run appliances. (Around 60% of the electricity we use in Canada comes from hydroelectric plants. Although

this is a "clean" source of energy, it does disrupt environmental water flows and disturb aquatic habitats. Another 25% comes from burning fossil fuels, contributing to pollution, the greenhouse effect and global warming, and nearly 12% comes from nuclear power, which comes with the as-yet-unsolved problem of radioactive nuclear waste.) Finally, around 10% of the water we use in our homes is used in the kitchen. Much of this is used for cleaning and dishwashing. Both the amount of water we use and the water we put down the drain have an effect on the environment.

Good green food

All our own food-related activities and those that bring food to stores have an impact on the environment. Every bite we eat comes at an environmental cost, but it also represents a chance to be

The year 2003 saw the mad cow disease scare reach North America, with the first case in Canadian cattle reported in May and the first US case in December. Some have suggested that the commercial bison (or buffalo) meat industry may attract new customers looking for an alternative to beef, should further cases be reported.

healthy, each meal being an opportunity to recharge our bodies with food that will make us feel good and look good. Being green in the kitchen is about looking after the inner environment of our bodies as well as the outer environment of the planet.

How food is produced

Before we look at how we can be greener with the food we eat, we need to understand where it comes from. Many Canadians (77%) now live in the city. It's easy to lose touch with the land and the way food is made when you're surrounded by high-rises and traffic. Those with a vegetable garden may have more of an idea, but it won't give you a full appreciation of the giant task of feeding Canada's population and the associated environmental implications.

Take, for example, the humble loaf of bread. Most people looking at the loaf would say that the only environmental problem with a bag of sliced white bread is the bag itself, because it's not biodegradable and is even more of a problem if it's littered. In fact, that loaf of bread represents an investment of many resources. It took topsoil and water to grow the wheat, energy to grind the wheat into flour, more energy and water to make it into a loaf, and fuel to deliver it.

Similar quantities of land, water and energy are used to produce the food in your local stores. Fresh

How food is produced

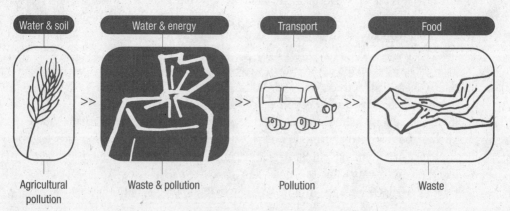

Water & soil — Agricultural pollution >> Water & energy — Waste & pollution >> Transport — Pollution >> Food — Waste

>>

How far can a grain go?

Not all of the grain grown in the world is turned directly into food for humans. Some of it becomes livestock feed to produce other foods. For example, grain is fed to cattle to produce beef.

According to the Worldwatch Institute, it takes:

>> 7 kg of grain to produce 1 kg of beef

>> 4 kg of grain to produce 1 kg of pork

>> just over 2 kg of grain to produce 1 kg of poultry

>> less than 2 kg of grain to produce 1 kg of farmed fish

products, such as eggs, fruit and vegetables, meat, fish and poultry, use fewer resources than the aisles and aisles of processed food in the average supermarket.

Food tips for a healthier inner and outer environment

There are a few general rules that are good guides to choosing foods that are better for your body and kinder to the planet.

Eat less meat to use less land. Try to replace one meat meal each week with a vegetarian alternative, such as a Chinese tofu stir-fry, an Indian lentil curry or Mexican bean tacos and burritos. In Western societies we eat far more meat, poultry and fish products than we need to, given their nutritional value. This taste for meat, along with fatty takeout foods and general overeating, is making these societies increasingly overweight and unhealthy, particularly in the United States and Canada.

You would expect the world's grain crops to be grown to produce food for people to eat. This isn't always so. A lot of the grain grown is used to feed animals on ranches and intensive livestock farms, which in turn are used for meat and other animal food products. Animal rights considerations aside, you can produce more food with a given patch of land by growing plant foods than you can by grazing cattle or by producing food to rear food animals. A significant amount of the land cleared in South America is intended to provide more grazing land for cattle that will one day end up as beef patties (probably smothered in special sauce, with lettuce, cheese, pickles and onions in a sesame seed bun).

There's no need for everyone to become a vegetarian, but we should question the amount of meat, particularly beef, we consume and look at other protein sources. Too much natural vegetation is being cleared to provide grazing land for beef cattle.

Buy seafood from sustainable sources and avoid farmed salmon. Seafood is becoming an increasingly popular protein food, particularly among people who wish to avoid red meat. Many have also heard of the health benefits of omega-3 fatty acids, commonly found in cold-water fish. However, the increasing demand for seafood is causing the depletion of fish stocks around the world. Sustainable seafood is harvested in limited quantities from carefully managed stocks. This ensures that individual species aren't overfished, marine habitat is preserved and pollution is prevented.

Canada, Norway and Chile produce cheaper salmon through intensive fish farming. Salmon is farmed in floating netcages, each containing tens of thousands of fish. These farms release vast amounts of waste, parasites, residue antibiotics and other drugs into the surrounding waters, spreading disease and parasites among wild native salmon and other marine species. Many of the farmed species are alien in the areas where they are farmed and are a threat to native species, competing with them for resources and impacting their habitat. Exercise some consumer power and avoid farmed salmon.

The Monterey Bay Aquarium Seafood WATCH program publishes the "Choices for Healthy Oceans" guide to sustainable seafood choices for people in the United States and Canada, listing the seafoods to look for and those to avoid. Visit www.montereybayaquarium.org to view or download the guide, which is regularly updated.

Buy fresh local produce in season. Advances in ways of harvesting, preserving and packaging fruit and vegetables have meant that they don't have to be consumed locally. Many varieties of fruit are picked before they are ripe so that they can be transported over long distances, ripening along the way. Harvesting and transportation are carefully timed so that the fruit looks its best when it's finally on display in a store. The end result is that these foods have used

Food additives to avoid & their E code numbers

>> ARTIFICIAL SWEETENERS: aspartame (951) and saccharin (954) – thought to be potentially carcinogenic

>> GLUTAMATES (620–635), particularly monosodium glutamate, or MSG (621) – a flavour enhancer that some people are particularly sensitive to

>> SULPHITES (220–228) – can cause severe asthma attacks and other breathing difficulties in sulphite-sensitive asthmatics

Try the 21-day challenge

did you know...

It takes around three weeks of repeating something daily to form a habit. Take recycling, for example. If you put in the effort to make sure you're recycling or composting all that you can as part of your normal routine, after a few weeks it will become habit and you'll barely notice the effort. There is a smorgasbord of greener lifestyle options – select something easy for starters and go back for more, as you're ready.

huge amounts of fuel to travel great distances. To make matters worse, they often have a lower nutritional value and don't taste as good as locally grown produce. How often have you bitten into a supermarket tomato and found it disappointingly tasteless?

Buy locally grown fruit and vegetables whenever possible. Picked in season, they taste better and are often better for you. Buying them also supports our nation's farmers. Buying local produce in season will reduce the range of choice, but you can still enjoy variety by using these foods in different ways. The change in availability of produce through the year is part of what makes the seasons interesting. Do smaller grocery shopping trips more often, so that you don't need your purchases to last longer than is natural.

Eat less processed food. Processed food has had a lot of changes made to it. The apricots in the fresh produce section, for example, are different from those in the canned fruit aisle and

vastly different from those in a jar of apricot jam. Processing food involves precooking the food, chopping it up, or adding extra ingredients or preservatives. Processing usually requires more energy and water use, and so has an additional cost to the environment. Some of the fibre (and goodness) may be removed from grains, such as rice and wheat, to make them whiter and softer. Processing in some cases means that the food can last longer or is easier to use. Unfortunately, some of the nutritional value of food can be lost when it's processed.

Avoid products with a lot of additives. Have a look at the ingredient list on the pack and avoid products with a long list of additives, artificial colours and flavours, particularly if you have food sensitivities or allergies. Colouring is added to foods to make them look more appetizing. Flour and other products are sometimes bleached to make them whiter. Preservatives are added to foods to give them a longer shelf life. Special additives can also keep oil and water mixed in a salad dressing or keep powdered spices from clumping together. A host of additives are put into foods to make them smell nicer and taste stronger, to change their colour and artificially increase their nutritional value. Additives can also cause allergic reactions, can make food harder to digest, can be bad for your health and can even cause hyperactivity in children.

Avoid irradiated foods. Food can also be irradiated. Irradiation either kills the germs and bugs in food or makes them unable to reproduce. Irradiation exposes food to X-rays and gamma rays from radioactive materials. It is also called cold pasteurization. While the World Health Organization and other organizations have declared irradiated food safe for human consumption, objectors argue that any technology that uses radioactive materials poses an occupational health and safety risk. Irradiation has also been shown to decrease levels of essential vitamins A, E and K and some fat-soluble cancer-preventing vitamins.

Use a water filter. Remove impurities and added chemicals from your drinking water by using a water filter or purifier. Make sure you change the cartridge regularly.

Get your vitamins and minerals from fresh food, not supplements. Some food additives are good for us, such as vitamin C. However, they are generally better absorbed from sources in which they occur naturally. Your body can become used to getting these vitamins and minerals from concentrated sources. This can slowly affect your body's natural ability to absorb these nutrients from food.

Go organic. It's worth going organic for the good of your health and the environment. If the cost concerns you, ease into buying organic foods. Start by buying organic broccoli, grapes and other foods that have a large surface area. With conventional farming, plants with larger surface areas collect larger amounts of residue from pesticides and other chemicals.

Organic farming produces food without the use of artificial pesticides or fertilizers. A number of crops are grown, instead of a single crop that can deplete the soil. Many organic farmers keep livestock alongside their plant crops. The manure provides natural fertilizer to keep the soil healthy and productive. Food crops are rotated with soil-enriching plant crops such as legumes, which replenish the nitrates in the soil. Organic food contains no artificial fertilizers, pesticides, hormones, growth stimulants, antibiotics, added waxes or finishes or other chemicals. It is also free from genetically modified content and is not irradiated. For consumers, this means that they are putting fewer pollutants into their bodies and into the environment.

Organic food is now available in many larger supermarkets. As well as fresh produce, there are ranges of canned organic food, organic pasta and baby food.

Make sure it's really organic. There are few restrictions on the use of the word "organic." From a chemistry perspective, anything that has carbon atoms in it can be called "organic." Some products call themselves "organic" to mean that they are plant-derived as opposed to synthetic. Check the labels on your food to be sure that it really is organically or biodynamically grown. Manufacturers know that people will pay more for organically grown products, so the word "organic" has suddenly become popular in all manner of product names and descriptions. Look for products that state "certified organic" on their labels. This means that their farming and production methods have met the criteria of independent organic certifying bodies.

Buy free-range and organic animal products. Don't forget that there are also alternatives to conventionally farmed animal products. Buy free-range, vegetarian eggs instead of those laid by battery hens fed with feed that contains hormones and animal content. Free-range, hormone-free chickens and organic meat are available from some butchers, supermarkets and health food stores.

Avoid genetically modified (GM) foods. The main GM products on Canadian supermarket shelves are made with modified canola, corn (or maize), soy, and cotton or cottonseed ingredients. Organic standards prohibit the use of GM ingredients.

Since GM foods are already out there on the supermarket shelves, the people who eat them are unwittingly part of an unofficial field trial. If you don't want to be part of the GM food experiment, look for foods labelled "GM-free," "not genetically modified" or "certified organic." In April 2004, the Standards Council of Canada announced the adoption of the Standard for Voluntary Labelling and Advertising of Foods That Are and Are Not Products of Genetic Engineering as a National Standard. This means that manufacturers can choose to declare that their products are GM-free, with standards that ensure the truth of such claims. However, manufacturers using genetically modified ingredients can equally choose to not disclose their use of GM ingredients.

Greenpeace Canada has produced the "How to Avoid Genetically Engineered Food" shoppers' guide to help consumers identify GM-free brands. Particularly use this guide when buying products made from soy, corn, cottonseed oil or canola. For more information, go to www.greenpeace.ca/shoppersguide.

For more information on the environmental impact of GM foods, see Hot Topics, pages 254–5.

Double-use energy while you cook. If you have a baby, steam-sterilize food containers in the top of a double boiler while cooking veggies or noodles in the lower part.

Electric burners

Energy-smart cooking

Cooking accounts for under 5% of our personal greenhouse gas contribution. This may not seem like much, particularly compared with transportation, which is responsible for nearly half of our personal greenhouse impact. However, every little bit adds up. There are now over 30 million people living in Canada. If each individual were to cut his or her greenhouse contribution by 1 tonne each year – the target encouraged by the Government of Canada – we would generate 30 million tonnes less greenhouse gases each year. It's worth making an effort to save energy while cooking.

The first step is to make sure your cooking appliances are energy-efficient, instead of power-hungry, inefficient models. The next step is to make sure you're using your appliances in an energy-efficient way. Even if you're not in a position to change your cooking appliances, you can still save energy and money through energy-efficient cooking.

Ovens, stovetops and cooking appliances

As a general rule it is cheaper and more energy-efficient to use natural gas than electricity to produce heat. This goes for space heating and heating hot water, as well as cooking. However, smaller electric appliances, such as deep fryers, frying pans and sandwich-makers, can be more efficient because they need to heat less space and less material.

Comparing gas flames with electric cooking elements, gas is better environmentally, is generally cheaper and it is easier to cook with. However, gas can also cause breathing difficulties for people with asthma or respiratory sensitivities. If you choose to go electric, choose a more energy-efficient type of burner. The EnerGuide label program covers electric ovens and stovetops, so don't forget to look at the EnerGuide labels when comparing products.

The program estimates that the most efficient range will save you around $321 on energy bills over its life.

If you are considering buying a new stovetop and you're in an area connected to natural gas supplies, then you might be weighing natural gas stoves against electric models. Here's a quick look at the environment case for each of these options.

Electric cooking

Pros:
• Heating elements distribute heat more evenly on the bottom of pots.
• Does not contribute to indoor air pollution.
• Are sometimes easier to clean.

Cons:
• Inefficient – use a lot more fuel to provide the heat energy.
• Elements take longer to heat up and cool down, giving cooks less control and increasing the risk of burning.
• Some of the energy is lost in transmitting the electricity from the power station to the home.
• Fossil fuel and nuclear power plants have detrimental effects on the environment. Even hydroelectric plants reduce river flows and harm habitats.

Gas cooking

Pros:
• Stoves and ovens generally cost less to run.
• The heat can be controlled instantly and is quick to produce a high heat.

• Gas is a more efficient use of energy, consuming less natural fuel resources and producing less pollution.
• Canada has its own reserves of natural gas.

Cons:
• Contributes to indoor air pollution – both unburned gas and its combustion gases can cause respiratory irritation.
• Slim chance of gas explosions.
• Natural gas is a fossil fuel and is not renewable.
• Not all areas are connected to natural gas supplies.

Induction stovetops

Induction cooking is a new system which uses electromagnetic technology and is possibly the way we'll cook in the future. Electricity fed to an inductor coil inside the stovetop produces a magnetic field. When a pot made of magnetic material is placed on the stovetop, the induction currents from the coil's magnetic field heat up the base of the pot itself, which then heats the food. The stovetop surface stays cool and just provides a surface for the pot to sit on. This cuts down on the amount of energy both used and lost to the surroundings. The stovetop is also easier to clean, as spills don't get baked onto the surface.

Induction stovetops are the most energy-efficient type of electric burner. They are already used by many of the world's top chefs, who enjoy the fine temperature control they offer. They produce heat very quickly. Most people accidentally burn the first few dishes they cook while getting used to the new method.

Not all types of cookware can be used with induction stovetops. The cookware must be magnetic, such as enamelled steel, cast iron and some types of glass cookware with iron-alloy base insets. Aluminum, earthenware and other non-magnetic cookware can't be used.

Choosing an oven

There are three types of oven currently available: conventional, fan-forced and microwave. Whichever type you buy, make sure you get the right size for your needs. The larger the oven, the more space has to be heated and the more energy used to reach the desired temperature. Why buy an oven big enough for a whole turkey when Christmas comes only once a year? Larger ovens are more expensive to buy, use more energy and cost more to run.

Conventional ovens have gas burners or electric elements that provide heat. Hot air rises, so these ovens tend to be hotter at the top. Conventional ovens are no longer as commonly available new, as most people prefer the more energy-efficient and evenly heating fan-forced ovens.

Fan-forced (or convection) ovens

incorporate a fan that circulates the hot air evenly around the oven. The even heat allows all shelves to be used simultaneously. These ovens heat up

faster, can cook food more quickly and use up to 35% less energy than conventional ovens. Some models come with a feature that allows you to turn the fan off, allowing for foods like pastry to be browned.

Microwave ovens use microwave radiation to heat the food directly. They are highly efficient, as they do not waste energy on heating the food containers or the oven itself. They can also cook food in a fraction of the time it takes a conventional oven. There is some concern that microwave cooking may alter food molecules, making them less nutritious or possibly unhealthy; that microwave ovens can leak harmful radiation; and that traces of plastic can migrate from the packaging or container into the food. Research into the health implications of microwave cooking has come up with mixed findings. If you do have a microwave oven and want to minimize the possible risks of using it, then stand 1.5–3 metres (5–10 feet) away from the microwave oven while it is in use. Use only microwave-safe plastic, glass or ceramic containers.

Self-cleaning ovens use intense heat during their cleaning program, so you would expect them to be less efficient. However, self-cleaning ovens are generally better insulated, using less energy when they're cooking. Considering that the oven will be in cooking mode regularly but self-cleaning only two or three times each year, the self-cleaning oven will have a lower net energy use than the equivalent regular oven.

Other cooking appliances

Ovens and stovetops aren't the only cooking devices in kitchens. Many people have electric kettles, electric frying pans, rice cookers, crockpots, toasters, deep fryers, toaster ovens, sandwich-makers and pressure cookers. It seems that each Mother's Day someone comes out with a new cooking device.

It makes little sense to heat a large oven just to warm up one piece of pizza. Use smaller cooking appliances for smaller cooking needs. They are generally very energy-efficient and cheap to run. For example, an electric frying pan uses around one-quarter of the energy of a conventional burner to cook the same meal.

Tips for energy-efficient cooking

• Cook or reheat small meals in smaller appliances such as toaster ovens or microwave ovens.
• Use less energy to thaw frozen food by standing it in the refrigerator overnight or on the counter instead of using a microwave or oven defrost function.
• Match the pot size to the size of the burner that you use.
• Use only enough water to cover the food when boiling. Don't waste energy heating excess water.
• Keep lids on pots and use a lower heat setting, instead of using a higher heat with the lid off. Lids help to keep the heat inside the pot.
• Use steamers and double boilers to cook a variety of vegetables at once.
• Keep the oven door shut. When you open the oven door, you let out over 20% of the heat, which then has to be replaced using more energy.
• With gas stovetops, make sure that the flame isn't too big for the size of the pot. If you see the edges of the flame beyond the side of the bottom of the pot, then you're wasting energy.
• Avoid prepared meals and cook from scratch yourself. Prepared, packaged meals use more energy – for processing, precooking, packaging and transportation – than those that you prepare yourself.
• If possible, use the full oven space by cooking several dishes in it at once. Leave around 5 cm clearance between pans to allow heat circulation.
• Consider using a pressure cooker for stovetop cooking. This can cut energy use by up to 50 to 70%.
• Turn the oven off a few minutes before cooking is finished and leave the oven door closed. The cooking will finish using the residual heat in the oven.
• Keep the surfaces of your cooking appliances clean to ensure that maximum heat is reflected. Keep the seals of oven doors clean so that they fit snugly.
• Clean self-cleaning ovens only when necessary. Use the self-cleaning function right after you've used the

oven so that you can use the residual heat.

Green machines for the kitchen

Rewind to a few minutes before you put the veggies in the oven. You probably got them out of the crisper section of your fridge. Fast forward to after you've eaten and you may be putting the dirty dishes into a dishwasher. Both of these appliances run on electricity and are manufactured using energy and resources and so have an impact on the environment. In fact, 7.5% of the average household's greenhouse gas emissions come from fridges or freezers. Dishwashers also use water and therefore have an effect on our precious water resources.

Choosing energy-efficient and water-efficient appliances will save you energy and water each week. This also means lower energy and water bills. You can use less water and energy by using these appliances in the right way.

Fridges and freezers
Energy-saving tips
• Set the fresh food compartment to around 1.7° to 3.3°C (35° to 38°F).
• Set the freezer to a temperature around −18°C (0°F).
• Make sure that the seals on your fridge and freezer doors are airtight.
• Place your fridge or freezer in a cool position, away from heat-producing appliances such as a dishwasher or oven.
• Keep the condenser coils clean and dust-free.
• If you have a second fridge or freezer, turn if off and leave the door ajar when it's not in use.
• Regularly defrost your fridge if it isn't a "frost-free" model.
• Make sure that the back of the fridge has adequate airflow. Allow a gap of at least 8 cm (3.15 inches) between the back of the fridge and the wall.
• Don't put hot food straight into the fridge or freezer. Allow it to cool first.

>>

Free cooling

Because we heat our homes, our fridges still have to work hard even in the cold Canadian winter. If there are freezing temperatures outside, you can use the cold weather to help your fridge do its job. Fill a plastic bottle with water, allowing a little room for expansion, and leave it outside until the water freezes. Place the bottle of ice in the fridge. The added cold from the frozen water will reduce the cooling load on the fridge over the time it takes for the ice to melt and for the water to meet the fridge temperature. You can then take the bottle outside and allow the water to refreeze again (and again and again).

Buying a fridge or freezer

• Look for an energy-efficient ENERGY STAR–qualified model. It may cost more to buy up front, but it will repay the money in reduced energy costs over its lifetime.

• Also use the EnerGuide label to choose the most efficient model. NRCan estimates that the most efficient fridge saves around $288 in energy cost savings compared with the least efficient, and that, similarly, the most efficient freezer saves around $62.

• In most cases, the larger the fridge is, the more energy it uses and the more it costs to run. However, you will need a fridge with enough interior space to allow both room for the food contained and space for cold air to circulate so that your fridge can operate more efficiently. Buy the right size for your household's needs.

• Two-door fridges with a top or bottom freezer are generally more efficient than side-by side models.

• Avoid automatic ice-makers and drink-dispensers, as they increase energy consumption and cost more to buy.

• Many frost-free refrigerators are less efficient. Remember to check the energy rating.

• If buying a stand-alone freezer, choose a chest freezer that opens at the top instead of an upright model with a vertical door. Chest models do a better job of retaining the cold air when the door is opened.

Dishwashers

Dishwasher or handwashing: which uses less water? It's a question that's almost too scary to ask because we're afraid that the answer will favour handwashing, the more labour intensive method. It all depends on how you handwash dishes and on the dishwasher model you're considering. Here's a rundown of the options:

Modern dishwashers use around 10–45 litres of water per load, depending on their efficiency and the setting used.

Two-drawer unit dishwashers are available that use as little as 9 litres per drawer. Each drawer is like a half-load, giving a half-sized wash option.

For dishwasher loads that aren't heavily dirty, use a couple of teaspoons of baking soda instead of conventional detergent. For dirtier loads, look for the less harsh alternatives that are available at health food stores and "green" retailers. You can also put a dash of white vinegar into the rinse aid compartment to give you sparkling clean glassware.

About 80% of the energy needed by dishwashers to operate is used to heat water. Buying a dishwasher that uses less water means less water to heat and less energy needed to heat it.

Older-model dishwashers vary in their water consumption, using up to 90 litres per load.

Dishwashing by hand, using two sinks full of water (one for washing, one for rinsing), uses around 15–20 litres per load. It may be more for larger loads, such as after a dinner party. The amount of water used goes up considerably if you rinse dishes under running tap water instead of using a filled sink or bucket.

Energy-saving tips for dishwashers

• If your dishwasher has an energy-saving, economy or "eco" setting, use it.
• Wash only full loads.
• Regularly clean the filter.
• Use the no-heat or air-dry option on your dishwasher if you have it. Air-dry loads overnight with the door ajar.
• Remember that a dishwasher is designed to wash dishes so that you don't have to – so don't bother rinsing or half-washing them in the sink before putting them into the dishwasher. Just scrape excess food off the dishes. The machine should be able to do the rest.

Buying a dishwasher

• Look for an energy-efficient ENERGY STAR–qualified model.
• If you have solar-heated or natural gas–heated hot water, then choose a dishwasher that has a dual water connection (i.e., a connection to both hot and cold water taps).
• If you have a small household, consider buying a machine that has a

half-load washing option. Or if there's only one or two of you, consider washing by hand.

Food packaging

Packaging has received a lot of bad press over recent years. We've seen lots of packaging in the mountains of garbage sent to landfill dumps. Much of the garbage that pollutes our streets and harms wildlife is packaging litter. But the visible drawbacks of packaging are only part of the picture.

Giving credit where credit is due, packaging has allowed food to be contained and preserved for longer than fresh food would otherwise keep. Packaging has meant that food can be preserved until times when it is out of season, stockpiled in times of plenty and transported to places with inadequate food supplies.

The problem with packaging is what happens to it when it's no longer wanted. Packaging is a big contributor to household waste. When this waste is sent to landfill, it rots, giving off greenhouse gases such as methane. However, plastic packaging and other synthetics don't break down quickly. Many are not biodegradable and sit in landfill for years, leaving the waste problem for future generations.

Many people focus their efforts on recycling packaging waste after it's been used. However, "precycling," or avoiding the creation of extra waste by buying wisely in the first place, is even better for the environment. You'll

Cork It!

When people are about to open a bottle of wine, very few of them realize the environmental story behind the stopper that's coming between them and their drink. Over recent years we've started to see corks disappear, to be replaced by plastic alternatives. This is an environmental tragedy.

Cork is a wonderful, sustainable resource. The cork oak survives without chemicals, fertilizers or irrigation. Cork trees aren't cut down; only their outer bark is harvested every nine years. Following harvest, the tree regenerates itself. Cork is also fully biodegradable and recyclable.

Over half the world's cork comes from cork-oak forests in Spain and Portugal. These forests are home to the endangered Bonelli's eagle and the Iberian lynx. As the world buys more wine with plastic stoppers, these forests are losing their markets and the farmers are having to clear the land in favour of more profitable crops.

The rise of the plastic wine-bottle stopper is using a non-renewable resource and threatening the survival of Bonelli's eagle and the Iberian lynx. You can make a difference by buying cork products and wine with real, natural cork.

often hear this spoken of as the **3 Rs** of waste minimization:

Reduce your waste-producing behaviour.

Reuse items that would otherwise be garbage wherever possible.

Recycle materials instead of throwing them away.

Precycling saves you from having to think about recycling or responsible waste disposal later. You can reduce the waste and packaging problem by being careful about what you purchase at the supermarket.

Tips for precycling

Buy in bulk. Buying products in bulk quantities means that less packaging is used per unit of product. It's also often cheaper to buy in bulk.

Buy products that come in refillable or reusable containers. Many manufacturers now make products and packaging that can be reused. For example, Colgate makes a toothbrush with a replaceable head, and cookies often come in a retro-style cookie tin that can be kept and reused. Think about the waste that will be generated as a result of your buying that item, and choose products accordingly.

Buy goods in recyclable packaging. Make sure that the products you buy have recyclable packaging that can be recycled in your local area.

Avoid overpackaged products. Don't buy individually wrapped items or those with unnecessary packaging.

Types of food packaging

As a rule, the best types of packaging are those that are paper-based. These include cardboard, paper, waxed paper, and milk and juice cartons. These are made from a renewable resource, preferably plantation pulp or recycled paper and cardboard. They are also biodegradable and some are recyclable. However, they don't suit all food types.

Steel, aluminum and glass are good for packaging foods with a high liquid content that need to be kept for a long time. Although they are made from mined, non-renewable resources, they have established recycling systems and can be recycled indefinitely. Extracting and purifying the valued ingredients from the raw materials takes a huge amount more energy and water, but this process needs to happen only once. Recycled materials have already been purified, so making new steel, glass and aluminum from recycled containers saves a lot of energy.

Plastics are a complicated range of synthetic materials. As packaging, they offer a flexible, lightweight, sometimes see-through alternative that can be made in a range of decorative colours and finishes. Plastics are not biodegradable and take many years to break down in landfill. They are generally made from petrochemicals and so are not sustainable in the long term. While many types of plastic claim to be recyclable, in reality only a few types are commonly recycled. More environmentally responsible types of plastic are being developed. These will be more biodegradable or made from plant ingredients such as cornstarch.

There is concern about the safety of some plastics, particularly PVC, which can contain the toxic elements lead or cadmium, and other types called endocrine disrupters, which can mimic hormones. Limit your use of plastics and recycle them wherever possible.

Basic types of endocrine-disrupting substances

>> Pesticides (excluding natural alternatives such as pyrethrum).

>> Heavy metals, such as lead, mercury and cadmium.

>> Organochlorines – these are compounds made from carbon, hydrogen and chlorine. Examples include dioxins (often associated with chlorine bleaching), PVC and PCBs.

>> Plasticizers and surfactants – often used to make plastics. Examples include phthalates (such as polyethylene terephthalate, which is used to make soft-drink bottle plastic), polycarbonates and styrenes.

"Endocrine disrupters" – chemicals that mess with your hormones

There are some kinds of plastic that do a very good impersonation of hormones. These plastics are often called "endocrine disrupters" because there is evidence to suggest that they can influence and damage the endocrine systems of the animals and humans that ingest them. Small amounts of plastic can sometimes leach into the foods they package.

The body's endocrine system includes glands, such as the pituitary, adrenals, ovaries and testes. It also includes the hormones that they produce – little chemical messengers sent through the body via the bloodstream.

Endocrine disrupters can reproduce the effects of hormones, most commonly the female hormone estrogen, when they enter the body. Too much estrogen can reduce fertility, harm fetal development and produce female physical characteristics in males. However, it appears that small amounts of a single endocrine disrupter have little effect.

The cause for concern with endocrine-disrupting plastics is that there are so many of them and they surround us. Researchers at Tulane University in New Orleans reported that when a number of weak endocrine-disrupting chemicals were combined, they became many times more potent. Endocrine disrupters are also fat-soluble and so can accumulate in the food chains, and they have a long biological half-life.

Tips to avoid exposure to endocrine disrupters

• Fats tend to absorb endocrine disrupters, so to avoid the migration of these substances into food, avoid storing fatty food in plastic containers or plastic wrap.
• Don't heat food, particularly fatty food, in plastic containers.
• Avoid oily fish and particularly shellfish harvested from polluted waters. Shellfish tend to accumulate heavy metals.
• Avoid pesticides in the food you prepare by buying organic food where possible. Thoroughly wash or peel non-organic fruit and vegetables.
• Avoid pesticides in your home and garden.
• Ask if pesticides are used at your workplace or your child's school. If they are used, politely suggest some non-toxic alternatives. For more information on these alternatives, see Green Laundry Room, pages 98–102, and Green Garden, pages 170–4.
• Don't give children (particularly teething babies) soft plastic toys or teething rings. Avoid toys made from PVC, especially if your child tends to put toys into his or her mouth.

Recycling

Recycling takes waste and turns it into a usable material resource that can be made into new products. It's also one of the easiest ways for a person to actively help the environment.

When you put your empty bottles and cans into a recycling bin, you might not think that you're doing very much. You need to remember that thousands of people like you are doing exactly the same thing. More than 750 million new drink cans could be made from the aluminum recovered by just Ontario's municipalities in 1998 alone.

Making new products from recycled materials uses a lot less energy and water. For example, it takes 75% less energy to make steel from recycled cans than from raw materials, so the overall environmental benefit is huge. However, billions of recyclable cans, jars, bottles, newspapers and boxes are still being sent to landfill when they could be recycled.

There's a bigger picture to recycling than the part we see when we're putting our newspapers, cans, boxes and bottles into our bins. In the last 50 years, the global population has nearly doubled, with an estimated 236 000 people being born every day. Recycling is no longer optional; it is a necessity if we are to manage our planet's resources sustainably.

You'd be surprised at the range of items that are made from recycled materials and how far a material can go. For example, office paper can be made from recycled materials. Once it's used, it can again be recycled into tissue products, printing and writing paper, or paperboard packaging.

In a nutshell, there are two easy ways to bring some environmental action to your home through recycling. First, make sure that you're recycling all that you can in your local area. Second, finish the recycling you started and buy back the products made from recycled materials.

For more information on buying recycled products, see Green Shopping, pages 199–208.

What materials can I recycle?

In Canada, and in many countries with developed curbside recycling programs, municipal councils often provide recycling services. They determine the range of materials that are collected, the recycling bins that are used and the frequency of collections. Unfortunately, this

Saving energy

did you know...

The energy saved by recycling just one aluminum can would power a TV for three hours.

means that recycling services can vary greatly from one town or city to another. One municipality may provide a blue box for newspapers, office paper and magazines, while another will ask residents to put these items out in bundles tied with string.

Remember that just because there's a recycling symbol on a product's packaging, it doesn't mean that it or the packaging can be recycled in your area. However, there is a range of materials that are commonly recycled in Canada's major population centres. In regional or remote areas, this range is smaller. The easiest way to make sure that you're recycling all the material that you can is to call your municipal council and find out about its services.

It's important that you put the right thing in the right bin. A lot of things that shouldn't be put into recycling bins in the first place are ending up in them. This makes it harder to sort and recycle the recyclable materials and can also pose a health risk for the people on the garbage trucks that collect the materials. People, either ignorant or irresponsible, have placed everything from live grenades to live puppies and from used diapers to used syringes in recycling bins. If in doubt, leave it out.

Rinse the food residue out of cans, jars, bottles and drink cartons using old dishwashing water, rather than using fresh water from the tap. Then put them into your recycling bin.

The ultimate recycling guide

On the next page is a quick overview of the materials that are commonly recycled through local collections, the types that can be recycled, what they get turned into and some tips for recycling them. It's worth checking with your local council because not all municipalities accept the same recyclables.

The ultimate recycling guide

MATERIAL	TYPES COMMONLY RECYCLED	RECYCLING ADVICE	WHAT THEY'RE MADE INTO	DID YOU KNOW …
Glass 	Clear, brown, green and blue bottles and jars	• Don't put oven-proof glass, ceramics, or wine and drinking glasses in your recycling bin as they can cause problems at recycling factories.	New glass bottles and jars, filtering material, sand-blasting material and "glasphalt" roadfill material	Recycling just one glass bottle saves enough energy to power a 100-watt lightbulb for four hours.
Aluminum 	Drink cans, foil trays and foil wrap	• Foil potato chip bags should not be included in your recycling bin.	New aluminum cans	Recycling 20 aluminum cans uses the same amount of energy as is required to produce one new can from raw materials.
Steel 	Steel food cans, pet food cans, aerosol containers, paint tins, coffee tins, bottle tops and jar lids	• Take the plastic lids off aerosol containers before recycling. • You can see if a can or jar lid is made from recyclable steel by checking with a fridge magnet – if it sticks, it's steel.	New cans, structural steel for buildings, car parts, bicycles, railway girders and a range of new steel products	Canadians have an admirable steel recycling rate of 65%. Every tonne of steel recycled saves 1131 kg of iron ore, 633 kg of coal and 54 kg of limestone.
Cartons 	Milk cartons and juice cartons	• If your munici-pality doesn't collect milk cartons, reuse them in your home or give them to a local school or kindergarten's art room.	Hand towels, pencils, paper plates and cups	Milk cartons have lost weight! The amount of material used to make the average milk carton has been reduced over 20% since 1970 through better design.

MATERIAL	TYPES COMMONLY RECYCLED	RECYCLING ADVICE	WHAT THEY'RE MADE INTO	DID YOU KNOW ...
Plastic 	Soft drink bottle plastic (PET or type 1) and milk bottle plastic (HDPE or type 2) only *Note: Many supermarkets also collect plastic supermarket bags.*	• Leave the lids off. • Don't put plastic bags in your municipal recycling bins. Recycle them through the special recycling bins provided in supermarkets.	New soft drink bottles, fabric, garbage and compost bins, landscaping materials and plastic lumber products	Some curbside recycling bins are made with up to 50% post-consumer plastic from recycled HDPE bottles. PET and HDPE make up 85 to 90% of all plastic bottles found in the household.
Cardboard 	Greeting cards, cereal boxes, larger cardboard boxes	• Many municipalities don't want cardboard contaminated with food spills, such as pizza boxes. Check with your own local council.	New cardboard packaging, tissue products, gift wrap and roofing felt	Nearly 90% of the fibre used to make corrugated cardboard boxes in Canada comes from recycled boxes and/or timber-processing waste. Nationally, we're also recycling about 77% of our corrugated boxes.
Paper 	Newspapers, magazines and waste office paper	• Don't include foil gift wrapping and self-carbonating paper.	Cardboard, egg cartons, insulation materials, kitty litter and new newsprint	Making new newsprint from recycled fibres uses six times less energy than making it from virgin pulp. If the average household recycled a 90 cm stack of newspapers, it would save the equivalent of 14% of its average household electricity bill.

Don't waste your waste

If your municipality doesn't collect a certain material, it doesn't mean that you can't reuse it. Many garbage items are being sent to landfills when they could be useful around the house. Here's a list of great ways to reuse some common household items.

Newspapers and magazines

• Shredded newspaper can be used as mulch over the summer months. It will reduce evaporation and lessen the amount of watering plants need.
• The colour comics pages of newspapers and old comic books can be reused as a fun gift-wrapping paper for children's presents.
• Newspaper with a little bit of vinegar is an effective and cheap window and mirror cleaner.
• Newspapers can also be used for lighting fires, mopping up spills, wrapping food scraps and protecting surfaces while painting.

Milk and juice cartons

• Plant seeds and seedlings in milk cartons, with some drainage holes punched in the bottom. The carton will protect the young seedling from weather and pests and will biodegrade as the plant grows.
• Give your cartons to your local school or daycare. They have dozens of craft projects that use milk and juice cartons.

Cans

• Stainless steel and chrome household items are currently very popular. Steel food cans with their labels removed are an affordable way to make this look for yourself. Food cans can be used as vases and pencil holders. Larger food cans and paint tins can be made into umbrella stands and garbage cans. Condensed milk tins with holes punched in make great tea-light lanterns.
• Small cans, such as baby-food tins, with both ends removed, make great cookie-cutters.

Bottles and jars

• Plastic bottles with handles can be made into scoops by cutting the tops off. Two-litre plastic milk bottles in particular make great poop scoopers for those with pet dogs!
• Plastic soft-drink bottles with the bottoms taken off can be used as a watering device for plants in the vegetable garden. Insert the open neck of the bottle into the dirt near the plant and fill with water.
• Glass bottles and jars can be reused to bottle preserves and other homemade foods.
• Glass jars are great see-through storage containers for things like popcorn kernels, drawing pins, sewing bits and pieces, rubber bands and garden seeds.
• Baby-food jars are good for carrying small portions of salad dressing or milk on picnics. They're also ideal for storing hair clips, hair elastics and safety pins.

Clothes and textiles

• Old clothing can be given to charities, such as Goodwill or Salvation Army stores, either to distribute to people in need or to resell. Even if the clothes or fabric aren't in good condition, they may still be wanted – cotton and woollen items of poor quality can be recycled into other products, such as blankets and soundproofing materials.

• Old electric blankets can be used as underblankets after the wires have been removed.

• Old towels can be turned into facecloths, hand towels or bibs.

• Old sheets can be used to protect furniture while painting.

• Old towels and sheets can also be used as cleaning rags.

Composting

A plate of raw potato peelings, brown overripe bananas and the dregs from the bottom of your coffee plunger may not sound very appetizing. But these are just some of the possible ingredients for making your own plant food using a compost bin. Composting is nature's way of recycling dead organic matter into new, nutrient-rich soil. Food scraps from your kitchen can be put into a compost heap, along with lawn clippings and other green garden waste.

Composting is an easy way to cut down the amount of waste that you send to landfill, where it's no longer useful. Up to 50% of the waste that people put into their garbage bins consists of food scraps and garden waste that could be composted.

Food scraps can also be put into a worm farm, where earthworms break them down and, as in a compost bin, turn them into plant food in the form of nutrient-rich worm castings. Worm farms don't take up much room, so they're a great alternative for an apartment with a balcony but no garden.

For more composting information, see Green Garden, pages 163–6.

Compost it!

Here are some of the more unusual items that you can put into your compost bin:

>> vegetable oil
>> tea bags
>> coffee grounds
>> vacuum dust
>> eggshells
>> hair clippings from a haircut or hair removed from a hairbrush
>> ash from wood fires
>> shredded paper and cardboard
>> dried flower arrangements

> ### Seven uses for baking soda in the kitchen
>
> 1. Mix a little with water to make a paste to clean baked-on spills on your stovetop.
> 2. Place an open box in the back of your fridge to absorb food smells.
> 3. Remove stains from coffee and tea cups by rubbing them with a paste made from baking soda.
> 4. After cutting meat on a chopping board, scrub it clean with a brush and baking soda.
> 5. Sprinkle a little into the bottom of your garbage bin to absorb odours.
> 6. After chopping onions, remove the onion smell from your hands by rubbing your hands with a baking soda paste while washing them.
> 7. Add some baking soda to some white vinegar in a bucket. Add hot water and mop the kitchen floors with it.

Cleaning up

Cleaning in the kitchen can involve a lot of unnecessary chemical cleaners and use a lot of water. We've all seen news stories about food poisoning, so we tend to get a bit obsessed with cleaning surfaces and killing germs in the kitchen. In fact, this can actually do more harm than good.

Germ warfare

Watch TV advertising to see the many ways that advertisers portray bacteria and germs as nasty miniature monsters, hell-bent on making cute smiling babies sick. This is to make you urgently need to buy products X, Y and Z to protect your family from evil germs.

The truth is that antibiotics and antibacterial cleaning agents, while vitally important where they are truly needed, are being grossly overused.

In the health care system, antibiotics are being used so widely that some strains of bacteria are building up resistance to them. These superbugs are effectively immune to antibiotics. Prescribing antibiotics to fight infection is the "nuke them" approach to treatment. It simply kills all bacteria, both the bacteria causing the infection and the beneficial bacteria that our bodies need for good health. The loss of "good" bacteria is what leads to thrush, which many women develop after a course of antibiotics.

The same goes for your home. Don't embark on germ warfare and buy every antibacterial soap, toothpaste, spray, cleaner and other product under the sun. There is a saying that "what doesn't kill us makes us stronger." Our bodies need the small challenges of fighting a little bit of disease to build up strong, healthy immune systems. If you want to make your home healthier, don't fill the air with pollutants from cleaning agents. You'll only depress your own immune system and help to breed superbugs. Instead, practise simple good hygiene, by washing with soap and water after blowing your nose or using the toilet and before meals. Use heat to kill the bacteria in food. Reduce the risk of food poisoning by cooking or reheating your food thoroughly.

Down the drain

Assuming you're on a sewer system (and not a septic tank, such as those used on farms and isolated properties or in small to medium-sized country towns), all the water that goes down the kitchen, bathroom and laundry sinks or is flushed through the toilet goes to a local treatment plant, where it is treated before being released back into the environment. Make sure that you use phosphate-free detergents and green cleaners to keep phosphates and other chemicals out of our waterways. For more information on green cleaners, see Green Laundry Room, pages 93–8.

Let's get one thing straight – the toilet and the sink are not meant to be garbage disposal units. Water treatment plants are designed to treat water with a certain level of impurity. Landfill dumps and garbage collection services are designed to contain waste. Food scraps that can't be composted should be put in the garbage. Food waste washed down the sink (or flushed down the toilet) only adds a large load of solid material to wastewater, making the water treatment process more difficult and more expensive. The solid food waste, once it's separated, is sent to the dump anyway. The difference is that it has needed more energy and resources to separate it from the water and it has increased the cost of processing by going via the sewer system. In short, it's not good for the environment and it increases water rates by increasing the cost of treatment.

Getting rid of fats

Instead of pouring fat down the sink or flushing it down the toilet, pour it into an empty milk or juice carton, fold down the top and put the lot in with your general garbage. If it is particularly runny, first put some shredded newspaper or kitty litter into the carton to absorb the bulk of the oil. Use paper towelling to wipe off excess fat from cookware and dispose of it in the general rubbish. It you have a lot of used oil – for example, from deep-frying – check with your municipality about how it suggests you dispose of it. Some councils or waste management authorities have special collection programs for waste oil and other liquid wastes.

Try also to limit the amount of melted fat or greasy water that goes down the drain. Fats solidify on cooling and can build up on the inside of pipes. Many plumbing blockages are caused by fat and food scrap buildup.

Water-saving tips for the kitchen

Given that 10% of the water we use in our homes is used in the kitchen, it's worth considering some ways of conserving water.

• When washing dishes by hand, fill a second sink or a large basin with rinse water instead of rinsing dishes under running water.
• Don't use running hot water to defrost frozen food. Instead, leave it to defrost overnight.

• Wash vegetables and fruit in a bowl or sink of water instead of under a running tap. When you're finished you can use the wash water to water plants.
• Collect the cold water that comes out of the tap while waiting for hot water to arrive. Use this water for refilling water purifiers, watering plants, washing fruit and vegetables and small cleaning jobs.
• Check taps for leaks and fix dripping taps.
• Install flow regulators or aerating devices on taps. They don't cost a lot but can reduce water flow by up to 50%.
• When boiling foods in water, use only enough water to cover the food.
• Use the boiled water from steaming vegetables to make vegetable stock or, once it's cool, tip it in the garden or compost bin.

FOR A GREENER KITCHEN:

EAT healthy foods.

BUY well.

USE energy-efficient appliances.

RECYCLE your waste.

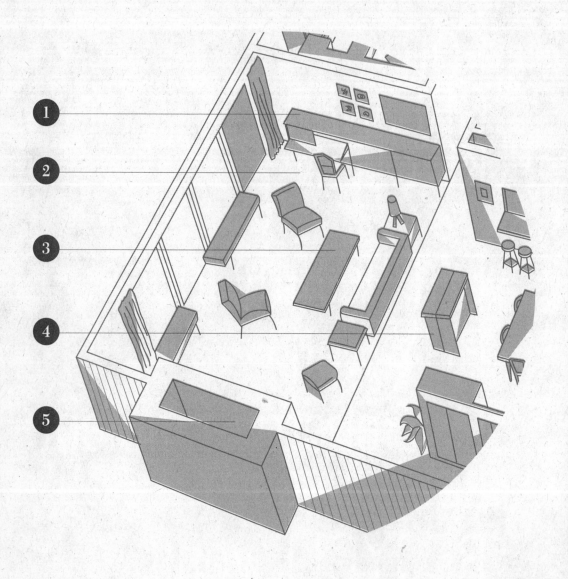

1 Good timber
2 Light from south-facing windows
3 Second-hand furniture
4 Energy-efficient entertainment
5 Green heating

>> The green living room

Many of us finish our busy days relaxing, so we want our living rooms to be comfortable – warm in the winter and cool in the summer. The living room is also where we entertain guests, so naturally we also want it to look good and to reflect our personal style.

Our home, particularly our main living area and the way we decorate it, says something about who we are. It shows our tastes and expresses our individuality. Being green in the living room doesn't mean that you have to furnish it with rough hessian rugs and packing crates. Being green is more about heating, cooling and lighting your living space with minimal energy use and greenhouse gas contribution, and carefully choosing furnishings that are softer on the environment. It also involves choosing and using any home entertainment gadgets in a way that reduces the waste of electricity.

All of this can be done without cramping your style. In fact, many greener interior design features are coming right back into fashion. For example, bamboo is again in fashion in a big way. We've also seen the return of seventies decor, which included sustainable cork flooring and lots of indoor plants to clean the air.

There are many ways that you can keep your home a comfortable temperature throughout the year, minimizing heat loss and gain while thinking about how different heating and cooling systems compare environmentally. There are also energy-efficient lighting options and electronics that help to entertain us, such as television sets and sound systems. It's sometimes as simple as understanding what those little blinking lights really mean.

Window heat loss
Canadian homes waste more energy due to badly sealed and poorly insulated windows and doors than the combined energy output of the Darlington and Pickering nuclear plants.

Keeping warm in winter and cool in summer

The first thing many of us spend money on in the living room is soft furnishings, such as plush throws and cute cushions. But what's the use of looking fabulous if you're freezing? You can Martha Stewart the place from wall to wall, but you're not going to enjoy being in the room if you're uncomfortably hot or cold. The benefit of a greener, more energy-efficient home is that it's more comfortable. So get comfortable first, and decorate later.

With our hot summers and cool winters, keeping our homes at a comfortable temperature is a major concern for Canadians. Many of us unwittingly spend heaps of money on electricity and gas to heat and cool our homes, only to have the heat escape out the window. Some people pump even more money into replacing perfectly good heating systems, and still find that their homes don't stay a comfortable temperature. You can spend thousands on a new heating and cooling system and hundreds more on

Winter heat loss

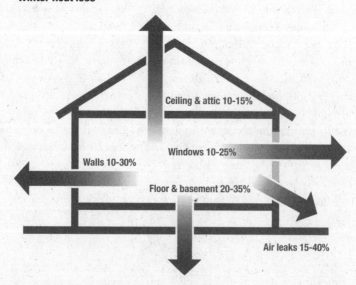

Ceiling & attic 10-15%

Windows 10-25%

Walls 10-30%

Floor & basement 20-35%

Air leaks 15-40%

Filling the gaps

Caulking fills a gap between two materials that meet but do not move relative to one another.
Weatherstripping closes a gap between two materials where one surface moves in relation to the other, for example, the gap between a door frame and a door.
Sealing makes an airtight (sometimes watertight) barrier or closure between two spaces, for example, around plumbing holes and pipes.

energy to run it, but you'll be throwing your money away if your home isn't airtight and well insulated.

Heating and cooling account for over half of the average Canadian home's energy use. Consequently, this energy use accounts for a good part of our greenhouse gas emissions. This can be greatly reduced by stopping winter warmth from escaping and summer heat from coming in.

Heat energy moves from areas where there's more heat to where it's cooler. Your heating and cooling costs and your impact on the environment can be greatly reduced if your home is well insulated and draft-proofed. Insulation helps to reduce the unwanted movement of heat into and out of your home. Heat can escape through poorly insulated or uninsulated ceilings, walls, floors and uncovered windows. Drafts and other air leaks can also allow heat to escape and cold air to come in.

In winter, cold outside air is very dry, so draft-proofing your house will also prevent indoor air from becoming uncomfortably dry. Cooking, bathing and other activities can create enough moisture in a draft-proofed house to

ensure an ideal winter humidity level without needing a humidifier.

Controlling heat loss

• Add weatherstripping to exterior doors to seal the gap between the door and its frame. You can also use a door snake at the base of the door.
• Locate any air leaks and drafts using a lit candle. Move it along baseboards and other joins; drafts will make the flame flicker. If you're concerned about the fire risk of using a flame, use a downy feather or thin piece of tissue. Once you've found the gaps, seal them with gap-filler. Ask your hardware store for advice on the right product for the job.
• Do an outdoor inspection as well as an indoor inspection for gaps and cracks. Carefully look over the house's exterior surfaces, particularly around window and door frames, at the end of winter and again at the end of summer. The changes in temperature and moisture levels can cause some building materials to expand or contract, causing new gaps to form.
• Install dampers in chimneys. Block off the chimneys of any fireplaces that you don't use.

• Choose windows, with low-emissivity (low-E) coatings, which help to reduce the heat loss.

• If you are using a room heater, keep the doors to unused rooms closed, especially those such as the bathroom with exhaust fans that open to the outside.

• Keep the curtains of south-facing windows open during the day to capture heat from the sun. Once the sun has gone down, close the curtains to keep heat in.

• Multiple layers of glazing improve the thermal resistance of the window – its ability to block the movement of heat. Windows in Canada should all be double-glazed at least. Consider adding a third layer of glazing. Storm windows can provide an extra layer of glazing to block heat movement, as well as providing protection from fierce weather.

• Assess your home's insulation and consider increasing the level of insulation if it's currently inadequate. In particular, check attic, basement and crawlspace insulation as these are the areas that are commonly poorly insulated and allowing heat loss. If the insulation in the attic is 150 mm (6 inches) or thinner, then additional insulation will make a significant difference.

• Make sure that any attic hatch door is insulated itself, that it closes tightly and that the hatch is weatherstripped.

• Rubber provides the best seal for weatherstripping and is waterproof. Rubber may be more expensive, but it

Sources of drafts

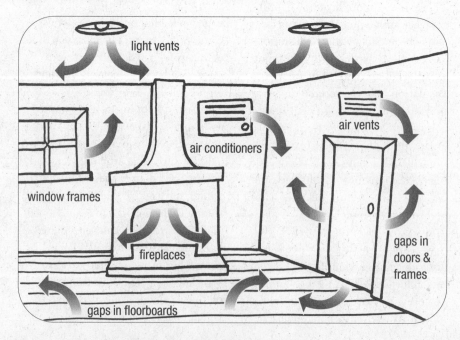

light vents

air conditioners

air vents

window frames

fireplaces

gaps in doors & frames

gaps in floorboards

lasts longer and is more effective and easier to clean than foam, felt and brush-edge weatherstripping.

• Mail slots in the front door, laundry chutes (particularly those that end in an uninsulated basement utility room), firewood chutes and pet doors can all let a huge amount of heat escape. Close them up completely if you don't use them.

Energy-efficient window dressing

Some of your winter heating, and the money you spend on it, could literally be going out the window. Up to 25% of the heat loss of the average home is through windows.

You can reduce the loss of heat through your windows, and the gain of heat in summer, by carefully choosing your window coverings.

• Choose drapes made from tightly woven fabrics.

• Line curtains with a reflective backing to reflect summer sun.

• Have curtains made to a snug fit for the windows. Make sure they are wide enough to stretch to both sides of the window. It is better for curtains to be too big for their window than too small. Gaps will allow cold drafts to flow into the room.

• Choose curtain rails or tracks that curve around at each end, bringing the edges of the curtain right up to the wall.

• Place boxed pelmets over the top of the curtain.

• Make sure that the curtains are long enough to fall well below the bottom of the window. Consider floor-length curtains where possible.

• If you choose holland or roman blinds, make sure that they are made from thick, closely woven fabrics and that they are well fitted to the window.

• Louvre, venetian, timber venetian and vertical blinds are not good insulators. They can effectively block summer heat but do not significantly prevent heat loss in winter. They should be used only in warm climates or in the homes of severe asthmatics, where fabric curtains can increase dust and dust mite levels.

The ultimate heating guide

Methods to retain heat within your house and better use your existing heating system are called "passive measures." Even with well-designed, energy-efficient houses, a lot of energy is needed to heat our houses in our cold winters. Many people live in less efficient, older-style homes with no immediate opportunity to build or buy a greener, warmer house. This is when we look at heating systems to help us keep warm in winter.

First, you need to take a good look at your house, the people who live in it and how they use it. This will affect your heating needs. For example, a family of four building a new home may decide to get hydronic floor heating or ducted heating to a number of rooms, while a single person renting an apartment may need little more than a portable room heater. Make sure you've exhausted the options of insulating better and blocking drafts, then ask yourself if you really need a change of heating system or whether passive measures will suffice. Then decide which rooms in your house need frequent heating; consider how big they are, how often they need to be heated and for how long. If possible, make sure heated rooms or zones of the house can be closed off from the rest of the house and are well insulated. The next step is to decide which heating system best suits your needs, is better for the environment and is more economical.

It is well worth consulting a home heating and energy expert, such as an energy efficiency adviser licensed by the NRCan EnerGuide for Houses program, before you make a major change to your home's heating systems. These advisers view your house as a system. Heating is an important part of this system and influences and is influenced by other parts of the home system, such as water heating or ventilation. The best solution to your home heating needs may not be the most obvious.

For more information on the environmental impact of power sources, see pages 252–53.

Tips for more efficient heating

• Wear a sweater! Central heating wasn't invented so that you could set the thermostat to 25°C in winter and wear a T-shirt. Wear clothes that are appropriate for the season, instead of turning up the heating.

• Set your thermostat to a reasonable temperature of 17°–20°C (63°–68°F). If it is programmable, set the thermostat to 20°C in the daytime and 16°C or lower during the sleeping hours. Some thermostats have this as a feature – called a "setback" option – which automatically lowers the temperature at night. As a general rule, each 1°C setback done on a regular basis represents a 1–2% saving on your fuel use.

• Regularly clean any heating ducts or filters. This will allow them to operate more efficiently, reduce the buildup of dust and other allergy triggers, and help to reduce fire risk. Clean or

---

How much heat does our furnace deliver?

did you know...

Some of the heat generated by furnaces is wasted – lost as radiant heat before it can be transferred to the rest of the house. Below are estimates of the efficiency of furnaces of varying ages and designs:

• Old (WWII-era or earlier) coal furnaces, converted to oil or gas – 50% efficient

• Furnaces 30–40 years old – up to 75% efficient

• Modern units – 80–95% efficient

replace furnace filters at least when the season changes, preferably once a month at the times of year when the furnace is heavily used.

• If you're finding that heat is accumulating around the ceiling, leaving the lower part of the room cold, install a ceiling fan to circulate warm air. A ceiling fan with a reverse function can help convective heaters to heat more efficiently. When the fan turns slowly in the reverse direction, a gentle updraft is created. This re-circulates the hot air trapped at the ceiling to provide even heat throughout the room.

• If you live in a two-storey house, use any upstairs living areas in winter, rather than heating downstairs living rooms. Upper storeys will be warmer because hot air rises.

• Heat only the rooms that people are in. Use a small portable room heater if only one room is being used.

• Close the windows and doors of rooms where a heater is on.

• Keep baseboard heaters and radiators clean.

• Maintain your heating system and have it serviced as recommended by the manufacturers. Oil-fired boilers should be professionally serviced annually. Gas-fired heating equipment should be checked and serviced every other year.

Types of heating systems

We use energy in various forms to heat our homes. Depending on your household's needs, you can choose a heater or heating system to heat a single room, a zone of your house or the entire house.

All heaters provide heat by one of two methods: the radiation of heat or the convection of warm air.

Radiant heaters heat people and objects by the direct radiation of heat from a hot surface. Examples include bar radiators, heated concrete slabs and open fires.

Space or **room heaters** warm a single room or zone of a house, rather than the whole.

Convective heaters transfer heat by warming air and circulating it. Fan heaters and ducted central heating work this way.

Central heating systems produce heat at a central point and distribute it as heated air through ducts or as heated water or oil through pipes, potentially to the whole house.

General rules for heating systems

While there is a range of different heaters and heating systems, with individual models having their own features and efficiencies, a few generalizations can be made. The size and shape of a room will determine the type of heater that will most efficiently heat it. Because convective heaters warm the air itself, rooms with a lot of air (in other words, large rooms) or with open stairwells and other openings are not suited to convective heaters. Remember also that hot air rises, so a convective heater in a room with a high ceiling will not provide heat efficiently for people at ground level, although a

Comparing central heating systems

	GAS OR ELECTRIC FURNACE, FORCED AIR	ELECTRIC HEAT PUMP SYSTEM	HYDRONIC FLOOR HEATING
Upfront costs:	$2000–$4500 to buy, plus $2000–$6000 to install	$4000–$7000 (for roof-space unit) to add to existing forced-air system	$6+ per square foot installed
Running costs:	Low if gas, high if electric	Medium	Medium
Greenhouse emissions:	Low	Medium	High (unless solar heated)
Safety:	Childproof in heated rooms – keep children away from furnace	Childproof – fuse-protected installations	Childproof in heated rooms – keep children away from furnace (if used in chosen system)
Notes:	A gas system is more efficient if vents are in the floor – floor vents generally can't be fitted after the house has been built.	Air-source heat pumps are a good supplementary form of heating (and cooling) when used with an oil or electric furnace system; they will reduce heating costs. They generally can't meet a house's entire heating needs alone economically.	Provides steady, even heating; very slow to heat up and cool down.
Look for:	• Systems that can be zoned to heat different areas separately. • Well-insulated ducts. • Electronic ignition rather than a pilot light. • Programmable timer & thermostat controls. • Electronic or high-efficiency bag-type air filters for better indoor air quality. • Two-speed fan.	• Systems that can be zoned to heat different areas separately. • Well-insulated ducts. • Programmable timer & thermostat controls.	• Zone controls, allowing you to provide different levels of heating to different parts of the home. • Programmable timer & thermostat controls.

Thermostat settings

Set your thermostat to reflect your activity.
Sedentary – e.g., entertaining, reading, watching TV: 20°C (68°F)
Active – e.g., working around the house, vacuuming: 18–19°C (64–66°F)
Sleeping – 14–16°C (57–61°F)
Unoccupied – e.g., to prevent pipes from freezing while on vacation: 13°C (55°F)

ceiling fan can help to recirculate the warm air that collects at ceiling level.

• Convective (air) heaters are better for heating small rooms quickly or for heating a number of rooms at once using a duct system. They are not very effective at heating large spaces.

• Radiant heaters can take a while to warm up, but are better for larger spaces and drafty rooms.

• Pilot lights in gas heating systems can cost up to $25 per year extra. Choose systems with electrical ignition instead, or at least turn the pilot light off in summer when the heater is not in use.

• Flued gas heaters can be a little less efficient than unflued models. However, unflued models release unburned gas and combustion gases into the home, contributing to indoor air pollution. They also tend to cause a lot of condensation.

• Gas heating and reverse-cycle electric heat pumps are more efficient, accounting for a third of the amount of greenhouse emissions of other electric heating systems.

• With all heating and cooling products, look for models that are ENERGY STAR qualified. If you're looking at central heating systems, also look for ENERGY STAR–qualified programmable thermostats.

For more information about choosing a power source and household greenhouse gas emissions, see Keys to a Greener House, pages 3–12, and Hot Topics, pages 257–8.

It's worth considering the main types of central heating systems, taking into account the purchase and installation costs, the ongoing running costs, the greenhouse gas emissions, any safety issues and where they are best installed. The running costs and emissions given on page 52 are based on the more efficient models of a given system and are intended to indicate the relative cost of each option. Cost estimates include installation, unless otherwise stated. The associated greenhouse gas emissions will depend on your fuel choice and the efficiency of the way you use that fuel.

Comparing fixed space heaters

	DUCTLESS WALL-MOUNTED HEAT PUMPS	ELECTRIC BASEBOARD HEATERS
Upfront costs:	From $2600 for a standard wall-mounted unit to $5000+ for a "minisplit" unit with two diffusers	From $120 per unit depending upon the output
Running costs:	Moderate–high (if summer cooling is heavily used)	High
Safety:	Childproof	Relatively childproof
Notes:	• "Minisplit" systems are available, with a compressor installed outside and one to three diffusers (outlets) inside. • Depending on the number of diffusers, can heat 1–3 rooms or a small home. • A good option to consider in areas without natural gas supplies.	• Fairly common because they are cheap to buy. However, they are expensive to run. • Baseboards allow rooms to be heated separately.
Look for:		

Space heaters can be used to heat one or two rooms. They are cheaper than installing a ducted system for the whole house and can more easily be fitted into an existing house. Some space heaters are fixed; others can be moved from room to room.

ELECTRIC FIREPLACES & STOVES	GAS WALL HEATERS, STOVES & FIREPLACE INSERTS	ADVANCED WOOD STOVES, HEATERS & FIREPLACES
• Stoves: $350–$700 • Fireplaces: $1000–$2000	• Gas fireplace inserts: $2500–$3500 • Gas stoves: $1500–$2500	• Advanced wood stoves or fireplace inserts: $1000–$3000 • Masonry fireplaces/flues: $2500
High	Low	Low (high for old-fashioned fireplaces)
Surfaces can become hot, posing a burn risk.	Surfaces of wall units become warm, but not too hot; exposed flames can be a fire and safety risk, particularly with small children.	Surfaces of wood heaters become very hot, posing a burn risk; fire risk from sparks and embers when stoking the fire or adding wood.
• Operate like an electric fan heater but with realistic-looking, glowing fake logs, coals and flames. • These devices are intended mainly to provide the look of an open fire – the heat is an afterthought.	• Can heat up to two rooms. • Gas log fires provide the atmosphere of an open fire without the ash, solid fuel or high greenhouse emissions. • Require venting.	• Installing a wood heater may affect your home insurance costs. • Certified wood heaters are far cleaner, more effective and more efficient than traditional open fireplaces and wood stoves. • Fuel costs are more stable than electricity and gas. • Must be operated properly to ensure safety, lower pollution and efficiency.
	• Child locks on closed systems • Oxygen depletion and overheating sensors are desirable • Direct venting or power venting for better efficiency • Electronic ignition rather than a pilot light	Buy only wood heaters that are certified as energy-efficient and low-emission by CSA International or the US EPA.

>>

Wood heating – no smoke without fire

There's nothing quite like an open fire to provide a warm, relaxing and romantic atmosphere. Just ask the 3 million Canadian households that burn wood. However, there are good and bad wood heaters. Older-style wood heaters and the traditional brick fireplace are very ineffective. Some even rob heat by drawing heated air up and out the chimney while inadequately heating the remaining indoor air. They burn through a lot of wood for only a little heat. They can also produce harmful combustion gases, including poisonous carbon monoxide, and emit fine combustion particles that can penetrate deep into the lungs, causing respiratory irritations.

The good news is that there are good wood heaters available too. Modern certified woodstoves, fireplaces and fireplace inserts allow you to heat with wood with greater efficiency, lower fuel costs and less pollution. If properly used, a certified wood heater can give you the same heat as an older model while using a third of the wood and producing up to 90% less pollution, with almost no smoke coming out of your chimney. So it's worth replacing an old wood heater with a new certified wood heater or installing a separate, greener heating system.

When you do use an open fire or a wood heater, there are a number of things that you can do to reduce the amount of polluting smoke produced.

>> Only use good-quality, dry firewood or fuel briquettes. Wood needs to be clean and to have been dried (or seasoned). Wet wood is harder to burn and produces more polluting gases.

>> Never use wood that has been treated with chemical finishes or varnishes. Never burn particleboard, plywood or other wood composites, which contain glues and other bonding agents. These woods can produce toxic gases, which are bad for your health and can trigger asthma attacks.

>> Use wood that comes from sustainable sources. Don't take dead fallen logs from parks or forests, as they provide homes for wildlife. Don't use driftwood because it may contain chemical treatments or preservatives.

>> Don't burn glossy magazines, plastic, cardboard or household garbage.

>> Install carbon monoxide detectors and smoke alarms indoors and keep a fire extinguisher within easy reach.

>> Never use oil, kerosene or other accelerants to get a fire started. They can lead to explosions or serious house fires.

>> Store firewood stacked under cover in a dry but ventilated area.

>> Use smaller logs instead of one large log.

>> Keep the fire burning brightly. A smouldering fire produces more smoke.

>> Check your chimney or flue once a year for blockages. Have it swept if necessary.

>> Recycle the ash – fire ash is great for the garden, so put it in the compost bin.

For more information about heating with wood, visit www.burnitsmart.org.

Geothermal heating

Over 80% of Icelandic homes are heated by clean geothermal energy. Below the surface of the earth, geothermal activity heats the groundwater. This hot bore water is piped to homes to provide heating.

Rotorua, in New Zealand's geothermal belt, has thermal pools and spas – a popular tourist destination for the spa lover.

In Canada, 10°–20°C groundwater is used directly or with heat pumps to heat more than 30 000 buildings, including Carleton University in Ottawa and factories in Nova Scotia. In the Yukon, geothermal energy keeps city water pipes from freezing.

Source: GEO

The ultimate cooling guide

While we want warm and cozy winter evenings indoors, we don't want sweltering, sleepless summer nights. Summer comfort starts with taking steps to prevent your home gaining heat in the first place, rather than trying to cool it down once it's heated up. If your home is well insulated and protected from the sun's heat, you may be able to get away with not using additional cooling.

Keeping cool in summer

• During the day, block the sun's heat by closing drapes, curtains and blinds, particularly where there's direct sunlight.

• Still air can feel "hotter" and more uncomfortable. Install ceiling fans to circulate air.

• At night, once the air outside the house is cooler than the air inside, open curtains and blinds and windows to let the cooler air circulate. However, don't open windows while an air conditioner is operating.

• If you live in a multi-storey house, spend time on lower floors where the air is cooler.

• Consider fitting external window blinds and shutters.

• Fill any gaps or air leaks. Just as they let heat out and drafts in during winter, they also let hot air in during summer.

• Lights, dishwashers, cooking appliances and dryers all produce heat. Avoid using them during the heat of the day. Hang clothes outside or use a fold-up airing rack instead of a clothes dryer to dry laundry.

• Plant shade trees around the house to shade both the roof and the windows.

• Put temporary shading on the south side of your house by putting up shade cloths that you can remove during winter, or by planting deciduous trees or vines on a pergola.

• Avoid putting paving outside south-facing windows as it can reflect a lot of heat and light into the house. Groundcovers, lawn, low shrubs and water features can help to cool the hot air outside.

• Use low-emissivity (low-E) coated glass on the inside surface of the outer pane of double-glazed windows. This coating helps to keep heat in during winter and keep radiant heat from the sun out in summer.

• Now is the time for T-shirts and miniskirts. As in winter, dress appropriately for the weather.

Tips for more efficient cooling

If you do need to use additional cooling or air conditioning:

• Keep windows and doors closed while running an air conditioner.

• Keep furniture and drapes clear of air conditioning vents.

• Regularly clean any filters and vents. Clean outer condenser coils once a year.

• Set thermostats to 25°–27°C (77°–81°F). As with heater thermostats, every degree cooler will have a corresponding increase in your electricity bills.

• Use air conditioning sparingly. Don't leave it running overnight or while you're out.

• Install a timer or use a programmable system.

• Use portable or personal fans wherever possible, particularly if you're the only person in the house.

• Have your ducts checked for leaks. There's no point using electricity to create cool air that leaks into the roof space.

• Find other ways to cool down. Put your feet in a cool footbath, have a cool drink or spray yourself with a refreshing mist.

Types of cooling systems

So you've done all that you can to insulate and shade your home, yet somehow your house has turned into an oven. You may wish to install an active cooling system to get rid of the heat that you haven't been able to keep out. As with heating, decide which rooms in your house need frequent cooling. Take into account how big they are, how often they need to be actively cooled and for how long. Where possible, make sure rooms that get particularly hot can be closed off from the rest of the house.

There are four types of cooling systems, any of which can provide cooling for a single room or the entire house. They generally run on electricity.

Electric fans have the lowest energy use and the lowest running cost and are the cheapest to purchase of all the types of cooling system. However, they do not actually make the air colder.

Evaporative cooling works by drawing in hot air from outside through a water-moistened filter. These coolers are best suited to hot and dry climates as they can make little difference to the temperature of already humid air. They are uncommon in Canada with our muggy summers.

Comparing cooling systems

	FANS	HEAT PUMPS	AIR CONDITIONERS
Upfront costs:	$20–$170 for a portable fan; from $50–$200 for a ceiling fan, plus installation costs	From $2600 for a standard wall-mounted unit to $5000+ for a "minisplit" unit with two diffusers; central roof-space heat pump unit – $7000; installation of new duct system – from $2500	Portable – $600–$1800; fixed – $200–$1600, plus installation; Split – $2000– $8000, plus installation; Central A/C unit – from $2800; installation of new duct system (if no existing ducts for heating) – from $2500
Running costs:	Low	Moderate–high	Moderate–high
Greenhouse emissions:	Relatively low	Relatively high	Relatively high
Safety:	Fitted fans need a ceiling higher than 2.7 m (around 8' 11"). Remember that children can tip fans over.	Childproof	Childproof
Notes:	Fans cool by moving air; they don't reduce temperatures. They suit warm, humid climates where temperatures don't get extremely hot. Ceiling fans can incorporate a light.	"Minisplit" systems are available, with a compressor installed outside and one to three diffusers (outlets) inside. Depending on the number of diffusers, can cool one to three rooms or a small home.	Central A/C is designed for larger houses. A well-placed room A/C may be enough for smaller houses. Window-mounted units are the cheapest, though not the most effective. Work best if ceiling-mounted. Can be noisy, particularly outside.
Look for:	• Curved blades that produce more air movement. • Variable speed control. • A reverse function for winter use (in ceiling fans). See page 51.	• Adjustable louvres on the vents. • "Setback" and "sleep" modes that adjust the thermostat setting.	• Programmable timer and thermostat. • Adjustable louvres on the vents. • "Setback" and "sleep" modes that adjust the thermostat setting.

Refrigerated **air conditioners** work by taking the heat from the indoor air and moving it outside. They also remove moisture from the air. Air conditioners have the greatest capacity to cool air but also have the highest energy use, running costs and purchase price, and account for more greenhouse emissions than other cooling systems. Central air conditioners provide cooling for the entire house. Room air conditioners can be mounted in a window or into the wall. As with room heaters, a well-placed unit may be able to provide enough cooling for more than one room. Portable models are also available.

Heat pumps are basically air conditioners with a reverse function that takes heat from outside the house and uses it for winter space heating.

As for heating appliances, use the EnerGuide labels to compare the efficiency of various options and look for models that are ENERGY STAR qualified. If you're looking at central cooling systems, also look for ENERGY STAR–qualified programmable thermostats.

Lighting

According to Natural Resources Canada, an average Canadian home has 30 light fixtures that consume an estimated $200 worth of electricity each year. This can be halved by maximizing your use of daylight, choosing the right light fittings and bulbs, and remembering to turn lights off when you don't need them.

Maximizing daylight

Artificial light uses electricity, which costs money and generates greenhouse gases. Daylight, on the other hand, is free and clean and, as an added bonus, is much more flattering. Knocking a hole in the wall and putting in a new or bigger window isn't the only option for increasing natural light. You can also put in a skylight or a solar light tube.

The energy saved from recycling one glass bottle would light a 100 watt incandescent light bulb for four hours.

Source: Northern Regional Waste Management Group.

Types of artificial lighting

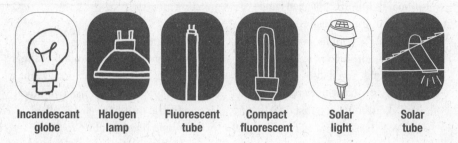

| Incandescant globe | Halogen lamp | Fluorescent tube | Compact fluorescent | Solar light | Solar tube |

A large traditional skylight is effectively a rooftop window. While skylights provide extra light, they can allow heat to be lost in winter and gained in summer. They can also look large and imposing on a rooftop and can cost several hundred dollars to install. Because of their large size, traditional skylights cannot always be placed over the area that needs light. Modern solar light tubes can be installed fairly easily to bring in daylight and transform dark and uninviting interiors.

Solar light tubes

A solar light tube consists of a small rooftop dome (around 25–40 cm or 10–16 inches in diameter), a highly reflective tube that passes through the roof to the ceiling and a light diffuser at the ceiling end of the tube. Basically, it collects a large amount of light from the outside and reflects it into the house. The benefits of solar light tubes are that they provide natural light without affecting your privacy, the light they provide is free during the daytime, they do not produce the heat that a normal incandescent bulb or halogen lamp produces, and they do not allow the relatively high amount of heat transfer that windows and skylights permit. They take just a couple of hours to install and most are designed to obstruct the sun's UVA and UVB rays. Solar light tubes can be fitted with optional exhaust fans for bathrooms and kitchens. They can also be fitted with an electric light kit that allows the room to be lit at night from the same point. Solar light tubes are a great way to bring natural light to hallways, bathrooms and other areas. Depending on their size and rooftop location, they can provide lighting at the same level as incandescent bulbs of between 75 and 300 watts.

Providing night light

There are four types of artificial lighting that can brighten up your home at night and, more importantly, help you to see what you're doing.

Incandescent lighting is provided by traditional lightbulbs. **Halogen lamps** are also used. Fluorescent tubes and the increasingly popular compact fluorescent lightbulbs provide **fluorescent light**. You'll also occasionally see **solar-powered lights**, often used outdoors at a distance from a house and its electrical wiring.

Incandescent lighting

Incandescent lamps and bulbs are the most commonly used type of household lighting. They come in clear or pearl glass finishes, screw or bayonet fittings, and 25, 40, 60, 80, 100 and 150 watt sizes. They are cheap to buy but use a lot of electricity and last only around 1000 hours. They end up costing more through their high energy use and short lifespan. However, they can be used in light fittings that have a dimmer function.

Note that there are "long life" incandescent lightbulbs available that last 1500 to 10 000 hours. Don't be fooled into buying them – their extended life means thousands of extra hours spent providing light while guzzling electricity.

Halogen lamps

Halogen lighting uses around half the electricity of incandescent globes, but the globes are more expensive to buy. However, the purchase cost is offset by their long lifespan of up to 2000 hours. Halogen lights are often used for lighting a specific area, such as a painting or a work area, rather than for general lighting.

Fluorescent lighting

Fluorescent lights are expensive to buy but will more than pay back the purchase price through energy savings and their longer life. They use about a quarter of the energy of incandescent bulbs to produce the same amount of light, and can last up to 8000 hours.

Fluorescent lights come in long, straight or circular tubes. They are often used in garages, workshops, kitchens and commercial and public buildings. Compact fluorescent lightbulbs are designed to fit into

Lights of the future: cold cathode lights

The same technology that lights up a laptop computer screen is being adapted to light up our homes. This new lighting technology is called the "cold cathode" lightbulb. Although it's shaped like an old-fashioned incandescent lightbulb, the similarity ends there.

Cold cathode lightbulbs use 90% less electricity and last up to 20 times longer than incandescent bulbs. They also produce less heat, making them safer to use and even more energy efficient. They can also be used in recessed downlighting fittings without the need for draft-causing roof venting. They are still very new, but expect to start seeing them in the near future.

Recycling fluorescent bulbs

Fluorescent bulbs are usually the first choice of the eco-conscious person because of their long life and vastly improved energy efficiency. However, they contain mercury, which can leach from landfill sites and contaminate groundwater. Environment Canada estimates that the 23 mg of mercury in the average four-foot-long fluorescent tube can contaminate 30 000 litres of water. For this reason, we definitely want fluorescent bulbs kept out of landfill. Unfortunately, only around 2% of the 6 million bulbs we discard annually are currently recycled.

Recycling fluorescent bulbs not only recovers recyclable materials from used bulbs (up to 98% of the bulb), it prevents pollution by keeping the mercury out of landfill and recycling it into new products. The other recovered materials are also recycled into new products. For example, some of the glass from the bulbs is made into fibreglass.

Used bulbs generally shouldn't be put into municipal household recycling bins. The glass from lightbulbs is a contaminant in the recycling of glass bottle and jars. Check with your municipality for advice on where you can recycle fluorescent bulbs. Some municipalities have depots where they can be dropped off. Ikea stores in Canada also collect fluorescent bulbs for recycling.

conventional light fittings and so can replace normal incandescent bulbs.

Some compact fluorescent lights are a two-piece light, and the actual bulb (the glass tube part) can be replaced without having to buy a whole new unit.

Frequently turning a fluorescent light on and off reduces its lifespan, so they aren't suitable for bathrooms.

Solar lighting

Solar lights have a solar panel on the top that produces electricity during the day and stores it in a battery. This battery powers the light during the night. Once a solar light is bought, the energy that powers it is free. Another benefit is that solar lights don't have to be connected to a household electricity supply, so they are often used in gardens. Solar lights are available through hardware and gardening stores, solar equipment specialty stores and some lighting outlets.

Planning and using lighting systems

Choosing the right lighting system is just as important as choosing the right bulb. General lighting provides soft light for a whole room; task lighting provides focused light over specific areas. The options are pendant lights, recessed lights, lamps, and fittings with multiple globes.

Pendant lights hang down from the ceiling. They produce the most light from a single globe and so are well suited to providing general light. Lights that are recessed into the wall or ceiling are often called "downlights." Downlights produce bright pools of light rather than general lighting. It takes up to six downlights to provide as much light to a room as a single pendant light does. Downlights are also often vented to the roof to prevent the light from overheating. Vented downlights are a source of air leaks and can reduce the energy efficiency of a house.

Lighting tips

• Remember to turn the lights off whenever a room is not being used.

• It sounds obvious, but open the curtains during the day instead of turning on lights.

• Limit your use of light fittings with multiple globes as they take more energy to produce the same lighting effect. It takes around six 25 watt incandescent globes to produce the same light output as a single 100 watt incandescent globe.

• If you like the warmer look of incandescent lighting but want to reduce your energy use, use warm-toned compact fluorescent lights.

• If you're painting a room, remember that lighter colours reflect light while darker colours absorb light.

• Choose your light fittings and lampshades carefully so that they don't block out too much of the light produced.

• Once in a while, carefully clean your fixtures and bulbs. A buildup of dirt and dust can reduce the light output by up to 50%.

• Have separate switches for each light, rather than one switch operating a series of lights. That way you can control the amount of light you have on and reduce energy wastage by overlighting.

• Although downlights can create a beautiful mood, they use a lot of power when providing general light. Limit their use to lighting decorative features and task areas, such as a kitchen counter or reading chair.

• Where you have a dimmer control, remember that lower (darker) settings use less electricity.

• For front porch or outside lights, use compact fluorescent lights if you want the area to be constantly lit. If you want the light on only when people are near, use an incandescent or halogen light fitted with a motion detector. That way the light goes on only when it's needed.

• Use compact fluorescent lights in areas where the light stays on for long

ENERGY STAR light bulbs

did you know...

The next time you replace a bulb, buy an ENERGY STAR–qualified compact fluorescent bulb, which will quickly pay for itself through reduced electricity costs. If every Canadian household replaced just one 60 watt incandescent bulb with an ENERGY STAR–qualified 20 watt compact fluorescent bulb, the environmental benefit would be equivalent to taking 66 000 cars off the road.

periods of time, such as the kitchen or living room. Reducing how frequently you turn the light on and off will extend the life of the globe. Use halogen or incandescent lights for rooms that are used only briefly and in fittings with a dimmer control.

Entertaining electricity

Most living rooms are full of gadgets, gizmos and electronic devices that (theoretically) make our lives easier and entertain us. Most homes have a television set, video and sound system. Many also have DVD players, game stations, electrical musical equipment, electric toys and home computer systems.

All these appliances use electricity and so contribute to the greenhouse effect. They also produce electromagnetic fields; for more information on this, see Green Bedroom, page 114. Like all modern products, where the environment is concerned not all electric equipment is created equally. Some equipment uses more electricity than others. You can reduce the amount of energy your electric techno-gadgets and gizmos use by carefully choosing the models you buy (again, look for the ENERGY STAR symbol), changing the way you use them and occasionally choosing not to use them at all. For more information on the ENERGY STAR rating system, see pages 11–2.

Entertainment without electricity

The ultimate way to cut down the energy use of a television set is to turn it off and not watch it. Western societies are seeing a rise in obesity, due to a poor diet and our sedentary lifestyles. Basically, we don't get out and exercise enough!

Instead of staying inside watching the TV:
>> Go for a walk.
>> Join a sporting club or become a member at your local tennis courts or gym and use the facilities.
>> Take Latin dancing lessons with your partner. It's fun, great exercise and great for your figure.

There will be nights that you want to spend indoors, and reading is to the mind what exercise is to the body. Exercise your brain:
>> Play Scrabble – it's fun and it increases your vocabulary.
>> Read a book (or even write one).
>> Have a conversation. Get to know your family. When you're bored with them, invite friends over and chat with them.
>> Take up yoga. As well as being good exercise, yoga helps you to relax and reduces stress levels.

Standby wattage = standby wastage

Have you ever got up during the night and stumbled around the house in the dark? Depending on how awake you were, you might have noticed the occasional tiny green light, or perhaps a blinking red one. These tiny lights are the sign of waiting electronics, ready for use. The convenience of having your television and stereo at the beck and call of your remote control comes at a cost to both you and the environment. The home is full of energy-using appliances, and some of them continue to use energy while on "standby" or even when they're switched off. This standby power quickly adds up. In fact, it's estimated that electronics on standby waste more electricity than the amount used by the fridges in Canadian homes.

The main culprits are televisions and VCRs in standby mode. The simple solution here is to turn them off manually when they're not in use. Other audio and video items also use a significant amount of energy in standby mode. Wherever you see one of those tiny lights, electricity is being used to power them. While it is only a tiny amount, it does add up over a long period of time. Computer equipment, printers and some other electronics can also use small amounts of electricity even when switched off. This power serves no function and is often due to poor product design. The only way to prevent this is to unplug the equipment from the wall when it's not in use. You can also reduce standby wastage by avoiding poorly designed products. Electronic equipment that is ENERGY STAR–qualified has limits on the amount of electricity it draws on standby.

Telltale signs of standby power use

Certain product features of electronic equipment need power to run. The outward signs of these features are listed below. Avoid them where you can or look for low-wattage models or the ENERGY STAR symbol on products, such as heating thermostats, that need a small constant power supply.

An appliance probably uses standby power if it has one or more of the following features:

>> There is no "off" switch.
>> It has a remote control.
>> It has a soft-touch keypad or controls.
>> It is warm to touch near the switch when turned off.
>> It charges the battery of a portable device.

To reduce standby and leakage power waste, do the following:
>> Switch electronics off rather than leaving them on standby.
>> Switch off at the wall and unplug the equipment you use only occasionally.

FOR A GREENER LIVING ROOM:

USE energy-efficient heating and cooling.

INSULATE to reduce heat loss.

MAXIMIZE the sun's free heat and light.

TURN OFF what you're not using.

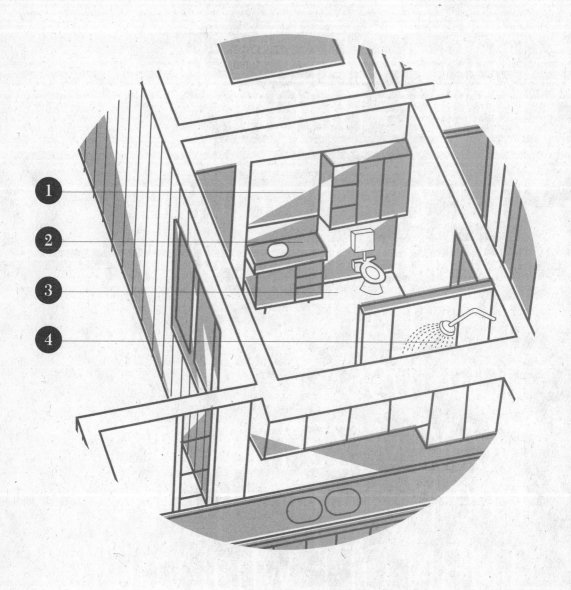

1 Green grooming products
2 Water-efficient basin
3 Green toilet
4 Green shower head

>> The green bathroom

The bathroom is where necessity and functionality meet luxury and sanctuary. It's the home of the beauty regime and the aromatherapy bath, and sometimes the art studio of makeup application. On the less exciting and more practical side, it's also the scene of body cleaning, tooth brushing, and shaving, and where the toilet is located.

Even the simplest, most functional bathroom of modern times is luxurious compared with the bathing practices of the past. At the beginning of the last century, bathtubs were status symbols, the BMWs or Gucci handbags of their time, and only the well-off could afford them, or a bathroom to put them in. Water was heated on the kitchen stove and ferried jug by jug to the bath or the sink.

Nowadays, we have hot and cold running water on tap, convenient plumbing and sewer systems, and there's a plethora of toiletries and personal care products on the market. It's easy to take all these things for

granted. However, our bathing habits do have an impact on the environment, so we should resist the temptation to overconsume in the name of hygiene and beauty.

The main areas of environmental concern in the bathroom are water heating and use, cleaning, waste disposal and toiletries. Toiletries, cosmetics and other grooming products represent a whole new environmental can of worms, such as animal testing, the source of ingredients, and packaging. For more information on these products, see Green Grooming, pages 211–29.

Green bathroom tips

Being green in the bathroom isn't only about water use and the hardware. The software can make a difference too, as can other bathroom habits. Here are some general tips for greening up the bathroom.

• Towels are bathroom software products that can be more environmentally friendly. Look out for organic cotton towels, preferably coloured with vegetable dyes or, better still, undyed. Also, don't throw away old towels. The outer edges, which are usually less worn, can be made into hand towels or washcloths and the rest can be cut up and used as rags around the house.

• Similarly, chlorine-free, organic cotton wool products are available, such as cotton swabs, cotton balls, tampons, nursing pads and sanitary napkins.

• Buy cane, bamboo or ceramic bathroom accessories instead of plastics.

• Go for ceramic or enamel bathroom fixtures rather than plastic or fibreglass, as they will generally last longer and hold the heat in water better.

• Avoid overpackaged toiletries and bathroom products. Bars of soap do not need to be individually wrapped. Toothpaste is toothpaste whether it comes out of a simple tube or a pump that has used up more resources in its production.

• Use a washcloth rather than a natural or synthetic sponge. The harvesting of natural sponges disturbs the marine environment, and synthetic sponges are generally made from non-sustainable plastics.

• Choose reusable instead of disposable products. For example, don't buy plastic disposable razors; instead, get metal razors with replaceable blades. Colgate produces a toothbrush with a replaceable head.

• Reduce the need to use chemical drain cleaners by keeping the drain in the shower or bath clear of soap scraps and hair. If possible, sit a sink strainer over the drain.

• When it's not too cold, open a window after your bath or shower. This will allow your bathroom fan to operate more effectively, and in warmer, drier weather perhaps eliminate the need to use an electric-powered fan altogether. It will also help to prevent the buildup of mould and so reduce the need for mould-removing cleaners and prevent the contribution of mould to poor indoor air quality, often a trigger for allergies.

• Avoid overpackaged deodorants and antiperspirants, especially if they contain aluminum, which has been linked to a number of health problems. Rock crystal deodorants made from mineral salts are a greener alternative to conventional deodorants and antiperspirants.

• After cleaning, put a tiny bit of almond oil on a cloth and run it over the shower glass and tiles. This fine layer of oil will hold off the buildup of soap scum so that your shower will need cleaning less often.

Saving water

Can one bathroom really make a difference? Considering that the average person has one shower or bath a day, brushes his or her teeth twice and goes to the toilet several times, a lot can be done in the bathroom to save water. Sometimes the smallest changes can have the biggest effect, particularly when we change things we do daily. Remember the 3 Rs of water efficiency: **reduce** the amount of water you use in daily living, **repair** leaks or faulty water-using devices to cut out wastage and **retrofit** your home with water-efficient fittings when you have the opportunity.

Water-saving tips for the bathroom

• **Install a water-saving shower head.** The shower is the second highest user of water inside the house. It takes one trip to a plumbing supplier or hardware shop to buy a new water-saving or "low-flow" shower head, and just a few minutes to install it. A standard shower head has a flow rate of around 15 to 20 litres per minute, while a water-saving head has a rate of around 9.5 litres per minute. Compared with a 20 litre per minute shower head, an average eight-minute shower with the low-flow shower head will use 84 litres less water. With one shower a day, after a year you will have saved 30 660 litres of water (30 744 if it's a leap year!). Those showers will probably have been hot, so you'll also have saved the cost of heating all that water. Most shower heads and faucets approved by the

Canadian Standards Association are stamped with their flow rates. Look for shower heads with a flow rate of around 9.5 litres (2.5 gallons) per minute.

• **Install a tap-flow regulator.** Put a tap-flow regulator or an aerator onto the end of your tap. Both reduce the flow rate of the tap. Don't bother with an aerator for the bathtub tap as aerating the water will allow it to cool, increasing the amount of heated water you need for your bath to be the desired temperature.

• **Have a shower instead of a bath.** Since few people enjoy a shallow bath, baths use more water than quick showers, particularly if the shower has a water-saving shower head. Save baths for when you have the time to enjoy a soak.

• **Shave with the plug in.** Whether you're a guy shaving or a girl doing some armpit deforestation, don't rinse your razor under running water. A running tap releases around 10 litres of water per minute, so it's better to partially fill the sink with warm water for rinsing the razor.

• **Don't brush your teeth while the tap is running.** You need only a cup of water to rinse out your mouth, your toothbrush and the basin after brushing your teeth. Use a cup when brushing your teeth instead of leaving the tap running and wasting around 5 litres of water in the process.

• **Fix dripping taps.** Make sure you fix dripping taps right away, as the drips quickly add up. Periodically change the washers in your taps to prevent leaks from starting, and to make it easier to turn taps on and off properly. Alternatively, most taps can be fitted with a ceramic washer system. Ceramic washers last longer and make the taps easier to turn on and off. But don't use them in shower taps, as they provide cruder adjustment of the water flow, making it harder to get the right temperature.

• **Check for leaks.** You can use your water meter to check for water leaks. At night, before going to bed, write down the meter reading. In the morning, check with the people you live with whether or not they've used any water during the night and, if they haven't, record the meter reading again. If the water meter reading has changed, it means there is a leak that needs to be traced and fixed. You may need to get a plumber in.

The green toilet

Nearly a third of the water we use at home is flushed down the toilet. Even in the smallest room in the house you can make a difference by saving water.

Water-saving tips for the toilet

• **Buy an ultra-low-flush (ULF) or dual-flush toilet.** If you need a new toilet, buy a modern ultra-low-flush toilet, which uses around 6 litres of water each flush. Building codes in some provinces and municipalities now require 6 litre toilets by law. Better still, look for dual-flush toilets, which are increasingly being used in new developments. Dual-flush toilets can use as little as 3 litres for a half flush and 6 litres for a full flush, compared with 18 litres for the old single-flush systems. Many municipalities have subsidized toilet-replacement programs, so check with your municipal government or your water provider about its programs.

• **Use the right button.** If you have a dual-flush toilet, make sure you use the appropriate flush button. Generally, try to use the half flush and use the full flush button only when necessary.

Drip, drip, drip

Imagine a leaky tap, slowly dripping at around one drip per second. It doesn't seem like much, does it? However, all those drips add up to about half a litre per hour. The longer you leave a leak unfixed, the more water you will waste. Leave it dripping for a year and you will waste enough water to:

>> fill 28 000 glasses
>> wash 28 loads of clothes
>> provide 56 showers
>> flush 700 toilets
>> clean your teeth 14 000 times

> ## Toilet-water wastage
>
> Older toilets use around 18 litres per flush. More recent water-conserving toilets use 13 litres per flush, while new ultra-low-flush toilets use 6 litres per flush. Let us assume an average toilet usage of five flushes per person each day. A person using an older-style toilet uses around 32 850 litres of water for toilet flushing each year, compared to 23 725 litres using a water-conserving toilet and 10 950 litres using an ultra-low-flush toilet.
>
> The toilet is also one of the most common sources of leaks. Check for a leaking cistern by adding a few drops of food colouring to the water contained in it. Do not flush the toilet. Wait a few minutes to see if the colour starts to appear in the water in the bowl. If it does, then the cistern leaks.

• **Use a toilet-flush regulator.** If you don't have a dual-flush toilet, you can buy a toilet-flush regulator from a hardware or plumbing store. These devices fit inside your toilet cistern and allow you to control the amount of water used each flush by shutting off the flow of water when you remove your finger from the button. The longer you hold the flush button down, the more water will be used.

• **Improvise a half-flush.** As an alternative to a flush regulator, you can simply put a water-filled plastic bottle inside the cistern (the top bit that stores the water) of a single-flush toilet. This will reduce the capacity of the cistern by the volume of the bottle. For example, if you put in a 1.25 litre filled plastic bottle, then each time you flush you will use 1.25 litres less water.

Septic tanks

If you're not in a sewered area, chances are you have some form of septic tank system to treat your household wastewater. Septic tank systems collect sewage and use bacterial, biological, chemical and physical processes to treat it. Most people are unaware that it is a range of good bacteria that do all the hard work of breaking down excrement in septic tanks. Composting toilets and grey water recycling systems that treat the wastewater in some way are classified as septic tank systems.

Septic tank systems have to be installed and maintained in accordance with provincial government requirements. To install, modify or expand a septic system, written approval is needed from your provincial environment ministry or municipal government or health unit acting on behalf of the ministry and its requirements. It is important to use septic systems with care to avoid overflow, as this can contaminate rivers, streams, lakes and groundwater.

Tips for septic tank systems

• Limit your use of harsh chemical cleaners, strong detergents, diaper treatments, disinfectants and bleaches, as they will kill the bacteria that do the biological decomposition that makes the tank system work. Instead, use simple soap-based cleaners and other green cleaners. For more information on these, see The Green Laundry Room, pages 93–8.

• To look after the system's bacteria cultures, avoid acidic cleaners and treatments and those that contain chlorine.

• Do not flush tampons, pads or disposable diapers down the system.

• Avoid putting excess oils or fats from the kitchen into the system, as they are difficult to process and can increase odours. Instead, wipe out excess fat from cookware and dishes using paper towelling or newspaper.

• Reduce the amount of food scraps and hair going into the system by putting sink strainers over the kitchen and bathroom sink drains.

• Do not use garbage disposal units.

• Don't overload your septic system as this can lead to an overflow (and you don't want that to happen). If you have house guests, put a time limit on showers.

• Reduce the overall demand on the septic tank system by getting some water-efficient habits. If you reduce the amount of water you use, you'll automatically reduce the amount of wastewater you produce – another reason to save water.

• Flush a cup of garden lime down the toilet to reduce odours.

• Inspect the system once a year and clean the tank at least every three years.

What not to flush down the toilet

The flip side of saving water is keeping it clean, and that still applies in the bathroom, despite the material we're dealing with in this room. If you're careful about what you flush down the toilet, you'll help prevent the pollution of our oceans and waterways, make the job easier for the water-treatment facilities and prevent blockages in your own plumbing.

• **Feminine hygiene products.** Pads and tampons are responsible for a huge proportion of toilet and pipe blockages. They should go in the garbage.

• **Food waste.** Food scraps should be put in the garbage, buried in the garden or composted. Food scraps that are flushed down the toilet only make the water treatment process more difficult and more expensive.

Other eco-tips for the toilet

Buy recycled toilet paper

Quilted, scented and gorgeously decorated toilet paper made from virgin wood pulp really has to be the height of consumerism run rampant. It makes better use of our planet's resources to use wood and the high-quality fibre from wood for making furniture and higher grades of printing paper or card, and to use recycled wastepaper to make toilet tissue instead, where the higher quality isn't needed. Greenpeace Canada has produced a shoppers' guide to buying greener tissue products. The guide "Ancient Forest

Friendly Tissue Products" lists toilet paper, facial tissue, paper towel and paper napkin brands to look for and those to avoid. According to Greenpeace, if each household in Canada replaced one roll of toilet paper cut from ancient forests with one roll of recycled toilet paper, we could save 47 962 trees in a year. More info: www.greenpeace.ca/tissue.

Avoid heavy-duty cleaners and cistern additives

Many of us are paranoid about the presence of germs in our bathrooms and toilets. Simple cleaners used often are the best way to keep your toilet clean without harming the environment. Additives that colour the water are unnecessary and use resources and energy in their production. Avoid using powerful or concentrated antibacterial agents in the toilet, as they kill all the bacteria, including those needed to break down excrement in the sewer system, and they help to breed antibiotic-resistant superbugs.

Take care of the smells naturally

Air fresheners do not clean or freshen the air. They just send in a smell that's hopefully stronger to the nose and theoretically, but not always, nicer than our natural human gases. Just open the window, weather permitting. If you feel you must have a nice smell, then keep an aromatherapy oil burner in the bathroom, supplied with water, a candle, oil and a box of matches. The candle will also help to burn some of the smelly methane gas out of the air.

Use the fan only when necessary

Fans use electricity. If you have a fan installed in your bathroom, turn it on only when you absolutely have to and when a blizzard prevents you from opening a window. If your fan is wired up so that it comes on automatically when the light is turned on, consider having it rewired to a separate switch, or simply disconnect it.

Reusing grey water

All the water that comes through our taps is drinking-quality, or "potable," water. However, not all of our water-using activities in the home need drinkable water. "Grey" water is the used water from the bathroom, laundry room and kitchen. Either it is discharged from washing machines, dishwashers, baths, showers and sinks or it goes down the drain. It doesn't include the water from toilets or bidets. Toilet wastewater is often called "black" or "brown" water, for obvious reasons.

Many countries have developed methods of reusing grey water as an alternative to potable water to help meet the demand for water supplies. Most commonly, grey water is used for irrigation and toilet flushing. There are projects that use grey water for crop and public park irrigation in Florida, California and, increasingly, Australia. Water authorities in Korea and Tokyo have even offered incentives for grey-water installations.

We can reduce our demand on mains water by reusing grey water from the laundry room and bathroom on the garden or for flushing the toilet. However, as well as the obvious environmental benefits of saving water this way, there are also some environmental and health issues to consider.

Grey water contains a lot more bacteria than tap water, and these may include disease-causing organisms. It can also contain a high chemical content, depending on the use of detergents and other cleaning agents when the water was first used. These chemicals may be harmful to soil life and not all that good for your plants. Grey-water systems can be designed and set up to irrigate the yard in hot weather. However, the system has to be approved by local environmental health and water authorities. In short, grey-water recycling is not something to rush into without doing your research and getting some expert advice.

Getting a new hot water system

A hot water system is a big-ticket item, so it is tempting just to go for the cheapest option. However, you really need to choose carefully so that you have one that meets your needs, is soft on the environment and is cost-effective over its lifetime.

This is another area where saving the planet will save you money. Because we get charged for the amount of energy (gas or electricity)

we use, helping the environment by reducing your energy use will also lower your energy bills.

Water heating represents an average of 20% of household utility costs, as much as $600 each year for a family of four. Hot water is the second biggest energy user after space heating in the average Canadian home, so it's worth getting an energy-efficient water heater. You might have to spend big to get the new system, but that's a one-time cost. Your energy bills come every couple of months. However, with solar water heaters, up to 50% of the energy used is from the sun – it's clean and it's free, at least until some evil person works out how to bill you for it! Solar energy does not contribute greenhouse gases to global warming.

How water heaters differ

Before you go shopping for a new hot water system, there are two important things to consider. These will greatly influence the range of products to look at. One consideration is whether or not the water is stored in your home before delivery. In storage systems, water is heated and stored in an insulated tank ready for use at any time, while tankless systems heat flowing water on demand when it passes a burner or electric element.

The other consideration is what kind of energy the system uses to heat the water. As a rule, solar hot-water heaters (with a gas-powered backup system) are the best environmentally. Natural gas, liquid propane and heating oil are all fossil fuels. All fossil fuels used to heat water (directly or indirectly, by first producing electricity to heat the water) produce greenhouse gases, which contribute to global warming. According to the Canadian Solar Industries Association, solar thermal water heating can supply 30–60% of the demand for energy for heating water in Canadian homes, cutting 0.4–3.5 tonnes of CO_2 of the greenhouse gas emissions of the average family of four.

Ventilation also needs to be considered. Combustion heaters (those using natural gas, liquid propane or heating oil as the fuel) need proper venting so that combustion by-products are safely removed, ensuring healthy indoor air quality. Finally, size matters. It is important to get a heater that can adequately supply the hot water needs of your household, without wasting energy heating water that won't be soon used.

What size?

The size of the hot water system you buy will depend on the type of system you choose (storage or instant) and the number of people in your house, or, for instant hot water, how many outlets need to be served at once. If you have appliances that use a lot of hot water, such as a hot tub or dishwasher, then count them as an extra person. It's important to get the size right, particularly with storage systems. If it's too big, you'll be paying to heat water you're not using. If it's too small, you'll constantly be running out of hot water.

When you buy a system, consult with the supplier about the specific needs of your household and give a brief list of all the water-using appliances in your house. The supplier will be able to recommend a size. Also, think about whether or not you will have houseguests often enough for this to be taken into consideration.

Tankless versus storage water heaters

Storage water heaters The majority of Canadian homes use storage water heaters. In storage systems, cold water is taken from water mains or wells,

No more scalding

Each year an estimated 4300 children visit the emergency rooms of Canada's hospitals having suffered scalds from hot liquids. Many of these are caused by hot tap water in homes with water-heater thermostats set at an unsafe level. Safe Kids Canada recommends setting your water heater to a hot tap-water temperature of 49°C (120°F).

For more info on child safety, visit <u>www.safekidscanada.ca</u>.

heated, and stored in an insulated tank ready for use throughout the day. Storage systems can heat water using solar energy, electricity, gas or oil.

One of the drawbacks of storage systems is that they use additional energy to keep the water hot while it is on standby but not in use. It is well worth buying more energy-efficient storage water heaters to ensure that ongoing energy (and environmental) costs are kept down. All models have an energy factor (EF) as part of their product specifications. EF information helps you to identify water heaters that are more efficient by comparing the energy delivered in heated water to the total daily energy use of the water heater. Look at each option's EF on product labels, brochures or manufacturers' websites and choose a heater with a high EF.

Look for:
• Extra tank insulation to reduce standby heat loss. The R value represents the level of insulation – the higher the R value, the better-insulated the tank.
• Heat traps, which allow cold water to flow into the tank without allowing unwanted flow of hot water out of the tank.
• A high EF rating.

Tankless water heaters Tankless water heaters (also called instantaneous, demand or continuous-flow water heaters) heat water as required, so they don't need a storage tank and theoretically the hot water never runs out. Tankless water heaters cut the energy losses suffered through standby heat loss. Conventional tankless water heaters are generally not able to supply an entire home's hot water needs in larger or higher-demand households. Consequently, they are often used as a backup to other water-heating systems, particularly solar water heaters.

More recently, low-mass water heaters have become available. These are able to supply much more hot water and are generally more efficient, through the use of electronic ignition and power exhaust.

Tankless water heaters are a great option in homes with space constraints because they take up less space. They are also suited to homes with one or two occupants and therefore a low overall demand. They can be used as an additional water heater close to a tap or shower some distance from a larger house's main water heater. They are also a good option if your hot-water use patterns include long periods with no demand.

Look for:
• Gas tankless water heaters over electric, because they are more efficient and can provide hot water at higher flow rates.
• A high EF rating.

Energy sources for heating water

Your options for the energy source of your water heater will depend on where you live. Natural gas is not available in all parts of Canada, and many areas don't allow regular delivery of liquid propane or heating oil. Some households can improve their energy efficiency by choosing the same energy source for both space heating and water heating.

Solar water heaters, at around $3000 for a typical system, are more expensive to buy than gas or electric water heaters. However, they are cheaper to run and not subject to the price rises experienced by electricity and gas. Solar systems can provide 30–60% of the energy needed to heat water for the average household, though this can vary with differing climate conditions and household water-use habits. This can make a significant difference to heating costs, which over time helps to offset the high cost of buying and installing solar water heaters. They are also a good option in isolated areas without access to natural gas infrastructure or easy supplies of propane or heating oil.

Electric water heaters can be storage or tankless. Conventional electric water heaters use electric resistance heating elements. They tend to take longer to heat water than water heaters using the combustion of fuel as the energy source. This means that they have a longer "recovery" time – the time taken for fresh cold water taken from the mains to heat after hot water has been drained. This can be a problem if all the members of your household tend to shower around the same time of day.

One thing to keep in mind when comparing energy sources is that every time energy is converted from one form into another, a certain amount of energy is lost. Let's compare gas with electricity. Gas water heaters take a fossil fuel (natural gas) and burn it to produce heat energy to make the water hot. With electric water heaters, heat energy is produced at power plants, possibly by burning fossil fuels, then converted to electrical energy, fed through the electricity grid to your house, and then converted back into heat energy to heat the water. Each time it's converted, some of the energy is wasted. Because of the extra energy-conversion steps, electricity is much less energy-efficient than gas. Recent improvements in the efficiency of this type of water heater are due more to improvements in tank insulation than to any improvement in the electric element itself.

Electric tankless water heaters are generally more expensive to run and less efficient than gas tankless systems. However, more efficient models are available at moderate cost. They are often used in apartments and other units where there's not enough space for a storage system or where fluing is problematic.

Combustion (natural gas, liquid propane and oil) water heaters are available as storage or tankless systems. They generally heat water faster than electric or solar water heaters. They

Can I go solar?

Installing a solar hot water system is a great way to reduce your household's contribution to the greenhouse effect. It's also one of the few applications of solar energy that is readily available to the public. However, not all dwellings are suited to solar hot water systems. Your home must have certain features to effectively use a solar hot water system.

>> You need a section of roof that roughly faces south.

>> The area where the panel is to go should get direct sunlight for most of the day. You may have to remove any shading vegetation.

>> The roof needs to have a slope of 15°–30°. Roofs that are steeper than 30° are dangerous to work on. Special mounting frames can produce the ideal angle but add significant cost.

>> A 300 litre tank filled with water will weigh around 420 kg, so the roof also needs to be strong. Get an expert to assess the roof and its weight-bearing capacity.

>> Depending on your old system, you may be able to adapt it to solar panels. The key factors are the age and type of the existing tank. Get a competent plumber with experience with solar systems to look at your existing service and advise you.

are more efficient than electric systems that use a heating element. However, combustion water heaters need ventilation to get rid of unhealthy combustion gases, generally through a chimney or wall. The position of the water heater may also be restricted by access to the gas line or by the location of a new or existing chimney. With liquid propane or heating oil, you will need regular fuel delivery and space for a fuel storage tank. Natural gas is particularly suitable for low-mass tankless water heaters, especially where a tankless system is chosen because space is limited and a high energy efficiency is desired.

Look for:

• Electronic ignition, so that fuel isn't wasted keeping a pilot light burning.

• Features that reduce the loss of heat through the flue vent, such as a flue damper.

• Power exhaust.

• A high EF rating.

Ventilation is needed with water heaters that are powered by natural gas, propane or oil. If you are replacing a combustion water heater with an electric water heater or vice versa, then you must factor in the change to or from a ventilation system. If you have had a combustion water heater and are replacing it with an electric system, you will need to block or alter vents not needed for space heaters to reduce heat loss to the outdoors, increasing the amount of heating needed for the home. Changing from an oil heater to a propane or gas heater may also require changes to ventilation, such as changes to maintain drafts for direct venting or to avoid condensation in the vent. Homes previously relying on electric water heaters may not have an existing chimney that can be used for ventilation. This needs to be factored into planning for and choosing a new water heater.

Heat-pump water heaters are much more efficient than conventional electric water heaters. NRCan estimates that a heat pump system can save $1670 in energy costs over 10 years compared with a conventional electric water heater, which more than pays back the $800 approximate difference in purchase price. Heat-pump water heaters operate at optimum efficiency in areas with mild temperatures. They are less efficient when the temperature drops below 4°C (39°F) or rises above 38°C (100°F). They can cut the energy costs of heating water by as much as 50–60% and save even more energy when the cold air produced in air-source systems is used to supplement home air conditioning in summer.

Combining water and space heating

Space heating and water heating systems can be integrated, often saving money on the total system. With combustion systems, this means a single burner and a single vent, rather than one each for the water heater and the space heater. The drawback with integrated systems is that they are designed to produce enough heat to heat both water and a whole house in winter. This means that they are using the same high-capacity heater to heat just water alone in warmer months when space heating isn't needed, with a subsequent and marked loss of efficiency. This is often referred to as "low seasonal efficiency."

Look for combustion systems with a high-efficiency low-mass boiler. Integrated combustion systems that don't use a high efficiency boiler may be cheaper to buy, but this saving is soon negated by the relatively high energy use in summer months, when only water is being heated. Integrated heat pump systems are also available, though they can be expensive to purchase. However, the purchase price is paid back through energy-cost savings.

Hot water tips

• Install your system as close as possible to where you use the hot water – the kitchen, bathroom and laundry room. The farther the water has to travel through pipes to get to where it's needed, the more heat is lost on the way.

• If you are building a new house, consider investing in a ground-source heat pump system, with or without integrated space heating and cooling. Such systems are difficult to retrofit into an existing house.

• When you turn the tap on, the water is cold at first. This is the water that is already sitting in the pipes between the system and the tap. If your kitchen, laundry room and bathroom are not close together, then install the system nearer the kitchen, where hot water is generally used in smaller but more frequent bursts. This will help to cut down on the heat lost in the pipes and reduce the cold water wasted while waiting for the flow to warm up.

• Storage tanks can be further insulated to reduce heat loss, particularly in colder climates, with a foil-backed insulation blanket. If your tank is insulated to R-10 or less, consider installing an insulation blanket or jacket, often available from hardware stores. Make sure that flues and air vents are not blocked. Also, check your system's warranty to make sure that insulating the system doesn't void the warranty.

• Consider buying and installing a water-heater timer if you have a storage system and if your household uses hot water during relatively short and predictable periods of time each day. Most timers have a manual override switch to allow water heating at any time.

• Practise the water-saving tips outlined earlier. Not only will this conserve this precious resource, it will also reduce the energy costs (and associated greenhouse gas emissions) of heating the water.

Countries going solar

International Energy Agency figures show that as of the year 2000, Japan and Germany and many other countries had more solar thermal panels (measured in collector area) installed per capita than Canada. Yet Regina receives more solar energy year-round than Tokyo or Hamburg.

Source: Canadian Solar Industries Association

FOR A GREENER BATHROOM:

RETROFIT with water-efficient fixtures.

REDUCE water wastage.

CHOOSE an energy-efficient water heater.

BUY recycled toilet paper.

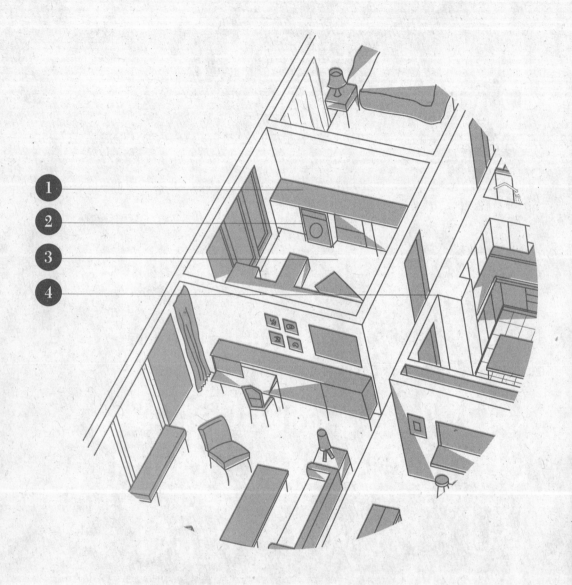

1 Cupboards with green cleaners
2 Water-efficient machine
3 Chemical-free floor
4 Green linen cupboard

>> The green laundry room

The laundry room doesn't have to be an energy-guzzling, water-wasting chemical warfare laboratory. It can be a low-energy, low-chemical cleaning centre for the home.

You can make a huge difference to the environment in the laundry room quite easily by choosing the right products and appliances and changing a few cleaning habits.

As with all water- and energy-saving practices, you'll also save money. Perhaps you can think of these financial and green benefits as your way of making housework more palatable.

Being green in the laundry room will give you a healthier home environment and cleaner air to breathe. Green-cleaning your clothes will keep them looking good longer.

Green appliances

Just how green is your washing machine? The washing machine and dryer you own, and how you use them, will go a long way toward making you an environmental friend or foe. They use water and energy and can be the means through which chemicals are released into waterways. However, if you get a green machine and use it properly, you'll reduce your reliance on complicated chemical detergents, reduce your water and energy consumption and save money in the process.

Front-loader or top-loader?

This is the first big decision when buying a washing machine. You may think that this consideration is purely about how easy it is to load and unload, or about fitting machines into small laundries. Wrong! When it comes to the environment and looking after the condition of your fabrics, the gap between front- and top-loaders is huge.

First, you have to understand how the two types of machines work. A top-loading machine is like a huge bucket that you fill with enough water to fully immerse the garments and add detergent. The machine agitates the load to create small currents that move the soapy water through the fabric. This method relies largely on the chemical action of the detergent to remove soiling and so needs more detergent. This action also places a lot of pull and drag on the clothes, which can wear them out and pull them out of shape much faster than hand-washing or a cycle in a front-loader.

Top-loading machines also use a huge amount more water than front-loaders. They also need enough room above them to allow the lid to open, which can prevent you from mounting a dryer above the machine in a small laundry space. The only real benefit is that their cycles are faster, but then who actually sits and watches their washing machine go through its cycle? If you're like most people and leave the machine to wash while you do something else, what's the difference between half an hour and a full hour? Front-loading machines also use less energy than top-loaders of the same capacity, despite the longer operating cycle.

The front-loading washing machine is also known as the "horizontal axis" washing machine, because its drum rotates around a horizontal axis. Front-loaders still use the chemical action of detergents to a degree, but they enlist the help of gravity to make a physical action that's like handwashing. Enough water is added to soak the fabric. As the drum turns, the fabric is lifted higher until, thanks to the force of gravity, it falls down to the bottom of the drum again with a nice squelchy thud. It's this squelchy thud that does the work. The weight of the wet fabric against itself pushes the soapy water through the fibres, removing dirt and grime without the drag of excess water. Clothes and linens are cleaned with less water and detergent and less wear and tear on the fabric. This is particularly important with fabrics that pill easily.

Buying a new washing machine or dryer

The first rule for buying a new washing machine is to look at front-loaders first. You'll also want a machine that uses water and energy efficiently. Following are some things to look for in a new washing machine. Some of these apply to buying dryers as well.

Low energy consumption

Look for the EnerGuide label when you're shopping for washing machines and dryers. In particular, look for washing machines that are ENERGY STAR–qualified. As of July 2004, standard-sized washing machines must be at least 36% more efficient than the minimum level required by government regulation to qualify for the ENERGY STAR symbol. ENERGY STAR–qualified machines are required to have other design features that deliver cleaning performance while using less energy and 30–50% less water. They must also extract more water from clothes during the spin cycle so that drying time is reduced, saving energy and wear and tear on your clothes. In short, all washers that bear the symbol are good choices environmentally. Again, choose front-loaders over top-loaders.

Low water consumption

The laundry accounts for around 20% of the water we use in the home. Washing machines can use 120–250 litres of water for each cycle. Look for machines that have a typical water consumption per cycle at the lower end of this scale. Also look for the ENERGY STAR symbol, as qualified machines must have water-efficient features. Remember that for hot- or warm-water washes, lower water use also means lower energy use.

Size matters

Each machine will state its load capacity. If you have a big family, you may wish to choose a larger washing machine and/or dryer. If you're one person

Real washer savings

NRCan estimates that the most efficient washing machines will save you around $955 in energy costs over their life, compared with the least efficient equivalent model. When you factor in a change from a top-loader to a front-loading washer and a switch to cold-water washes, you can save an additional $200 each year in reduced water, energy and detergent costs.

Why front-loaders are tops

When compared with top-loading washing machines, front-loading washing machines:

>> use up to 60% less water

>> use up to 40% less energy

>> use up to 50% less detergent

>> keep clothes looking newer for longer

>> reduce pilling in fabrics

>> can fit into a limited space

>> sometimes cost more up front to buy, but will save you money over their life

with a small wardrobe of outfits that you wear frequently, you may prefer a machine with a small load size so that you're not wasting water and energy with each wash. Choose a machine that reflects your household's usual washing needs. For unusually large loads, such as spring-cleaning blankets and quilts, you can always go to a laundromat. Many laundromats now have one large double-load machine.

A range of wash-cycle options

The closer you can tailor the cycle to the needs of the items being washed, the more efficiently your machine will run. Look out for features such as a range of settings for different fabrics, variable temperatures, variable wash times, adjustable load size, a low-energy or eco-mode option and possibly a suds-saving option.

Tips for using washing machines

If your washing machine is in good working order, chances are you're not going to fork out several hundred dollars to buy a new, greener one.

However, there are a few tips that will improve the efficiency of your existing washing machine, saving energy, water and money and probably producing a cleaner load. If you do get a new machine, these tips still apply and will help you to run your machine in a more environmentally friendly manner and maximize its life.

Follow the instructions. Make sure you follow the manufacturer's instructions for running and looking after your machine. If you've lost your manual, call the manufacturer's customer service number (usually in the phone directory), tell them the model number and ask for their advice or a spare copy of the machine's manual.

Have it serviced periodically. Just as a car runs more smoothly and efficiently when it's regularly serviced, so do large appliances. Follow the service recommendations in your machine's manual.

Clean the filter. Washing machines can get a buildup of lint, dirt, sand, candy wrappers and forgotten tissues.

>>

Retiring appliances

Your average washing machine or fridge is a bit too large to fit into the garbage bin. If you're lucky, the people who are selling you a new appliance may be happy to take away the old one. If not, don't dump it!

Call your municipality and ask for advice on where appliances can be taken. Some may have a collection service or know of one locally. The refrigerants in old fridges should be properly disposed of, as they may contain ozone-depleting CFCs.

Appliances are worth recycling. Steel, for example, can be extracted from old appliances and made into new steel products, such as food cans, car parts, building materials and even new appliances.

This can lead to poor performance and ultimately a machine that simply doesn't work. Some machines have a self-cleaning function. Again, check your machine's manual for instructions on how to clear the filter, and clean it regularly.

Use the right amount of detergent. Surplus detergent puts unnecessary chemicals into our waterways. Use the recommended amount of detergent for your machine (generally less for front-loading machines) and for the level of soiling of the load.

Soak heavily soiled or stained garments separately. It can be tempting to put a mega-dirty item in with a normal load to save the effort. People often then choose a more intense washing cycle and put in extra detergent. This extra washing power may get the dirt out of the item in question, but extra water, energy and detergent is being wasted on the rest of the wash. Soak the items separately, with a chlorine-free pre-wash soak if necessary, and then wash it in with a normal load.

Wash appropriate load sizes. Wait until you have a full load before washing. If you need to wash a small load, then use a lower water or load-size setting. Remember that washing one large load uses less water and energy than two small loads.

Use cold water. Wherever possible, use a cold-wash cycle, which uses up to 90% less energy than a warm- or hot-water cycle. Many detergents are now formulated to work just as well in cold water, although you may wish to pre-dissolve powder detergents.

Look after the machine. Like any machine, it will last longer if you look after it. Don't treat it roughly, use it to climb on to reach heights or let kids play with it.

Tips for drying clothes

Use a solar-powered clothes dryer (a clothesline!). Whenever the weather allows, dry your clothes on a clothesline using the power of the sun and the wind. In cooler weather you can always finish off the drying by hanging clothes in front of the heater if it's already on, or with a quick turn in the dryer.

Heat the home at the same time. Dry clothes on a drying-rack placed in front of a heater. That way you use the energy that has dried your clothes a second time to warm your house. If you have a fan-forced heater, which produces hot, dry air, the slight increase in humidity from the evaporated water may be quite a relief. However, do not place articles directly on a heater or too close to naked flames, particularly with flammable synthetic fabrics.

Spin-dry before using the dryer. The spin cycle of the washing machine removes excess water much more efficiently than hot, dry air in a dryer. Use the dryer only for damp (not dripping) clothes.

Get the load size right. Aim to dry a full load – your machine instructions will recommend load sizes. Smaller loads waste energy. Don't overfill the dryer, as there needs to be room for the warm air to circulate.

Dry fabrics of similar weight together. Fabrics will dry more efficiently and evenly when similar fabrics are dried together. For example, try to do a separate load for towels, another for bedding and table linens and so on.

Know when to stop. Don't overdry clothes, as this wastes energy and can weaken the fabric fibres. Also, don't add wet clothes to a partially dry load as you'll overdry some of the original load.

Dry two (or more) loads in a row. Rather than allowing the dryer to cool, dry two loads in a row to make use of the residual heat still in the machine.

Use the cool-down cycle. This cycle (just air without added heat) uses the residual heat in the dryer to finish drying the load. It's often called the permanent-press cycle, as loads dried with cool air crease less, reducing the need for ironing.

Clean the lint filter after each load. Fluff and lint can quickly build up in a dryer's filter, blocking the flow of air. Remove lint after each load to ensure that the machine runs efficiently.

Dry cleaning

Dry cleaning uses solvents instead of water to clean fabrics. This is particularly useful with fibres that shrink, roughen or deteriorate when washed in water. Conventional dry-cleaning uses the toxic solvent perchloroethylene, or "perc," which has been linked to liver cancer and is known to cause cancer in animals.

When dry-cleaned clothes are brought home, they continue to give off solvent residue in the form of gas, exposing the whole household to potentially harmful gases. Indoor air quality is particularly of concern, as most of us spend the bulk of our time indoors.

Avoid dry cleaning where possible by buying clothes that you can wash by hand or machine. Also remember that some clothing manufacturers will revert to dry-clean-only labels if they are unsure of the best way to look after a new fabric but know that it may be sensitive to wet washing.

Some dry cleaners are phasing out their use of perc and are switching over to carbon dioxide or wet cleaning processes. If you have clothes that must be dry cleaned, ask your dry cleaner about their methods.

If you do get a garment dry-cleaned with perc, don't put it straight into your wardrobe where it will emit gas into the room that you sleep in. Take the protective plastic off and allow the garment to air outside before putting it away.

The Environmental Choice Program, Environment Canada's eco-labelling program, has a category called Garment Cleaning Services. Dry cleaners that are EcoLogo-certified have a lower impact on the environment, through reductions in resource and energy consumption, material sent to landfill (recycling hangers and plastic garment bags, for example) and toxic emissions to the environment. More info: www.environmentalchoice.ca.

Choosing laundry products

A new washing machine is a choice that you have to make only once every 10 to 20 years. However, a new box or bottle of laundry power or liquid comes around every few weeks, so you don't have to wait long before making a change in this department.

If you take a walk down your local supermarket's cleaning aisle, you'll be bombarded with packaging information, with every product competing to be chosen by you. Every pack seems to have an eco-, bio- or enviro-name and a whole lot of scientific-sounding statements. It can be hard to read between the lines and find out what works, what is good for the environment and what is necessary for your own personal needs.

When people buy laundry detergents, soaks and treatments, they generally consider performance, price, environmental aspects and health aspects. For many people, it's not just about being "green." Their concern for the environment is born out of a need for a healthier lifestyle and living environment. People are becoming more and more aware of chemical sensitivities and the environmental causes of health problems.

For those of us without chemistry degrees, it's hard to read an ingredients list on a laundry product and distinguish between the ingredients that are necessary for good cleaning performance and those that may have an environmental or health impact. The following tips show what to look for and how these contents affect the environment and/or your health.

What to look for

Choose biodegradable products.
Buy only laundry products that state that they are biodegradable – preferably "readily biodegradable" or "easily biodegradable." This means that the product will readily break down into harmless substances through the natural decomposition process.

Avoid phosphates/phosphorous chemicals.
Phosphates are added to laundry products and other cleaners and toiletries to soften hard water and make it more alkaline. Algae find phosphates quite nutritious. They love them! However, this upsets the balance of aquatic life. The algae thrive, using more than their fair share of the oxygen in the water and starving other marine life. Phosphates lead to algal blooms, which kill fish and other marine life and contaminate drinking water. Look for laundry products that are completely phosphate-free.

Avoid chlorine-based bleaches.
Bleaches are used to sanitize, whiten and deodorize clothes. Many contain chlorine or chlorine compounds (often hypochlorite salts). The manufacture of bleach often produces as waste or by-products mercury and dioxins,

which are bad for the environment. Chlorine bleaches can also leave a dioxin residue in garments, which can accumulate in the body's tissues and are linked to a range of health problems. The sun has a sanitizing and bleaching effect, so, if the weather permits, line dry your clothes. Alternatively, a hot cycle (over 65°C) in the dryer will kill the bacteria that cause smells. Non-chlorine bleaches and soaks can be used to brighten clothes. They will usually use sodium percarbonate or hydrogen peroxide of sodium perborate instead of toxic chlorine compounds.

Avoid optical whiteners / fluorescers.
Optical whiteners are added to laundry products to give clothes that whiter-than-white brightness. They work by coating fabric fibres with white or slightly blue-white substances that reflect more white and so make the clothes look cleaner. They do not remove more dirt; they essentially whitewash it. Similarly, fluorescers work by absorbing ultra-violet light and re-emitting blue light to make the garment appear whiter. Producing and using unnecessary chemicals is not good for the environment, but another cause for concern with these products is that they can cause allergic reactions and skin rashes. People with sensitive skins should definitely avoid them.

Look for the EcoLogo.
Look for products that carry the EcoLogo, the symbol of the Environmental Choice Program. The program places strict requirements on participating manufacturers, limiting the chemicals that are used to make the products, investigating how the products are manufactured and requiring that the cleaning products are readily biodegradable. For more info, visit www.environmentalchoice.ca.

Don't be blinded by science.
Cleaning clothes is actually very simple. Most stains and spills are made up of tiny solid particles (like dirt, for example), water-soluble salts and compounds and/or fats or oils, which will dissolve with the help of detergent. It's all basically animal, mineral or vegetable! Yet advertising would have you believe that it's more complicated than that and that you need enzymes, disinfectants and a range of other additives. Our society's obsession with killing germs is increasing our use of chemicals. The use of unnecessary chemicals is bad for the environment and for people with sensitive skin and allergies. Enzymes, for example, can trigger allergic reactions. For every modern stain remover there is generally an old-fashioned equivalent that is just as effective, usually less toxic, and cheaper.

Avoid synthetic fragrances.
If you have asthma or are sensitive to inhaled scents, avoid added fragrance. The word "fragrance" on a products ingredient list can cover dozens of different chemicals, many of which

can trigger allergic reactions. Synthetic fragrances have been implicated in inhalation allergies. If you like a little bit of fragrance, look for products that are perfumed with plant-derived pure essential oils.

Avoid petroleum-derived ingredients.

Laundry washing liquids and powders often contain detergents or surfactants that are made from petroleum products. Petrochemicals are slow to biodegrade and can cause allergic reactions. Petroleum products are also not renewable. Look for alternatives made with surfactants based on plant oils instead of derived from petroleum oil (sometimes listed as "mineral oil"). These plant-based detergents break down quickly into harmless substances and are made from a renewable resource. Unfortunately, there is a huge range of petrochemical ingredients and it can be hard to spot them on an ingredient list without a chemistry degree. However, products that use plant-oil-based surfactants will often state this clearly on the packaging because it's a selling point. Commonly used plant oils are coconut, palm kernel and corn oils. They may also be listed as "vegetable oil."

Choose concentrated formulations with sensible packaging.

Buy a concentrated product so you need to use only a small amount per wash. This means that you can wash more loads per box or bottle, reducing packaging waste. Also, fewer packages have to be made and transported to

stores, so transport fuel and the associated greenhouse gases are reduced. Wherever possible, choose products with packaging made from materials that are recyclable and recycled in your area (for example, cardboard and some types of plastic). Check with your municipality if you're not sure what's collected in your area.

Choose products formulated to work in cold water.

That way you can capitalize on the energy savings of a cold-water wash, without poor results.

Choose products with a cause.

Some cleaning products assist the environment by helping to raise funds for environmental groups. This happens when a product manufacturer gives a green group some of the profits from sales. Make sure first that the product is a better environmental alternative, as marketers may use greenwashing to make a bad product appear environmentally friendly.

Green cleaners

There are six basic cleaning ingredients for general cleaning that you can buy from your local supermarket for very little money. Many of them form the basic components of much more expensive, heavily marketed cleaning products. Different combinations of these ingredients, along with a little water,

Around 54 000 tonnes of general-purpose cleaners are used in Canadian homes each year.

When using commercial cleaning products, make sure you read the instructions – they are generally written to help you, not annoy you. Many cleaners are unsafe to touch or give off toxic fumes. If the label says to ventilate the room while cleaning – DO IT! If it says to wear gloves or protective clothing – DO IT! If the directions are unclear, call the manufacturer to clarify. Better still, try to find a greener, less harmful alternative.

some elbow grease and perhaps a couple of drops of aromatherapy oil, can replace most of the commercial cleaning products in your laundry or under-the-sink cupboard.

You may have noticed that ominous-sounding phrase "elbow grease." Cleaning does take some degree of effort. How much depends on how long you leave it. In our busy lives, we tend to put off cleaning until the grime can no longer be ignored. By then it has become harder to remove, so we bring in the heavy artillery – the industrial-strength cleaners. Many cleaning products are simply more powerful, more concentrated or more chemically active versions of simple cleaners. Remember that the very properties that make these products effective cleaners for built-up dirt and scum are the same properties that make them harmful to the environment and your health. The key to green cleaning is a little bit of effort often.

The six-piece tool kit (basic ingredients you must have)

Bicarbonate of soda (sodium bicarbonate or baking soda)
Baking soda is abrasive and it softens hard water, so it cleans without scratching. It is also great at absorbing odours and is a mild disinfectant. There are dozens of uses for baking soda, both in cleaning and grooming, so buy it in bulk. For more information on baking soda for beauty, see Green Grooming, page 227.

White vinegar
Like all vinegars, white vinegar is slightly acidic, containing naturally occurring acetic acid. White vinegar dissolves grease, deodorizes and is a mild disinfectant. It is great for cleaning glass and shiny surfaces, so keep some in a labelled spray bottle.

Lemon juice

Lemon juice deodorizes, is a mild bleach, cleans and is mildly acidic. Plus it grows on trees, literally.

Borax

Borax is a mineral found in nature and is usually shelved with other laundry products in the supermarket. Borax cleans, deodorizes, is a mild bleach and a disinfectant and helps to control some household pests. Borax is poisonous if eaten, so keep it out of reach of children and away from pets. Avoid using borax on surfaces where you prepare food. Borax can irritate the skin and eyes, so wear gloves if you have sensitive skin and wear eye protection if you're spraying a solution that contains borax.

Pure soap

Pure soap is a 100% readily bio-degradable general cleaner. It can be bought in bars or flakes but dissolves better in flakes. You can make your own soap flakes by grating a bar of pure soap. Make sure you keep soap flakes dry, as they tend to clump.

Washing soda (sodium carbonate)

Washing soda cuts grease, disinfects, softens water and removes stains.

Similarly to baking soda, it also removes odours. It removes oil, grease and even wax without the fumes that normally go with many of the commercial products sold to do the same job. However, it can irritate the skin, so wear rubber gloves while you're using it.

Optional extras for special jobs

Tea-tree oil is a great natural cleaner and healer. Tea-tree oil disinfects and is antifungal.

Eucalyptus oil is very good at removing fat, grease and all manner of stickiness, as well as being great for relieving colds and the flu. However, eucalyptus oil is poisonous and can kill if swallowed, so keep it out of the reach of children.

Rosewater doesn't really do a lot, but it smells lovely.

Aromatherapy oils are relaxing or invigorating and smell a whole lot better than vinegar. Just pay attention to any precautions accompanying each oil and use as recommended.

Green cleaner hints and recipes

Floors with sealed surfaces

Mix $1/4$ cup of baking soda and $1/2$ cup of vinegar in a bucket. Add warm water

and a few drops of tea-tree oil. Use this solution to mop the floors. This is a great one to do with kids. They'll love the fizz created when the soda and the vinegar mix. A few drops of peppermint and grapefruit oils (or any favourite aromatherapy combination) can be added to freshen up the room and make the job more pleasant.

General-purpose cleaner

Mix 1 teaspoon of baking soda with 1 teaspoon of soap and a squeeze of lemon in $1/4$ litre of water. This is particularly good for cleaning countertops. Use some extra baking soda on difficult spots.

General-purpose spray cleaner

Dissolve 2 teaspoons of borax and 1 heaping teaspoon of soap flakes in 3 cups of water and store in a labelled spray bottle.

General disinfectant

Mix $1/4$ cup borax, $1/4$ cup white vinegar and the juice of half a lemon in hot water.

Dishwasher powder

Most dishwasher powders are formulated to be strong enough to remove baked-on or particularly tough food stains. They are highly toxic powders and should always be kept out of children's reach. However, their cleaning power is wasted on lightly dirty dishes. Instead, put 2 teaspoons of baking soda in the powder tray. For sparkling clean glassware, use a dash of white vinegar as a rinse aid. It really works and is a whole lot cheaper.

Removing smells

Body odour, cigarette smoke and other smells can be reduced or removed from clothing by adding a cup of baking soda to a washing load. You can also put a handful of baking soda into the bottom of your kitchen garbage can or leave an open box in the fridge to control food smells.

Laundry detergent

To make a cheap laundry detergent for lightly soiled loads, thoroughly

Caustic soda confusion

Washing soda is sometimes confused with caustic soda (sodium hydroxide), which is commonly used as a drain and oven cleaner. Caustic soda is corrosive and a very dangerous skin and eye irritant and is not recommended for this reason. Some argue that caustic soda is fine for unclogging drains provided it's used safely, as it reacts to produce fairly harmless salts and can be sufficiently diluted with water. However, these salts are harmful to our freshwater ecosystems. It's much better environmentally to prevent drains from becoming clogged in the first place. Once a week put $1/4$ cup of baking soda down the drain followed by $1/2$ cup of white vinegar. Allow the two to fizz for a couple of minutes, then flush with a few litres of hot water.

dissolve $\frac{1}{2}$ cup of pure soap flakes and $\frac{1}{3}$ cup of washing soda in half a bucket of hot water. Add cool water to fill the bucket and mix well. It will set to form a soft gel. Use two cups per wash in a front-loader, three for a top-loader.

Carpet spills
Sponge off excess liquid, then saturate the remainder with soda water and sponge off again. Generously sprinkle the damp patch with baking soda and allow it to dry. Vacuum the dry baking soda.

Grease and adhesives
Ever noticed the thick grease that collects on top of the range hood or above the stove? This can be removed with paper towels (with recycled content of course!) and eucalyptus oil. Eucalyptus oil is also good for removing the sticky patches left after you've taken off price tags and adhesive labels.

Showers
Soap scum can be cleaned off shower walls and doors using baking soda in the same way you would use a powder cleaner. Once the shower recess is clean, wipe the surfaces with a soft cloth with a little bit of baby oil or almond oil. The fine layer of oil makes it harder for soap scum to adhere to the wall and keeps the surfaces looking shiny. You can also add a favourite essential oil to the oil to fragrance it. Whenever you have a shower, the warm water will help to release the fragrance.

Windows
Clean windows with sprayed vinegar and a rag or old newspaper. If the window is particularly dirty, it may first need a clean with soapy water.

Toilet cleaner
Once a week give the toilet a rinse and quick brush with white vinegar.

Bedding freshener
Freshen up quilts, duvets and blankets on a hot day. Put them on the line in the sun, lightly spray with rosewater, and dry in the sun. This will also air the bedding. The sunlight has a naturally sanitizing effect and the rosewater will give your bedding a delicate fragrance.

Mould
Apply diluted hydrogen peroxide to mould and leave for a few minutes. Wipe away with a damp cloth. As with many cleaners and disinfectants, prevention is better than cure. Prevent mould from forming by regularly airing damp rooms and by using a fan when cooking or showering.

Chemical-free cleaning
From a scientific point of view (without wanting to scare you), most of what we do around the house consists of combinations of tiny physical and chemical reactions. Most of the green cleaners listed so far use a combination of physical and chemical reactions to dissolve grease, remove dirt, neutralize odours and kill germs.

However, some cleaning products have been developed that use few or no chemicals to do their job. The two main types are steam cleaners and fibre-technology products.

Steam cleaners and steam mops are electrical appliances. You fill them with tap water, plug them into a power outlet and give them a few minutes to build up enough heat to produce steam through the cleaning head. As well as cleaning surfaces, the high temperature of the steam sanitizes the surfaces. The most widely available type is a steam mop, such as the Bissell Steam Mop or the DeLonghi Scopa Steam Mop. Some are designed to also steam clean curtains, carpets, mattresses and upholstery. Small, hand-held steam cleaners are available as well.

Advances in fibre technology have brought us chamois cloths that can hold large volumes of water, Lycra that allows aerobics instructors to get really creative, and non-iron cotton, which allows some business-shirt wearers to sleep five minutes longer in the morning. Fibre technology has now produced a range of cloth products designed with cleaning in mind. Cloths have improved cleaning power because they use fibres of varying lengths, sizes and surface textures. Some are designed to pick up and hold dust particles; others are designed to be more abrasive to remove bathroom scum. With many of these products you can control how thoroughly you clean by how wet you make the cloth.

The best cloths and mitts generally don't require the use of detergents. Some particularly stubborn messes may need the help of a little detergent, but nowhere near as much as you would use with a conventional sponge. Mops with specially designed, padded microfibre mop heads are also available.

Pest control

"Control" is the operative word, not extermination!

We share the earth with a whole range of plants and creatures, and we are only just starting to understand the complex relationships between them, and how they are interdependent. We have to keep the creepy crawlies in our homes and gardens under control without harming the environment, other wildlife or our own health by using poisonous pesticides. This chapter looks at pests in the home.

For more information on garden pest control, see Green Garden, pages 170–4.

Traditional pest control involved nuking the pest with vast amounts of insecticides, baits and poisons. During "the golden years of Hollywood," actress Maureen O'Hara was filmed being sprayed with DDT to keep flies away while making a movie on location in Australia. Little did we know then that the poisons that killed the flies and mosquitoes were also killing us.

Poisoning is a chemical means of pest control, but there are alternatives.

The basics of green pest control

Enlist predatory allies. This method lets the animals that eat the pest do the job of keeping their numbers down for you. For example, leave some spiders that aren't harmful to humans (e.g., daddy-long-legs) around to catch flies and other insects.

Be a home-wrecker. Most pests don't like to feel exposed. Limiting the number of sites where they can live or breed will help keep them out of your house. Ventilate your house, as they tend not to like drafts.

Don't feed them. Pests go where there's food, so don't be surprised to get a pest problem if you're in the habit of leaving food out or not cleaning properly. Clean up food spills quickly and avoid eating in bedrooms, particularly if they are carpeted. Keep garbage in bins with well-fitting lids and wash them regularly.

Put up barriers. Physical barriers will help to keep pests out. Block cracks, holes and gaps that allow entry into your house.

Get some chemical help. Some substances are non-toxic to humans but poisonous to pests. Others simply repel them. Strategically place repellents around the house to keep pests away or, if all else fails, use a non-toxic insecticide.

Use brute force. Another option is to kill pests using old-fashioned traps and a trusty fly swatter.

Annoy the hell out of them. There is some evidence to suggest that certain pests don't like particular electrical and magnetic fields.

Be aware of seasonal variation. The pest problem may decline or be cyclical, particularly in the cases of mice, spiders, millipedes and ants.

Pest control tips – critter by critter

Ants

Don't leave out uncovered food or food spills, and wipe out your oven or grill after use. Keep your garbage bins away from the house if possible. Ants also like pet food, so be careful where you place your pet's bowl. Mix something sweet, such as jam or honey, with borax to make an effective ant poison. Put the mixture on small saucers or container lids and place them near ant trails or in cupboards where you have an ant problem. Make sure children know not to eat the mixture, and don't use it if you have small children or pets that may unknowingly eat it. If you find the ants' nest, you can kill the ants and destroy their nest by pouring boiling water into it. Ant-repelling herbs such as pennyroyal, rue or tansy planted in small, strategically placed pots or dried bunches provide a less gruesome way to keep ants away. You can also try to deter them by sprinkling a little cayenne pepper at the points where they enter the house. Mop floors with soapy water with a few drops of peppermint oil to erase the scent trail and deter the ants.

Cockroaches

Keep cockroaches out of the house in the first place by sealing cracks and crevices in walls and openings around pipes. Make sure your doors and windows fit snugly. Cockroaches are repelled by cucumber with the ends cut off, pyrethrum and vanilla beans. Try leaving these in cupboards that regularly get invaded, or wipe them with a little tea-tree, peppermint or citronella oil. Bait cockroaches with sugar laced with 5% borax, but keep this out of the way of children and pets. You can also make a trap using a glass jar, greasing the inside walls and half filling it with beer. The cockroaches won't be able to resist the offer of free beer and will fall into the jar, be unable to escape and drown. At least they'll die happy. If you must use an insecticide, use one based on natural pyrethrum.

Flies

Again, as with most pests, don't leave out food or food scraps, as they attract the flies. Fit screens to your windows and doors to keep them and other insects out of the house. Trap flies using traditional sticky flypaper (available from supermarkets and hardware stores). Sharpen your aim and reflexes by killing flies with a fly swatter. Grow insect-repelling plants such as eau-de-cologne mint or pyrethrum near doors and windows.

Flour beetles

These beetles are small black or reddish-brown specks that infest a range of dry goods, such as dried flowers, flour (as the name suggests) and other dry ingredients, and dry pet food. If you discover an infestation, throw out the affected food or material. Carefully inspect other food products stored in the same cupboard and throw out any other affected products. To be on the safe side, put the remaining food that appears clean into the freezer for a couple of days, as the beetles can't survive temperature extremes. Thoroughly vacuum and wash out the cupboard before restocking it.

Dust mites

Dust mites can cause asthma attacks, but their numbers can be reduced by regularly washing bedding, curtains and upholstery and vacuuming carpets. You may wish to remove carpeting from your house altogether, or at least from the bedrooms. Dust mites are sensitive to extremes in temperature and sunlight. Wash bedding at least once every two weeks in a hot-water wash of at least 55°C (131°F), adding a little eucalyptus oil to the wash cycle and drying outside in the sunlight. Air blankets and duvets in sunlight.

You can make your indoor air quality healthier and you can reduce the likelihood of anyone having an asthma attack in your household by taking measures to reduce dust mite numbers in your home. This is particularly important in the bedrooms of small children. There is evidence that early exposure of infants to allergens such as dust mite feces can contribute to the development of asthma.

Dust mites are sensitive to dry conditions, changes in temperature and sunlight (particularly UV light). This can be used to control them.

Mosquitoes

Summer 2003 saw an outbreak of West Nile virus in North America. This mosquito-borne disease made 142 people sick in Manitoba alone, with two eventually dying from the illness. The presence of the virus in Canada makes the control of mosquitoes – the carriers of the disease – even more important.

Mosquitoes become a particular problem when you've given them some nice still water to breed in, so get rid of stagnant water around the house. Make sure that any buckets or containers left outside are under cover from rain or left upside down, empty your pet's water bowl at the end of each day and refill it instead of just topping it up, and make sure water features in the garden have either moving water or a stock of fish. When you're entertaining outdoors, burn citronella candles to repel mosquitoes. Alternatively, make a personal repellent of one part lavender oil, one part eucalyptus oil, one part pennyroyal oil and three parts of a carrier such as moisturizer or almond oil. Combine well and rub onto exposed skin.

House dust mites hate changes in temperature and particularly cold, dry conditions, so why not give them the cold shoulder? Put soft toys into the freezer for 24 hours to kill dust mites. Dust mites' allergy-causing fecal matter can be removed by washing the toys at any temperature.

Actions to decrease dust mite numbers

>> Keep bedrooms well ventilated and well lit with natural light.
>> Use mattress sheets, duvet covers and pillowcases and regularly clean the covers.
>> Wash sheets, pillowcases and quilts in hot water (at least 55°C or 131°F).
>> Air blankets and duvets weekly, preferably in sunlight.
>> Regularly vacuum mattresses, furniture and drapes as well as carpets.
>> Invest in a vacuum cleaner with strong suction and a good filter system.
>> Dust with a damp cloth instead of a feather duster.
>> Limit the number of open storage areas in the bedroom where dust can collect, such as under the bed, on top of wardrobes and on open bookcases.

Moths

There are a number of natural fragrances that humans enjoy but that moths will avoid. Make muslin sachets of dried lavender, orange peel (or a combination of citrus peels), rosemary, cloves and mint and place them in your linen cupboard and drawers and hang them in your wardrobe. Lavender and rosemary are both quite relaxing scents, so place muslin bags of these in with your bed linens. Eucalyptus oil and Epsom salts also repel moths.

The natural oils in cedar are also great for keeping away moths and other insects, which is partly why it has been used in the past to make hope chests. Small balls made from cedar are also available to use in place of moth balls. For more information on why not to use moth balls, see The Green Bedroom, page 110.

Rodents

Keep benches and cupboards free from spilled or exposed food. Make sure food such as cereals, flour and chocolate (not surprisingly, a favourite with mice) is kept in sealed containers. Check your walls and floors for gaps through which rodents may be entering. Seal the gaps: steel wool makes a good unfriendly interim measure. Use old-fashioned mousetraps instead of poison to kill mice. Poison is more harmful to the environment and toxic for children and pets. Bait the mousetrap with a small bit of chocolate or peanut butter rather than cheese. It's much more effective.

Silverfish

Silverfish like warm, damp conditions, such as around pipes that carry warm water. Regularly vacuum such areas to remove food particles and silverfish eggs. You can also catch them in homemade traps. Simply wrap clear or masking tape around the outside of a glass jar to provide a surface that silverfish can grip to. They will climb up the sides and fall into the jar but will be unable to climb the smooth inside of the jar to escape. Trapped silverfish can either be let out outside (away from the house) or drowned in soapy water.

Spiders

Good weatherstripping and window and door caulking will help to keep spiders out in the first instance. Regularly clear cobwebs indoors. Get to know spiders to find out which ones you want and which ones you don't, as there are a number of beneficial spiders that can help you to keep other pests at bay. For this reason it is unwise to try to completely eradicate spiders from your property. Health Canada has a website with useful information about spiders commonly found in Canada, at www.house-spider.ca.

FOR A GREENER LAUNDRY ROOM:

INVEST in water-efficient appliances.

BUY green cleaning alternatives.

AVOID dry cleaning.

USE natural pest control.

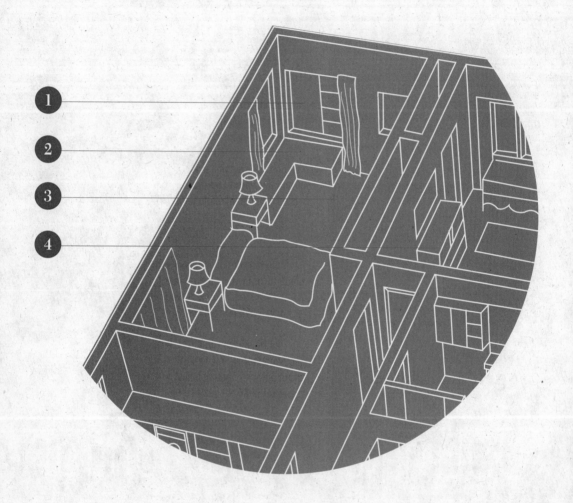

1 Insulating window coverings
2 Organic cotton cover
3 Green flooring
4 Good timber

>> The green bedroom

Our home is our sanctuary from the rest of the world, somewhere to return to after a hard day at the office or a big night out. The bedroom is the ultimate refuge, the place where we spend around eight hours each day sleeping, dreaming and recharging our batteries.

Sleep is vital for both our physical health and our mental well-being. Adequate sleep helps us to perform better during the day, to be more alert and responsive. It also helps us to recover from injury and illness and to remain in good health. A lack of sleep or a poor night's sleep can make it hard for us to concentrate, can impair our memory, can reduce our libido, can exacerbate depression and can even lead to accidents on the road and in the workplace.

While we're in deep sleep, our metabolism slows down, our temperature drops slightly and our body restores itself. This time is so important to our general health. It's vital that we give our bodies a healthy environment to perform this important function. We can do this by making sure that our bedrooms, bedroom furniture and bedding are made from healthy fibres, that dust and indoor air pollutants are kept to a minimum, that the air is kept clean and fresh and that the room is free from unhealthy radiation. While we're focusing on this inner refuge, let's not forget about the outer environment. We can also choose furniture, bedding and clothing made from materials that are better for the health of our planet.

Furniture

Good sleep starts with a good bed. Choosing the right one is important, as you'll spend around a third of your life in bed. Most modern beds are one of two basic types: mattress and base ensembles or slat beds. Futons are effectively a kind of slat bed. Depending on the design, slat beds are preferable to ensembles, as ensembles use more materials to manufacture and don't allow air to circulate under the mattress.

Choosing bedroom furniture

Choose beds that are made from sustainable or recycled materials, FSC-certified timber or plantation timber. The same applies to any furniture you are buying. Avoid furniture made from timber that comes from old-growth forests or endangered timber species. Recycled timber furniture is becoming more popular and widely available. For example, European manufacturer Ethnicraft use recycled teak from demolished warehouses in Java, Indonesia. Reclaimed timber that hasn't been retreated has the added benefit of having had time to outgas any fumes that might trigger allergic reactions or produce poor indoor air quality.

Look for furniture that is made from timber certified to the standards designated by the Forest Stewardship Council (FSC). Don't be afraid to ask where the timber comes from. You'll find that if a company has a good environmental record, they'll be very forthcoming with the information. Some furniture makers, such as Ikea, even have their own plantations where they grow some of the timber for their products. Ikea also sources some of the timber for its products from FSC-certified suppliers. Even if a furniture company doesn't use an environmentally preferred timber source, your act of asking the source of its timber will encourage it to change its sources. For more info about timber choices and FSC certification, visit www.certifiedwood.org and www.fsccanada.org.

Avoid "alternative" wood composites. These include fibreboard (MDF), particleboard and plywood. They can contain large amounts of adhesives and formaldehyde, which emit gas and pollute indoor air – not good if you have breathing sensitivities. These materials are also sometimes made from sawmill waste from old-growth forest products.

Look at second-hand or antique furniture. Second-hand trade gives you the option to turn someone else's trash into your treasure. Second-hand furniture pieces can have unusual designs that aren't commonly available. Older particleboard or treated wood furniture will also have lost most of its gas pollutants. However, check old painted furniture for paint containing lead.

Choose your mattress carefully.
Mattresses come in two types, those with springs and those with stuffing. Spring mattresses have an inner spring unit with layers of padding attached. Mattresses without springs can be filled with a wide range of materials, including synthetic foam and wool.

Avoid mattresses made from synthetic foam. These mattresses emit formaldehyde and other chemical gases, which you don't want to be inhaling while asleep. Ideally, look for mattresses made or covered with natural fibres, such as cotton or wool. They can be expensive and hard to obtain, but they are available. Willow Natural Home and Nature's Bedding are two Canadian manufacturers that make natural rubber "stuffed" mattresses and inner-spring mattresses with organic cotton and wool covers. Natural fibres are more widely available in bed linens, so you can have more control over what's up against your skin. If you do get a mattress made with synthetic fibres, let it air for a few days before putting it onto your bed. Then, each time you change the bed linens, leave the mattress to air uncovered for a few hours with the bedroom window open.

Bedding

When we talk about bedding, we're really talking about fabric. Many people will find this hard to swallow, but the fact that something is "natural" doesn't necessarily mean that it's "environmentally friendly." This is true of fabrics and textiles. Natural fibres are often better from a health perspective, but they can still adversely affect the environment in the way they're made.

It's estimated that a quarter of all insecticides used globally each year are used to make non-organic cotton – that's 25% of insecticides used on only around 3% of the world's crops.

Greener bedding options

Organic cotton bed linen is an alternative that is less harmful to the environment. Global concern for soil and land use along with pesticides and chemical fertilizers has led to a boom in organic farming. Cotton crops are thirsty and prone to pests, so they need large amounts of water and pesticides. Organic cotton bedding is now becoming available, through a few select sources.

Conventional cotton doesn't take dye well. If you're looking at buying cotton products, then, as a rough guide, darker-coloured bed linen will have needed more chemicals to dye the fabric and fix the dye. The dyeing process also produces polluted wastewater. On the plus side, however, cotton is fairly easy to care for and generally doesn't need dry cleaning. As well as making organic cotton bedding, many alternative bedding companies also offer undyed conventional cotton bedding.

**Warmer with wool
– above and below**

Many people wonder why they're cold even with extra blankets and quilts piled high on top of them. Extra bedding on top stops heat loss from that side of your body, but it doesn't stop the heat lost from underneath your body. Don't forget to insulate underneath as well as on top by using a wool underlay, extra blankets and/or a thicker mattress protector underneath the sheet covering your mattress.

Hemp is a strong, durable fibre and a fast-growing crop. Hemp crops have few pests and need less water and fewer pesticides than conventional cotton crops. One of the other benefits of hemp fibre is that it holds dye very well, unlike cotton, so hemp fabric can be dyed in a wide range of vibrant colours using less dye and associated chemicals in the dyeing process. Hemp has had a little bit of bad (or in some cases, good) PR, because of the association with marijuana use. Agricultural hemp, however, has negligible amounts of the narcotic tetrahydrocannabinol (THC), which is what gives marijuana its more recreational properties. Canada's ban on hemp farming was finally lifted in March 1998 after 50 years, opening opportunities for local hemp production. Hemp crops can be used to make a range of products, from bedding to hemp oil to cosmetics to rope and string. You can even get hemp ice cream.

Wool can help you to reduce your greenhouse emissions even though sheep farming and wool scouring do have an impact on the environment. Wool is very effective at retaining heat. Using wool blankets on your bed will take away the need to use additional space heating in your bedroom.

Generally avoid synthetics. More energy is needed to produce synthetic fibres than natural fibres. Also, because they are sourced from petroleum, of which there is a limited supply, they are not a renewable product in the long term. Like all petrochemical products, they do take a toll on the environment and contribute to the greenhouse effect. They are also more flammable than natural fibres and tend to be less absorbent and to emit small amounts of air-polluting fumes.

Clothing

Traditionally, the fashion industry has shied away from environmental issues. Fashion is one of the obvious features of our throwaway society. The plain truth is that the more strongly trend-oriented a label is, the more it will want you to buy a garment, wear it to death for six months and replace it with a newer fashion the next season.

Fortunately, the fashion industry is starting to improve. The eco-chic trend is growing right across the clothing industry, from mainstream casual fashion to active sportswear to designer labels. For example, Levi-Strauss has purchased over 330 000 pounds of organic cotton for its 501 jeans, and Nike is increasing its use of organic cotton and is blending it with conventional cotton. Giorgio Armani himself – fashion's emperor of upscale good taste – is using hemp in some of his clothing ranges.

Tips for your wardrobe

Less is more
Why do we always find ourselves with a wardrobe full of clothes and nothing to wear? These wardrobes are often full of cheap, fashionable impulse purchases that are now out of fashion or so poorly made that they haven't stayed in good condition. Any wardrobe consultant, whether environmentally aware or not, will tell you that it's better to buy a few well-made, basic garments with your hard-earned dollar than an armload of statement-making fashion pieces.

Go for alternative fibres
Look for garments made from organic cotton or hemp fibre and help to create a market for farmers who grow these greener crops.

Buy garments with easy care instructions

Dry cleaning leaves residual solvents in the garment that emit into the air at home, contributing to unhealthy, poor indoor air quality. Wherever possible, avoid buying "dry clean only" garments.

Share and share alike
Swap and share clothes with friends who have similar tastes and are a similar size. This swap system falls down only when someone fails to look after the clothes they borrow, returns them with obvious stains or forgets to return borrowed items promptly.

Buy recycled
Some polar-fleece clothes are made from plastic recycled from soft-drink-bottle plastic. Look out for garments made from fabrics marketed as Synchilla, Ecospun, PCR or Ecofleece, such as Patagonia's wide PCR range. Hempop, a recycled plastic and hemp blend fabric, is also available.

Buy second-hand

You can get some great retro clothing for a fraction of the price from charity stores and recycled-clothing boutiques. Buying second-hand clothes and other products makes better use of our resources and reduces the amount of waste being sent to landfill. When the second-hand store is run by a charity, the money you spend there goes to a worthy cause. You never know – you may even unearth a valuable vintage designer original.

Look after your clothes

You can keep your clothes looking newer for longer just by looking after them. Wear old clothes when you're doing housework or other grubby activities, do the fifties housewife thing and wear an apron to protect your clothes while cooking, use a front-loading washing machine (because it's gentler on clothes than a top-loader) and get minor tears or holes mended.

A healthy bedroom environment

It's all very well and good to get rid of the dirt, dust and grime that we can see. However, there are some things we can't see that can make the air unclean and our homes unhealthy. Our homes, and particularly our bedrooms, can contain odourless and colourless gases and airborne particles that can enter our bodies and cause illness or irritate our lungs and trigger asthma and allergies. Our houses' electrical wiring and the many gadgets the wires feed all produce small electromagnetic fields (EMFs). These can also adversely affect our health. Improving the air quality and minimizing EMF pollution in the bedroom will prevent unhealthy exposure eight hours a night.

>>

Moth-proof your wardrobe

There's nothing worse than pulling on a garment while you're in a hurry to get dressed and finding that it's been moth-eaten. In the past, the unpleasant alternative was to fill your wardrobe with smelly moth balls. Luckily, moth balls have gone out of fashion, as they are not a good green alternative for pest control. They are a petroleum-derived product made with a cocktail of synthetic chemicals, including the suspected carcinogen para-dichlorobenzene. They also bear an unfortunate resemblance to mints and so should never be left where a child might find them and eat them.

There are natural alternatives to moth balls. Cedar contains natural oils that repel insects. You can buy cedar balls to replace moth balls. You can put sweaters and spare bedding into old-fashioned hope chests made from cedar. You can also fill small muslin bags with dried herbs that repel moths. Use a combination of dried lavender, orange peel, rosemary and mint and hang it in your wardrobe. You may like to keep a spare sachet of lavender and rosemary near your bed, as these scents are relaxing fragrances.

Plants that clean the air

Bring the outdoors indoors! It's good feng shui and will help to make your sleep sweeter and healthier. All of these plants help to clean the air:

>> Aloe vera
>> Happy plant (*Dracaena varieties*)
>> Peace lily (*Spathiphyllum varieties*)
>> Gerbera
>> Chrysanthemum
>> Kentia palm (*Howea forsteriana*)
>> Butterfly or golden cane palm (*Chrysalidocarpus lutescens*)
>> Spider plant (*Chlorophytum comosum*)
>> Rubber plants
>> Aspidistra
>> Boston fern

Indoor air quality

Recent years have seen dramatic increases in asthma, allergies and multiple chemical sensitivities in people of all ages. Our modern lifestyle exposes us to a huge range of substances, while our hours spent indoors result in constant low-level exposure to indoor air pollutants. It's important that we protect our health by taking steps to provide clean air to breathe inside our homes. You can do this in three steps:

1. Prevent indoor air pollution.
2. Ventilate to remove pollutants.
3. Dehumidify to remove excess moisture.

Indoor air pollution comes from a variety of sources.

Gas pollutants are emitted by dry-cleaned clothes and the materials that some beds, furniture and mattresses are made from. Carpets, plastic products, clothes, books and other printed materials, foam insulation and small electrical goods can also release gas pollutants, including volatile organic compounds (VOCs). Try to minimize the amount of these products that you have in the room where you sleep. New homes, renovated or freshly painted rooms, or those containing new furniture or other products that emit gas should be thoroughly ventilated as often as possible for the first few months after you get them. Some building materials outgas a lot more VOCs and other pollutants than others, so factor this into your choices when building or renovating. As well as ventilating, keep a few potted plants in your bedroom. You can choose indoor plant varieties that have been shown to cut indoor air pollutants significantly.

Combustion gases from gas, propane, oil, kerosene and LPG heating and cooking are less of a problem in the bedroom than they are in the kitchen and living room. However, all indoor air pollutants can diffuse through the house, so remember to ventilate all rooms. Backdrafting from fireplaces can also put fine combustion particles and gases into indoor air. This occurs when unbalanced ventilation creates a pressure difference between the air outside and inside the home. The result is that air blows down the chimney, through the fireplace and into the room instead of flowing up the chimney. This can be avoided by choosing the right ventilation system for your house.

Cigarette smoke, unfiltered and passively smoked, is worse than the smoke drawn through the filter by the smoker. Smoking is bad enough for your health on its own. Avoid smoking in bed as well or you'll passively smoke the remaining fumes. Smoking in bed is also a major cause of household fires.

Toiletries, pesticides, paints and cleaners should all have limited use in the bedroom. This includes perfumed toiletries and spray deodorants. Use them in the bathroom, where you spend only short periods of time. Use only low-fume or green cleaners in the bedroom. Avoid using pesticides in the bedroom altogether, particularly children's bedrooms. Pests generally follow food, so you can prevent them from coming into the bedroom by making a general rule of not eating in the bedroom.

Airborne particles, particularly fine solid ones, can get in your lungs and irritate them. Take care when using powdered products or dusting in the bedroom. It's better to use body powder in the bathroom.

Natural pollutants are biological sources of irritants, such as dust mites, moulds and other fungi. Mould and fungi can be avoided by preventing a buildup of moisture inside. If you find that condensation forms on your windows on cold mornings, there's a good chance that your room isn't adequately ventilated. Make sure you air the room regularly and clean away any patches of mould that start to form.

Ventilation

Ventilation is the elimination of stale, moist air and indoor air pollutants from inside the house, replacing it with "fresh" air from outside the house. In recent years our homes have become much more airtight in an effort to reduce heat loss in winter. Cutting drafts from outdoors has also reduced a passive source of fresh air, making ventilation even more important. The National Building Code of Canada now requires that new homes include a mechanical ventilation system with a minimum capacity of one-third of an air change per hour. This means that one-third of the total volume of air in the home is replaced by outside air every hour.

Things to keep in mind when purchasing a ventilation system:
• Choose the right size range for your home's needs.

• Choose the option that is the quietest, most energy efficient and best performer within the chosen size range. The US-based Home Ventilation Institute (HVI) has a rating and certification program recognized as a method of assuring performance by the R-2000 Building Program and the National Building Code of Canada. Look on product labels for HVI ratings and compare noise levels and energy efficiency. More info: www.hvi.org.

• When installing, place the exhaust hood where moisture won't cause problems for exterior surfaces.

• If you have appliances with chimneys, make sure that the operation of your ventilator won't cause the associated appliances to backdraft.

Where indoor air is referred to as "stale," outside air is often referred to as "fresh" or "clean." But what if you live in an area with high air pollution? In such cases you may wish to also invest in an electronic air filter or air purifier, particularly if you're an allergy sufferer. Their noiseless operation allows people to keep the filter in their bedrooms, providing healthier sleep. Look for newer HEPA (high-efficiency particulate arrester) filtering systems. Unlike earlier systems commonly used, they do not produce ozone, require no cleaning and improve rather than lose their efficiency over time.

Controlling humidity

When you consider that our bodies are around 65% water, blood is 82% water and the lungs are 90% water, it's no surprise that our bodies need some moisture in the air to ensure our comfort. However, too much moisture is also a problem. Air that is too damp can also irritate skin and nasal passages. Humid indoor air can also cause condensation on windows and water damage to soft furnishings, promote the growth of mould and even rot wood.

Tips for excess moisture prevention:

• First check whether you have adequate ventilation. If you don't have a mechanical ventilation system and you suffer from asthma or allergies, chances are that your health and moisture problems may both be eased by investing in an energy-efficient ventilator.

• Use a bathroom fan to remove steam moisture from baths and showers. A good-quality, energy-efficient model will do so while reducing heat loss from the house.

• Air your house on dry, hot days rather than in muggy weather.

• Check for leaking pipes and water fixtures. Repair leaks promptly.

• Have clothes dryers vented to the outside air if indoor moisture is a problem.

• Poor site drainage on your property can contribute to moisture problems. Grade the soil so that water naturally flows away from your house, aided by gravity.

• Cracks in basement floors and walls can allow moisture from groundwater in. Repair and seal them promptly.

• If your cooking methods are producing a lot of steam, use a range exhaust fan. However, a too powerful or poorly designed model, as with a bathroom fan, may exhaust too much warm air from inside the house in cold weather, increasing the need for heating.

Humidity can be controlled to keep the relative humidity inside your house at an ideal level of below 50% in summer and 30% in winter. You can check your home's humidity with a hygrometer, which costs around $10 for a mechanical model and up to $60 for an electronic model. If your best efforts aren't keeping moisture under control, then you will need a dehumidifier.

Electromagnetic pollution (EMF fields)

One of the features of a flowing electrical current is that it creates a small magnetic field around it. The larger the current is, the bigger the electromagnetic field (EMF).

Recently there have been concerns that living very close to high-voltage power lines can increase the risk of childhood leukemia, though research so far hasn't been conclusive. This has led to concerns about the safety of EMF pollution from smaller electric currents, such as those related to the electrical appliances in our homes. EMFs have been linked with higher incidences of headaches, high blood pressure and stress. Some studies have linked EMF exposure to childhood cancer, though Health Canada's investigations into these studies have found the evidence weak. The full effects of EMF pollution may be felt only over a long period of low-level exposure, which is hard to experiment with in a laboratory. We are the first generations to live surrounded by such unnatural levels of EMFs, so it may be a while before we can be certain of their effects. The International Agency for Research on Cancer has classified ELF (extremely low-frequency) magnetic fields as "possibly carcinogenic" to humans based on studies of childhood cancer.

In the meantime, err on the side of caution and make sure that you reduce EMF sources near where you sleep. EMFs can pass through walls, so take into account the electrical devices that are on the other side of your bedroom walls. Think about the head of each bed in the house and make sure that none is on the other side of the wall of an electricity meter or fuse boxes or television sets.

FOR A GREENER BEDROOM:

CHOOSE sustainable materials.

AIR bedding regularly.

CARE for your clothes.

CLEAN the air with plants.

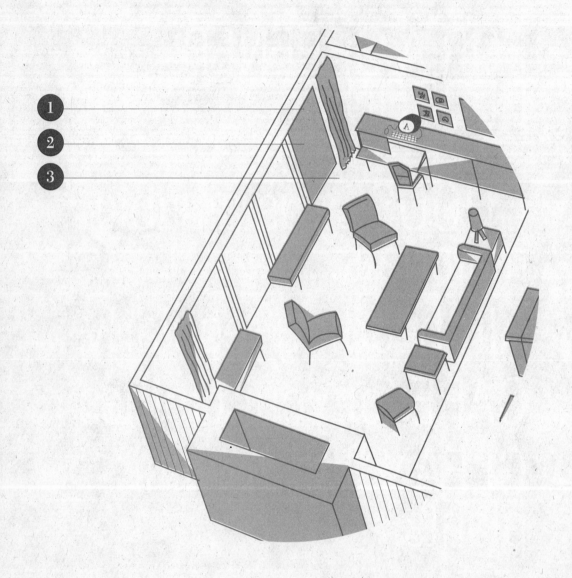

1   Energy-efficient computer
2   Green window coverings
3   Green flooring

>> The green office

You can make small changes to your lifestyle so that you live more lightly on the earth at home, so you can certainly do the same at work. It's even easier to make a difference if you have an office at home, where you are in control.

If you are employed outside the home, don't leave your values on the doorstep when you leave for work – while you may not be in a decision-making position, you can certainly contribute to a healthier workplace and healthier planet by looking at your own working habits and making small changes to the way you do things.

There are so many different kinds of workplace that it's hard to make environmentally helpful suggestions that apply across the board, but there are a few common elements, most of which relate to administrative tasks and energy consumption.

All businesses have some form of administration and paperwork, and they all use resources, produce waste and ultimately affect the environment. Many of us have made attempts at creating a paperless office and have looked into recycling office wastepaper and buying copy paper with recycled content, but there are other green issues in the average office, including energy use, water use and the core business practices themselves.

If you work at home, you have control over the way you work.

How to green up your office

The first step to greening up your office is to conduct an environmental review, taking a good look at the equipment used, the way people work and the purchases made for the business. Then decide what changes need to be made and set about making them happen. If you are your own boss, go for it!

No matter how small your home office is, you will have activities, areas or products that have an environmental implication. Issues surrounding lighting, heating, cooling and cleaning are the same as those for the green house.

Over 6 out of 10 Canadian households have a computer and over half use the Internet at home. Computers and monitors account for around 7% of electricity use in the average office. Other electronic equipment, heating, lighting, cooling, ventilation and kitchen appliances in the staff room also consume electricity.

Office consumables include copy paper, toilet paper, assorted stationery, lightbulbs, toner and ink cartridges, floppy disks, CD-ROMs and other products. All of these consume energy, raw materials and sometimes water in their manufacture. Some use these resources unsustainably. These products also end up as waste.

Office equipment (fax machines, photocopiers, computers, computer peripherals, printers, telephone and answering machine systems, any audiovisual equipment and paper shredders) uses electricity with the effects previously mentioned. Many of these devices use consumable products, such as ink cartridges, blades and disks, which can contribute to waste.

Office furniture uses material resources in its manufacture and can also give off gas pollutants, leading to poor indoor air quality.

The environmental impacts in all of these areas can be minimized through simple changes to the way we work and the products we buy.

Paper products and use

For those who control the office purse strings, paper represents a big cost. To the more green-minded, paper production uses a lot of energy and water, has often been bleached, pollutes waterways and is often based on virgin fibre from woodchips. The more paper an office uses, the higher the dollar costs and the environmental costs. To cut down these costs:

• Use e-mail instead of paper to send memos.
• Set up a filing system within your e-mail program and regularly make backups, instead of printing paper copies and filing them in filing cabinets.
• Where given a choice, subscribe to the electronic versions of newsletters, rather than the printed versions.
• Get your printing estimates right. Printing extra copies of literature only wastes paper, costs more money and takes up more storage space.

• Proofread and spell-check your documents onscreen. As a rule, make sure you at least run a spell-check before printing a document. Use the "track changes" function in word-processing programs to make editing notes.

• Where possible, avoid using cover pages when sending faxes.

• Set your printer and photocopier to print double-sided.

• Reuse paper that's printed on only one side to make notepaper or for printing draft documents. Keep a separate tray or bin for it next to your printer or photocopier.

• Reuse envelopes if presentation-quality envelopes aren't needed.

• Recycle paper that has been printed on both sides. Also recycle envelopes, newspapers, magazines and other paper products. Leave out self-carbonating paper as it contaminates the recycled product.

The paper you choose is as important as how you use it. The two main considerations are the fibre content and the way it is (or isn't) bleached. Ideally, aim to purchase paper made from recycled waste or sustainable alternative fibres, such as hemp or sugar-cane waste. There's nothing wrong with paper made from wood pulp, as long as the wood comes from sustainably managed timber plantations, not old-growth forests. There does need to be some virgin fibre used at some stage, as paper cannot be infinitely recycled. Eventually the fibre disintegrates.

However, paper does not need to contain 100% new, high-quality fibre. The bulk of timber grown in plantations should be used in building and furniture, where the structural strength of hardwoods is needed.

Look out for the following when purchasing office paper:

• Avoid papers that have been bleached with chlorine. Instead use varieties that are oxygen-bleached or unbleached.

Note that "manila" folders and envelopes are generally bleached then dyed to give them their colour. They are generally not unbleached products.

• Look for papers that have a high, preferably 100% recycled content. Remember that recycling still uses some resources. Buying recycled-content paper products does not justify overconsuming them.

• To be truly "recycled," office papers with recycled content should be made largely from recycled "post-consumer" waste – wastepaper that has been used at least once by consumers, after which it is collected and sorted. Pre-consumer waste is often offcuts from the production of other virgin papers or sawmill waste, which is essentially virgin pulp. Some of this may come from old-growth forests.

• Avoid papers made from plantation fibre from unknown sources. They're likely to come from poorly managed plantations in Indonesia, Thailand or Brazil.

• Look for paper products that are EcoLogo or Forest Stewardship Council (FSC) certified.

Screen savers

Screen savers do NOT save energy. They simply prevent a static image from being "burned" into the monitor's screen.
Use monitor sleep and hard-drive sleep modes to reduce energy use automatically when your computer is left unattended for a given length of time.

• For help with finding environmentally preferred papers, visit the Conservatree website (www.conservatree.org). Conservatree is a not-for-profit organization aiming to conserve resources and ancient forests by facilitating environmentally sound paper choices. Its website has a detailed listing of the eco-papers available, with detailed information about each including the content, whether or not it is chlorine-free or acid-free, the weights and finishes available and more.

• Look for recycled content and forest-friendly tissue products for your office, too. Greenpeace Canada's "Ancient Forest Friendly Tissue Products" shopping guide lists over 150 toilet paper, facial tissue, paper towel and paper napkin products available in Canada and whether or not each product is ancient-forest-friendly. The guide is available online at www.greenpeace.ca/tissue.

Equipment

Office equipment is one of the biggest drains of electricity in a home office. You can reduce this energy consumption by buying new appliances and equipment that have met the ENERGY STAR initiative requirements. For more information, see page 11. ENERGY STAR–qualified office equipment can reduce your work-related energy bills by over 50% by utilizing sleep modes and other energy-saving functions. The ENERGY STAR initiative can apply to fax machines, computers, monitors, scanners, photocopiers, printers and home entertainment equipment. With some ENERGY STAR–qualified devices, it's worth checking that the energy-saving features are enabled when you first use them. The following tips on how to use your office equipment will save even more energy.

Computers

• Monitors use most of the power when your computer is on. When you shut down your computer, make sure the monitor is off as well.

• Laptops can use up to 90% less energy than desktop computers. Depending on your budget and the way you use computers, consider a laptop instead of a desktop computer.

• Internal devices, such as modems or CD-ROM drives, are generally more efficient than external devices because internal devices run off your computer's own power supply. External devices generally have separate power connections.

- Remember when buying a monitor that the larger the screen is, the more energy it will consume.
- Remember to turn the printer off rather than leave it on standby.
- Inkjet printers use up to 95% less energy than laser printers.
- Share printers in an office environment, rather than having one for each computer.
- Save paper by using print preview functions to see whether you need to change some of the page setup or layout.

Photocopiers

- Photocopiers use huge amounts of energy, so choose the smallest size that will meet your needs.
- Choose photocopiers that can print double-sided.
- Check that the photocopier you buy can use recycled-content copy paper.
- Photocopiers run more efficiently when they print large amounts, so do photocopying in batches. For a small number of copies, use your printer or fax instead.

Fax machines

- Buy a plain-paper inkjet fax instead of a thermal fax machine.
- Consider buying a printer and fax machine in one, particularly for small offices or home offices. There are also models that act as scanners in addition to the other functions.
- Avoid using cover pages. Instead use a Post-it note on the first page for "attention to" notes.
- Fax modems are also available. These allow you to send electronic documents as faxes directly without having to first print them.

Electricity leakage

Standby wattage and energy leakage are issues in most parts of the house, and a home office is no

Electricity leakage
If you want to turn certain equipment off at the power outlet at night to prevent energy wastage, mark the different power cords or plugs with coloured dot stickers. Use a different colour for the equipment that should be left on so that you don't confuse them.
If some power outlets are hard to get at, consider plugging into a more accessible power bar. Plug-in timers can also be put into power outlets.

exception. Remember that some electrical appliances connected to the power outlet still draw small but continuous amounts of electricity when they're in standby mode or even when they're turned off.

Some equipment needs to stay connected and turned on 24 hours a day. This includes the kitchen refrigerator, fax machines, telephone systems and answering machines, and some kinds of photocopiers (which have a small electric element to prevent moisture from building up inside). However, other equipment can be turned off at the wall at night and over weekends to reduce the costs of electricity leakage.

Lighting

The same lighting principles that apply to your home apply to the office. As it's unlikely that you'll have office lights with dimmer controls, it's worth replacing all incandescent bulbs with compact fluorescent lightbulbs, preferably those that are ENERGY STAR–qualified. The continuous lighting for long periods typical of an office is ideal for using compact fluorescents. They last longer if used in blocks of six hours or more, instead of being frequently switched on and off. Use incandescent bulbs for storerooms, which are lit only for occasional, brief periods.

Do all that you can to bring natural light into your home office. It will lift your spirits and, what's more, it's free. If you can, choose office space with large windows. If you're renovating to

accommodate a home office, consider installing solar light tubes to bring daylight into areas away from windows. Increasing the use of natural light through these tubes and using more energy-efficient artificial lighting have the added benefit of generating less heat than traditional lighting. In summer this will make your office a more comfortable place.

Purchasing

Green purchasing aims to make a company truly "eco," by balancing the considerations of both ecology and economy.

Organizations such as the Buy Recycled Business Alliance (BRBA) in the US and government initiatives such as the Environmental Choice program are encouraging businesses to put their purchasing dollar behind products containing recycled content. This is helping to drive the demand for recycled products, which in turn helps to make North America's recycling industries more financially viable. For example, BBRA member companies support recycling by implementing purchasing policies in their operations that give preference to products with recycled content.

No matter how small your business is, you can adopt a purchasing policy and extend it to include energy-efficient products, products with lower chemical content, greenhouse-friendly products and products made from alternative green fibres, as well as recycled products. The reduced energy costs from buying energy-rated products and energy-efficient lightbulbs will save quite a bit of money. When it comes to energy, being green can keep you out of the red. Consider reinvesting these savings back into the environment by using the money to subsidize the sometimes higher cost of environmentally preferred cleaning products and recycled-content papers.

The money saved can also be put toward switching to a greener source of power.

For further information on green power, see pages 6–7. At first glance it might seem crazy to spend more money for electricity than you have to. However, choosing energy from special environmental programs does create business benefits and opportunities as well as helping the environment.

If you sign up for a green-power electricity product, you can:
• Position your company as a good corporate citizen.
• Gain a leading "green" edge over your competitors.
• Incorporate it into a broader environmental policy.
• Advertise your use of green power in your marketing communications. If the green electricity product you

purchase is accredited by the Environmental Choice program, you may be able to use the EcoLogo in your marketing.
• Count your company's reduced greenhouse gas contributions as Emission Reduction Credits (ERCs). This may help meet emissions targets required by legislation or by voluntary environmental programs, such as the Voluntary Challenge and Registry Program.
• Improve your environmental performance rating, with the potential to be included in environmentally screened or socially responsible investment funds.

A list of some of the Canadian utilities offering green electricity is included in Further Information, page 280. Friends of the Earth Canada is running a Green Energy campaign, encouraging individuals and businesses in particular to purchase green electricity. Its website has useful information about green electricity procurement and a number of case studies of businesses already using green energy to power their companies. Visit www.foecanada.org for more information.

>>

Basements in business

If working from home is an option, consider putting wasted space in the basement to work. It costs around $6000–$8000 for a moderate conversion from a 150 square foot (14 m₂) basement to a home office. If you were previously driving to work, think of the fuel costs you will save and the extra time to sleep in.

The Organisation for Economic Co-operation and Development (OECD) predicts that global paper consumption will have grown by around 77% by 2020.

Waste management

Offices generate waste through the use of paper, other stationery products and goods with packaging.

The computer age brought with it the potential for the paperless office, but some people still prefer hard copies of some documents. This may be for storage, security or legal reasons or where documents are being sent to people who do not have the facilities to read an electronic document. Sometimes it's just because people don't like to change their habits.

There are now many established businesses producing a market for recycling post-consumer office paper. 50% to 80% of the waste produced by offices is recyclable paper. Many paper-recycling companies comment that it is difficult to get reliable clean supplies of recycled feedstock, but say that the quality of paper from offices and manufacturers is much higher than from household recycling collections.

Some waste management and recycling companies in Canada provide free or low-cost collection services for white office paper, which is then recycled. Some also collect cardboard and newspapers. If you work from home and produce a relatively small amount of paper waste, you might be able to include it with other paper in blue box or other local recycling collections. Check with your municipal government to clarify what it collects. Some municipalities also have drop-off points to which larger quantities of paper waste can be taken, usually at waste transfer stations.

Larger businesses are probably already paying waste disposal costs. Such companies can have recycling built into their waste management contracts. If you first reduce the amount of waste your organization produces, you can dramatically cut your waste disposal costs.

Other office recycling

Paper isn't the only material in a business environment that can be recycled.

Cellphone recycling

did you know...

Cellphones and their batteries can be recycled to extract a range of marketable materials, including:

>> nickel – this is used in the production of stainless steel

>> cadmium – a component used in new batteries

>> plastics – used in furniture and to heat the furnaces to extract the metals

>> small amounts of gold and copper

Recycling around 50 000 cellphones recovers 1.5 kg of gold.

Cellphones and their **batteries** should never be sent to landfill. Cellphone batteries contain the heavy metal cadmium, which can leach into groundwater and threaten environmental health. The good news is that cellphones and their batteries can now be recycled in Canada through a number of reuse, recycling and charitable collections. For example, Bell Mobility has launched the Recycle, Reuse, Redial program, in which around 40% of cellphones donated are refurbished and reused, with the remaining 60% recycled, recovering the component materials. Of those reused, some are donated to Canadian charities and others are sold overseas. People with unwanted cellphones can drop them off at participating Bell World or Espace Bell outlets. There are also a handful of other commercial and charitable cellphone-recycling programs.

Printer cartridges (laser and inkjet) and **toner** bottles can be refilled, re-inked, re-manufactured or recycled. They should not be sent to landfill, as toner and ink can contain cadmium, carbon black and a range of other potentially hazardous materials. As a general rule, inkjet cartridges can't be remanufactured, but certain models of toner cartridge can. Some cartridge brands have collection programs for their product, including collection bins in stores and mail-back programs. Visit the website or call the customer service number of the brand you are using and ask if they take their cartridges back. For example, HP takes back and recycles printer cartridges through its Planet Partners program (www.hp.ca/recycle). It is one of the few companies taking back and recycling its inkjet cartridges. Many brands take back only toner cartridges. Some companies offer recycling bins and collection services for organizations that consume large quantities of toner and ink cartridges.

The used cartridge trade is a lucrative business, and there are a handful of "backyard" remanufacturers producing poor-quality cartridges – more interested in making a quick dollar

E-waste and techno trash in Canada

Our love for and fast uptake of new technology has a nasty side effect. A study conducted by Environment Canada's National Office of Pollution Prevention looked at trends in the waste produced by obsolete and unused computers, monitors, laptops, peripherals and other IT equipment (excluding mainframes and other large equipment). The study predicted that in 2005 there would be:

>> 67 324 tonnes of IT equipment waste disposed of,
>> 47 791 tonnes reused,
>> 11 948 tonnes stored, and
>> 43 428 recycled.

than in the environment, whatever their sales pitch may be. Poorly re-manufactured cartridges can cause extra wear and tear on the printer and shorten its lifespan. Make sure that any re-manufactured product you buy is recommended by your printer manufacturer or certified with the Environmental Choice program, or that the company offering the cartridges is EcoLogo, ISO9000 or ISO14000 certified.

Computers and computer parts can be recycled into new computer parts, or the valuable metals can be recovered for other purposes. There are a number of charitable computer-recycling programs that take unwanted computers from businesses as a kind of donation. The computer is "cleaned" and any old files are deleted, and the computer is given to schools, the disadvantaged or community groups. It's advisable that you first delete all your personal data and files, but leave the programs intact. Industry Canada's Computers For Schools program takes donations

of surplus equipment from the corporate sector and passes them on to schools and public libraries. Details of this and a selection of other computer-recycling programs are in Further Information (pages 287–8). Many of the charitable recyclers can give you a tax receipt for the donation of your old equipment. IBM's PC buyback program will even pay money for some items. IBM also sells certified refurbished second-hand PCs at a fraction of the cost of new models.

Office furniture can be sold second-hand, refurbished or recycled.

Disks can be reformatted or recycled.

Being green at work when you don't work at home

In any workplace, it doesn't take much to change some practices if you make it easy for people. The bigger the workplace, the bigger the positive effect small changes can have. If you have successfully made your home environment a greener place to live, talk to your boss about introducing low-impact changes at work, but remember, there's not a lot of use in setting up an environmental program that no one uses.

There are several areas where you can initiate small changes.

Transportation

Encourage your colleagues to take public transportation instead of driving, or to carpool where possible or ride a bike. See if your boss will offer company cars selectively to employees willing to car pool. Renegotiate start and finish times to outside peak hours and, for part-timers, renegotiate the number of days you work in order to reduce the number of times you make the trip.

Cigarette butts

One common litter problem that many businesses have is cigarette butts, which have been overlooked as a serious environmental problem for some years.

It's important for the quality of indoor air and workers' health that offices be smoke-free zones. A side effect of the increase in smoke-free restaurants, offices and other buildings has been a marked increase in outdoor smoking and consequently the direct disposal of butts into the environment.

If your office has a smoke-free policy but some employees smoke, consider setting up a proper smoking area outside. Choose an area that's away from doors, windows or other sources of fresh air for the building and definitely provide a bin for butts.

Educate colleagues

Once you have new systems in place, you need to educate co-workers to make it easier for them to use the systems. Those who are less green-minded won't have the same commitment to changing their work habits as you do, so make it as easy for them as you can. Put up signs with energy-saving tips specific to particular equipment near the equipment itself. Clearly label any recycling bins and reusable paper bins.

Hold an education session for staff and make it fun. If you put on a special

Polystyrene cups

did you know...

Polystyrene foam cups are not biodegradable and are rarely recycled. Take your own mug to get takeout coffee or tea. If you do get the occasional coffee in a disposable cup, find a café that uses paper-based cups instead of foam cups.

Starbucks and Tim Hortons have reusable "commuter mugs" available for their hot drinks and even offer a small discount to customers who use these mugs. In 2003 alone, Starbucks customers used commuter mugs 13.5 million times, keeping an estimated 266.2 tonnes of paper from landfills.

Cigarette butts

>> Cigarettes contain some 3900 chemicals. Many of these are considered dangerous to humans and other living organisms. As filters are designed specifically to trap some of the dangerous by-products of smoking, the cigarette butt is in fact a small poisonous pellet.

>> Butts are made from cellulose acetate (similar to rayon), which is biodegradable in periods ranging from one to two months in favourable conditions to up to three years or more in sea water. The New South Wales EPA (in Australia) states that butts can take up to 15 years to break down.

>> The butts contain not only cigarette tar and nicotine but also the residue of complex processes involving hundreds of chemical compounds, many of them bad for your health, including a quantity of radioactive polonium-210.

>> Butts littered on sidewalks and roadways are washed into stormwater drains. An unknown but significant proportion then find their way into waterways and onto beaches. Cigarette butts have been found in the stomachs of birds, sea turtles and other aquatic life.

>> Butts may seem small, but their numbers add up. CigaretteLitter.Org estimates that 4.5 trillion butts are littered each year worldwide. They are by far the most common litter item found by volunteers for the annual Great Canadian Shoreline Cleanup.

lunch or afternoon coffee break, you're more likely to have everyone turn up. While they're eating you'll have their undivided attention. Go through the systems that you have put in place and how staff should use them. Show examples of the signs you have put up and explain what they mean. Also outline the benefits for the environment and the importance of greening up the business sector. With a bit of imagination you can turn it into an enjoyable team-building exercise.

Monitor the changes
Document the "before" and "after" environmental assessment of your office. This will help you to measure the extent of waste reduction, changes in energy consumption and any savings made through greener purchasing or energy efficiency. Report this information on the (hopeful) success of the program to your boss and suggest it be included in any promotional literature or corporate profile documents.

Spread the word
Tell your friends in other businesses, suppliers and contacts about your successes and encourage them to green up their offices. With any luck you might find that the greening of the business sector is contagious.

FOR A GREENER OFFICE:

REDUCE your paper use.

BUY recycled paper.

CHOOSE energy-efficient equipment.

RECYCLE your waste.

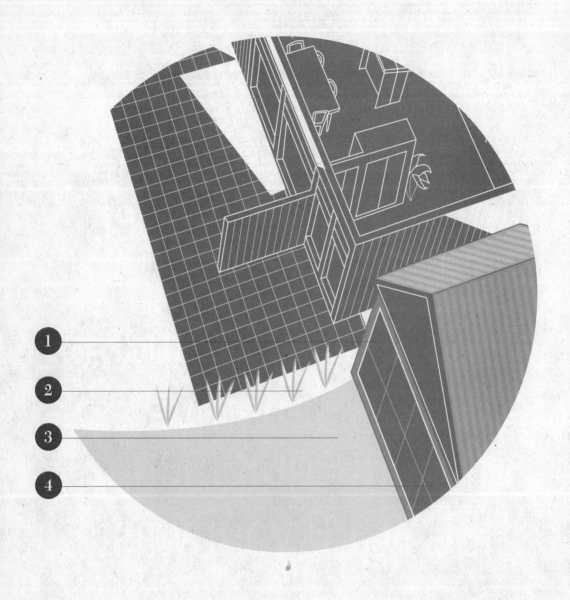

1 Bicycle
2 Air-cleaning plants
3 Swept (not hosed) driveway
4 Fuel-efficient car

>> The green garage

Cars are bad for the environment. There's no nice way to put it. Ideally, we should all stop using our cars, but in reality this is not going to happen.

When most people think about cars and the environment, they think about pollution. Car exhaust contains combustion gases, fine particle emissions and sometimes lead, all of which contribute to air pollution. These gases react with sunlight to form smog, which is bad for our health and can trigger asthma attacks. Smog and air pollution are particularly concentrated in urban areas. Urban air quality directly affects the health of a city's residents. It's estimated that in the year 2000 alone, 5000 people in Canada died prematurely because of air pollution.

The other problem is the greenhouse effect. Greenhouse gases such as methane, carbon monoxide and nitrous oxide float up into the atmosphere, where they act like a nice cozy blanket for the planet, preventing heat from escaping the atmosphere. This leads to global warming, which leads to climate change. One of the scariest things about the greenhouse effect is that it doesn't respect national borders and

can't be confined to a region. The effects of a few developed countries performing poorly on greenhouse issues are felt by the whole world. Canada, Australia and the US are among the highest producers of greenhouse gases per capita, making us very unpopular with our Pacific neighbours, particularly the vulnerable low-lying islands.

The natural world, farms, industry and households all contribute to the greenhouse effect. Passenger road transport accounts for nearly 50% of the average Canadian's personal greenhouse gas contribution. Though some of this is from public transportation, a high proportion is from private car use, which we can modify for the benefit of the planet.

In the past, ozone-depleting chlorofluorocarbons (CFCs) were used in the air-conditioning units in cars. The government has passed laws prescribing their gradual elimination, but some may still be found in the air-conditioning systems of older cars.

When you're buying a car, it's important to consider all aspects of a car and how they affect the environment. From an environmental perspective, your choice of car is more important than the way you drive it and maintain it. Once you buy a car, you're locked into that particular car's fuel-consumption and exhaust patterns for the entire time you use it. For more information on buying a new car, see pages 140–1.

Cars have a life cycle, each stage of which has different environmental implications. At the concept stage, cars can be designed so that they will run more efficiently and therefore be greener during their years on the road. The production of the car uses resources to make the materials that make up the car and its parts. Energy is required to mine or produce these materials, to transport them to the factory, in the manufacturing process itself and, finally, to transport the finished product to the buyer. The manufacturing process also generates pollution, which has to be monitored and controlled.

The consumer has control of the car during its use. This is where you, as a consumer and a car owner, can make a huge difference. While your car is on the road, its exhaust will contribute to pollution and to the greenhouse effect. Caring for and cleaning the car will use water, detergents and other chemicals. These environmental impacts can all be minimized.

Finally, once the car is no longer wanted for transportation and has reached the end of its life, it is dismantled. Reusable parts are removed for use by mechanics, steel and other marketable materials are collected for recycling, and the remainder is disposed of.

To make a difference in the garage, you need to look at how you can soften the environmental impact of your car, along with the latest green machines on the market, alternatives to cars and the future for car transportation and fuel.

Life cycle impact of cars

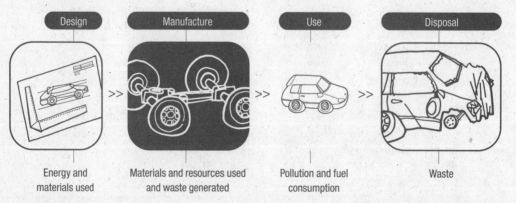

Design	Manufacture	Use	Disposal
Energy and materials used	Materials and resources used and waste generated	Pollution and fuel consumption	Waste

Tips for greener car use

The amount of fuel you use relates directly to the amount of greenhouse gas your car produces, regardless of which car you're driving or which fuel it's using. So, in short, no matter what car you currently have, it will help the environment to reduce your fuel use. The bonus is that it will also save you money.

Reducing fuel consumption

Reduce your driving.

Turn local trips (for example, to get milk when it unexpectedly runs out) into healthy exercise by walking, cycling or roller blading rather than driving. Try to avoid driving during rush hour, as the stop-start driving that you do in heavy traffic is very inefficient.

Sitting in rush-hour traffic can be stressful and unhealthy, particularly if you're sitting behind a large truck, taking in its dirty diesel exhaust. Also limit the number of trips you make in winter, as the fewer cold starts your engine has to make, the better.

Don't just sit there . . . stop idling!

Many people needlessly waste a lot of gasoline and produce a lot of pollution leaving their engine running to warm up the car in winter. Once your car is running, the best way to warm it up is to drive it. Late-model cars with computer-controlled, fuel-injected engines don't need more than 30 seconds of idling before driving. All that idling could be

one reason fuel consumption soars in winter by up to 50%!

Drive smoothly.

Don't push your car too hard. In manual cars, move up through the gears with comfortable acceleration. Don't drive in a higher or lower gear than necessary, as this wastes fuel. In both manual and automatic cars, try to maintain a steady speed and avoid rapid acceleration and deceleration, which guzzle gas.

A European study showed that aggressive driving – fast acceleration from traffic lights and hard braking – reduces travel time by only 4%. This is equivalent to only 2.5 minutes out of a 60-minute trip, resulting in 57.5 minutes of stressful and somewhat dangerous driving.

Don't speed.

Slower driving is also greener driving. High speeds use a lot of extra fuel. As a general rule, a cruising speed of 120 km/h uses 20% more fuel than 100 km/h, while cruising at 90 km/h instead of 100 km/h improves fuel efficiency by around 10%.

Keep the tires pumped up.

Slightly flat tires have increased resistance against the road, creating a slight drag on the car. This means that you need more fuel to go the same speed. Regularly check that your tires are at the recommended pressure, particularly in winter, when cold temperatures decrease the air pressure. A single tire underinflated by 6 psi can increase fuel consumption by 3% and take 10 000 km off the tire's life.

Turn off the engine when stationary.

If you're in a traffic jam and not moving, turn off the engine. Similarly, turn it off when you're stopping for more than half a minute or so. For example, when pulling over to collect someone, don't leave the engine running while waiting for them to show up.

Service your car regularly.

As with all machinery, cars run more efficiently when they are in prime working condition, whereas out-of-tune cars burn more fuel. Make sure that you get your car serviced and tuned at the recommended intervals.

Don't overfill.

Spilling fuel by overfilling at the pump and evaporation from a poorly sealed tank can both waste gas. Fill up to the first click and make sure your car's gas cap fits properly.

Lighten the load.

The more weight your car carries, the more fuel it requires to move it. Remove any unnecessary weight from your car. For example, when you get home after a trip, unpack your car right away. In winter, clear any snow piled on top of your car or that has built up under the bumper or in the wheel wells. Snow adds weight and increases the aerodynamic drag on your car.

Reduce the need for air conditioning and heating.

Using the air conditioner can increase fuel consumption by around 5–10%. On hot days, drive for the first few minutes of the trip without the air conditioner on, with the windows down to let the hot air inside the car escape. Then turn on the air conditioner. Switch over to the economy mode once the car is cool. Park in the shade or under cover wherever possible and put sun shades up in your car windows when you leave your car in the sun.

Conversely, leave the car in the sun in winter to heat up the interior in the same way a greenhouse heats up.

Use the trunk, not the roof.

If there's space in the back or trunk of the car, use this instead of putting loads onto roof racks. Items on a roof rack will increase wind resistance, reducing the aerodynamic efficiency of your car.

Consider using an engine block heater.

Block heaters offer a solution to the problem of getting a car's cold engine to turn over and start on a chilly winter morning, by using an electric element to warm the engine and lubricant oil. The result is a car that starts more easily, uses fuel more efficiently and produces less pollution. However, leaving the block heater on all night will negate these benefits by wasting electricity. Use a block heater in conjunction with an electric timer device. Set the timer to start the block heater warming the engine two hours before you plan to drive.

Green-clean your machine

It's easy to justify cleaning your car. Done properly, it will help to keep the paintwork in good condition, prevent rust and ensure a better resale value, should you eventually sell it. However, cars don't need most of the car cosmetics and products currently on the market. You should make sure that you're using water wisely and that you're not releasing extra chemicals into the waterways and the environment.

Reuse water on the car. Cars don't need to be washed with drinking water. You can reuse bath water to wash the car (provided it's not heavily laced with bubble bath, bath salts or other additives).

Avoid detergents containing phosphate. A solution of pure soap and water is all you need to clean the muck off your car. If you do use a detergent, avoid those containing phosphates. Just as phosphates in laundry detergents are harmful to our waterways, so too are the phosphates in car shampoos. This is particularly important if you're washing the car in the driveway or on the roadside and the water is going directly into the drain. It's also important to avoid abrasives, as they can damage the paint.

Use a bucket. You don't need gallons and gallons of water to clean your car. Use buckets instead of a hose for washing and rinsing. The hose attachments that you can buy for car cleaning generally waste a huge amount of water.

Don't put motor oil down the drain. Each year Canadians dump and spill the equivalent of seven *Exxon Valdez*

Recycling oil

Since used motor oil should be recycled, you may be wondering what it gets made into.
>> Recycled oil can be re-refined, restoring the lubricating properties of the oil while removing contaminants. Re-refining used oil takes about one third of the energy of refining crude oil to lubricant quality. Look for environmentally certified re-refined motor oil products, bearing the EcoLogo symbol. Recycled oil is also used to make asphalt for roads and can be burned to recover energy in furnaces with appropriate pollution controls.
>> Oil filters are made from various metals, which are shredded, re-smelted and made into new metal products, including nails and wire.
>> Empty plastic oil bottles can be recycled into new containers, bins and garden and landscaping products.

Free vehicle emissions inspections

Each summer, specially trained staff from Environment Canada work with local green and community groups to provide Let's Drive Green vehicle emission clinics in communities across the country. At these two- or three-day voluntary clinics, people can have a free test of their tailpipe's emissions and receive useful information on improving their car's environmental performance. Have your vehicle tested to make sure that you're not inadvertently producing any more air pollution than you need to. If you are part of a community group or other local organization and want to help your community even more, consider involving your organization as a local host for a clinic in your area. For more information, visit www.ec.gc.ca/ transport/clinics.

tankers of used motor oil into Canadian waterways. If you change the motor oil yourself, never pour it into the gutter, down a sink or drain, bury it or dump it. If not properly disposed of, it can lead to the contamination of soil, air, groundwater and other waterways. One litre of motor oil can contaminate a million litres of water. Motor oil is now being recycled in Canada, and many municipalities have drop-off centres that take unwanted motor oil and other liquid wastes. The website of western Canada's Used Oil Materials Recycling Associations provides details of the 1000 EcoCentres and collection points across British Columbia, Alberta, Saskatchewan and Manitoba that collect used oil through their programs, as well as information on recycling used motor oil, used oil filters and empty plastic oil containers. Visit www.usedoilrecycling.com. Your municipal government can also give you information about local used-oil collections.

Reining in road salt

Each winter, snow piles up on our driveways and roads. To counter this, around 5 million tonnes of road salt is used across Canada every winter. This salt is carried away by the melting snow, contaminating groundwater and surface water and harming wildlife and vegetation. Streams, small lake ecosystems and groundwater are particularly vulnerable to road-salt contamination. The main salt used is sodium chloride – the common table salt we use on food. Humans themselves can only complain of salty-tasting water from wells near roads, so road salt hasn't been banned. Environment Canada has invited environmental authorities, environment groups, government bodies, industries and other stakeholders to participate in the development of control strategies and alternatives for the use of road salt. The possibilities include improving salt-application technology and weather forecasting tools so that less salt can be used to accomplish the same

>>

Retiring old cars

Road vehicles contribute up to 35% of smog-forming emissions and 18.5% of Canada's total greenhouse gas emissions. Up to half of these emissions come from the 10–15% of Canada's vehicles that are old (pre-1988) or poorly maintained. Environment Canada sponsors a number of scrappage programs across Canada aimed at taking these older, more polluting vehicles off the road. There are programs operating in many major cities, including Vancouver, Calgary, Winnipeg, Toronto, Ottawa, Montreal and Fredericton. Owners who fit certain criteria can scrap their older vehicles through such programs in exchange for incentives, such as transit passes or rebates on new vehicles or bicycles. For more information, visit www.ec.gc.ca/transport/scrappage.htm.

results, thus reducing losses at salt storage sites; controlling the run-off from snow dumps; and using less harmful alternatives in environmentally sensitive areas. Aside from ensuring that you're not using excessive salt to clear your own driveway or using sand to clear snow instead, there's not much that the individual can do at this stage. However, some people are using hydronic heating in driveway snow-melting systems for salt-free and snow-free driveways.

Current fuels

It's great to use less fuel in your car, but what about the fuel itself? Gasoline, diesel fuel, propane and compressed natural gas (CNG) are all powering vehicles around Canada. They are all hydrocarbon-based fossil fuels, which are not renewable. Their combustion produces carbon dioxide, carbon monoxide and other greenhouse gases, contributing to global warming and poisoning the air. The good news is that clean, renewable hydrogen is sitting on the horizon as the most likely car fuel of the future.

The world's oil companies know that the writing is on the wall for the industry. While we've tapped only some of the earth's fossil fuel, much of it is not accessible without disturbing sensitive ecosystems. The industry estimates that, at our present levels of consumption, the world has reserves of around 50 years of crude oil and around 70 years of natural gas left. However, our consumption of fossil fuels isn't steady; it's increasing.

Another problem with oil is that oil reserves are limited to a number of oil-producing countries, many of which are experiencing political instability. Wars in oil-rich countries affect pump prices at gas stations around the world. The recent war in

Iraq saw gasoline prices in North America reach record highs in 2004 and a related shift in car sales toward more fuel-efficient models. Interest in SUVs was dampened, with a slowdown in sales of larger SUVs, while dealerships were selling Toyota Prius gas/electric hybrids as quickly as they could get them in. With both the limit to the world's oil reserves and the volatile political climate in the oil-rich Middle East, gasoline prices are expected to continue to rise.

The barrel of ready oil is running dry and the industry is having to look at alternatives. BP, for example, is now the world's largest manufacturer and user of solar cells and is looking to solar energy to produce a good portion of its income in the future. Additionally, as the public has become more aware of the health and environmental problems of car pollution, the fuel companies have improved their products so that they produce less pollution. The fuels of today are very different from those of 30 years ago.

Natural gas

Of the fossil fuels listed above, the best fuels environmentally are compressed natural gas (CNG) and propane. CNG allows for a reduction in greenhouse emissions of 30–40% for cars and 10–20% for heavy vehicles compared with gasoline, and has up to 60% less potential to form harmful ground-level ozone. Many buses now run on natural gas, which is the same gas that we use in our homes for heating and cooking. There are a small number of cars available with factory-fitted CNG engines, including some CNG/gasoline bi-fuel models. CNG engines can be retrofitted to cars, though factory-fitted CNG vehicles tend to be more efficient. Most of Canada's 30 000 natural gas vehicles are converted CNG/gasoline bi-fuel vehicles.

Conversions of existing cars cost $3500 to $4000 and conversion kits are available for most vehicles produced in North America. However, the purchase price is soon paid back as natural gas is around 40% cheaper than gasoline. Conversions usually result in a smaller trunk space, since extra room is taken up by the gas storage cylinder.

In 1999 there were only 130 natural gas refuelling stations available to the public. With the relative lack of refuelling stations, CNG/gasoline bi-fuel vehicles ensure that the car can still run on gasoline as a backup when the CNG runs out and a refuelling station isn't nearby. Private on-site refuelling is an option where natural gas is available.

Propane

Environmentally, the benefits of propane are similar to natural gas, offering reduced emissions along with reduced costs over gasoline. Like CNG vehicles, propane-powered vehicles can be factory-fitted or converted, with conversions costing around $2400 to $2800. Some car manufacturers offer propane engines as an option but generally charge a lot for them. Almost all of Canada's 150 000 propane vehicles are converted, and many are propane/gasoline bi-fuel.

Refuelling is much more convenient for propane than for CNG. Propane is commonly available at many gas stations throughout Canada and generally costs around 25–35% less than gasoline.

Gasoline

Gasoline is the most commonly used car fuel in Canada. Gasoline used to contain added lead to reduce engine knocking and give the gas a higher octane rating. Lead is poisonous, accumulates in the body and through the food chain, and is associated with a number of health problems. Because of this, lead has been removed from gasoline in Canada. Federal initiatives are now focusing on reducing benzene and sulphur levels in gasoline. Gasoline is also being blended with ethanol, an alcohol biofuel distilled from plant material.

Diesel

Diesel-fuelled cars generally require less mechanical maintenance than gasoline-fuelled cars. However, diesel engines put out much higher levels of particle emissions than gasoline engines. This is of particular concern in urban areas, where they contribute to smog and are linked with lung cancer. Both gasoline and diesel fuel contain sulphur, diesel more so. During combustion, sulphur compounds are formed, which in the atmosphere react to produce acid rain. Sulphur also interferes with diesel-fuelled cars' exhaust catalysts, which are meant to cut down the polluting particle emissions of diesel engines. Low-sulphur diesel supplies are being sought and regulated to reduce the pollution from diesel engines.

Biofuels

Biofuels are plant oil and alcohol fuels that can be blended with gasoline to reduce gas consumption and the

Greenhouse Grand Prix

Which is the leanest, greenest car? If you challenge a late-model SUV, a mid-sized sedan and a gasoline/electric hybrid to a year's worth or 20 000 km of driving, the hybrid comes in at first place, producing the least amount of carbon dioxide emissions, with the SUV in last place.

Over 20 000 km:

>> Hybrid produces 2 tonnes CO_2

>> Gasoline sedan produces 4 tonnes CO_2

>> SUV produces 6 tonnes CO_2

Remember that every litre of gasoline you save means 2.4 kg less carbon dioxide you've released into the atmosphere, reducing your contribution to the greenhouse effect.

pollution associated with it. Biofuels are less polluting and, because they come from plant crops, are renewable. Usually the alcohol ethanol is distilled from fermented plant matter. The best plants for making alcohol are those that contain sugars, starch or cellulose, such as sugar cane, sugar beet, cereals and kelp. Ethanol from grains such as corn and wheat is already being distilled in Canada.

Blending of 7–10% ethanol by volume is common in Canada and is sold at many fuelling stations, often under the name "gasohol." Ethanol content is designated by the letter E with a number representing the percentage, such as "E10." Look for gas stations that sell blends that are EcoLogo-accredited to ensure that the ethanol portion has been distilled from biomass sources. Some car manufacturers are making vehicles that can run on blends with even higher concentrations of ethanol. These E85 vehicles are not common, and E85 fuel is also not widely available.

Plant oils, including canola, olive oil and sunflower oil, can be used to supplement diesel fuel. Biodiesel fuels are being developed in countries such as the US and South Africa and are a possible transport fuel of the future. Some trials are even experimenting with making biodiesel fuel from waste cooking oil from fast-food outlets. The unwanted waste oil that once cooked your french fries may end up powering your car.

Crops can be grown specifically for the purpose of producing biofuels, but in the long term, the planet's growing population may need this land to grow food crops. Anticipating this, many biofuel projects get their biomass from the unwanted part of food plants, such as bagasse, the waste fibre from sugar cane.

Buying a new car

The size, weight and engine type (and consequent fuel type needed) will all affect the overall environmental performance of your car. These rules generally apply:
• Larger cars are less efficient because they are heavier and therefore need more energy to move them around. Sport utility vehicles (SUVs), being

Celebrity green machines

Leonardo DiCaprio, the official face of Earth Day, has become even greener by swapping his main vehicle for an electric hybrid car. Leo now drives a Toyota Prius and likes it so much he bought another three for members of his family. Other celebrities reportedly driving electric hybrid cars include Brad Pitt, Jennifer Aniston, Alicia Silverstone and Cameron Diaz.

New cars – the greenest and the meanest

Each year the American Council for an Energy Efficient Economy (ACEEE) publishes the *Green Book: The Environmental Guide to Cars & Trucks* – a buyers' guide for new vehicles on the market in the US that scores cars according to their environmental performance. When the book is released, ACEEE also names the top performers, or the "greenest" vehicles, and the worst, or the "meanest." More info: www.greenercars.com.

Environmental Defence adapts this information for the Canadian market as part of its Green Cars campaign. Each year it releases its 10 greenest and 10 meanest vehicles lists for Canada, as well as providing information on greener vehicle choices and the top-rated models within each class of vehicle. More info: www.environmentaldefence.ca.

generally larger, are also heavier and therefore more expensive to run. The Canadian government classifies SUVs as "light-duty trucks." As such, SUVs don't have to comply with the minimum fuel-efficiency standards that are in place for cars and can get away with being a lot more polluting than the family cars they are increasingly replacing.

• Newer cars are generally less polluting than similar-sized older cars, provided both have been well maintained.

• Cars with lighter paint and interior colours will tend to reflect light, while darker colours absorb light and heat.

• Compare each model's fuel consumption and opt for the most efficient model. The Office of Energy Efficiency has developed an EnerGuide fuel-consumption labelling system for all new cars and light-duty vehicles sold in Canada. The label for any given model shows estimates for both city- and highway-driving fuel consumption in litres/km and a dollar figure estimate of fuel costs over a year, based on 20 000 km travel, with 55% city and 45% highway driving and with the Canadian annual average fuel price for each type of fuel. Complete EnerGuide ratings for cars and light-duty vehicles are published in the "Fuel Consumption Guide." An interactive version of the guide is online at the Auto$mart website (http://oee.nrcan.gc.ca/vehicles). You can also order a free copy by calling 1-800-387-2000.

• If possible, choose an engine that runs on a less polluting fuel, such as propane or CNG.

• If carpooling is an option, make sure you buy a passenger-friendly car.

• Consider buying one of the latest green machines, such as the electric hybrids now on the market.

Electric, electric hybrid and solar cars

Every auto show trumpets some new mega-eco-car that's super-lightweight, runs on peanuts, emits a fragrant, rose-scent exhaust and/or can fold into a convenient suitcase. Concept cars are interesting, but not a lot of use until they are commercially available.

Now that legislators are convinced that global warming is a reality and that cars are contributing to it, we're finally seeing some of these concepts being developed into viable products, some of which are now available on the market.

The hydrogen car

Arguably the ultimate fuel of the future is hydrogen. Hydrogen burns with oxygen to produce energy. The by-product is not some scary carcinogen, but simple water. Unfortunately, hydrogen has had an undeserved bad reputation as a fuel since the 1937 explosion of the hydrogen-fuelled Hindenberg airship. Recent research has shown that the disaster was more likely to have been caused by the dangerous combination of a lot of electrical activity in the air (causing lightning) and the cotton-based fabric of the airship, coated with a highly flammable paint that contained powdered aluminum.

Hydrogen is used as the fuel in the fuel cell of an electric car. A fuel cell is like a battery, except that a battery is a sealed unit. Once the chemicals contained in it have been combined, no more energy (electricity) can be produced and the battery is "flat." With a fuel cell, you can keep feeding in the chemicals (in this case hydrogen and oxygen) that combine and produce energy. Sounds simple, doesn't it? The difficulty is in storing the hydrogen.

Hydrogen occurs naturally as a gas. As a fuel, it needs to be liquefied and stored in a large, heavy, pressurized and well-insulated tank, which doesn't leave much room in the trunk for luggage or shopping. This is the hurdle to overcome before hydrogen-powered cars become a reality on the road.

Electric hybrid cars

One solution is the electric hybrid, which combines a fuel cell with the traditional gasoline engine. While the car is running on unleaded gas, hydrogen is produced as a by-product. This hydrogen becomes the fuel for the fuel cell, so the battery recharges while the car is running on gas. The battery drives an electric motor when the car is starting up and slowing down, making it well suited to city driving. The car produces far fewer emissions when running in electric mode. The gas motor kicks in at higher speeds, when more power is needed.

Electric hybrid cars also shut down the gasoline engine when the car is stationary, for example, when stopped at traffic lights. The overall result is a car that produces up to 90% less polluting emissions.

Sounds like a fabulous concept car that will never be available, doesn't it? In fact, four electric hybrids have been released in Canada. You could buy one of these green machines tomorrow. They are the Toyota Prius, the Honda Civic Hybrid, the Honda Insight, and the Ford Escape Hybrid. The Honda Insight appears to be most efficient, but it is a two-door car and therefore smaller. The Toyota Prius and Honda Civic Hybrid are four-door cars and are designed to be comfortable passenger cars. Given that we'd like to see people sharing a ride, the Prius and the Civic Hybrid may be better choices. As mentioned earlier, SUVs should generally be avoided. However, some people and certain occupations have genuine need for SUVs. The Ford Escape Hybrid is an SUV with the environmental benefits of hybrid technology.

Solar cars

On the horizon (along with the sun) is the solar-powered car. Like the electric car, it is silent and clean, with little environmental impact.

However, there are still a few problems to overcome before solar-powered cars become a reality on the roads. The main one is the unreliability of the weather. What do you do when the sun goes behind a cloud? Research is continuing on solar-powered cars, but for the time being they will remain in the domain of solar-car race events and auto-show concept car displays.

Alternatives to using cars

Obviously, the best option is to try to reduce our reliance on cars in our daily lives. Urban planners, employers and individuals can all do a range of things that will help the environment by limiting the use of cars.

What urban planners can do

Civil engineers and urban planners can do a lot for the environment by being creative and thinking outside the box. Here are some ideas:
• Improve public transportation systems.
• Provide bicycle lanes on popular bicycle routes.
• Provide express lanes on freeways or main arterial roads for cars with two or more passengers or for selected environmentally preferred cars.
• Help fund public transportation improvement by charging a levy on downtown parking.

What employers can do

Employers can:
• Offer public transportaion vouchers instead of company cars and parking in salary packages.
• Make any shower facilities their site may have available to staff who walk, skate, jog or ride bikes to work.
• Look into the possibilities of online offices and video-conferencing so that

some employees can work from home full- or part-time. Many are already looking into this option for parents wishing to work from home after having babies.

What you can do

• **Use public transportation.** A person who lives 5 minutes' drive from a train station, but 40 minutes from work may consider driving to the station and taking the train the rest of the way into work. This will also save on downtown parking costs.

• **Move closer to work** or to a house with better access to public transportation. This is one of the benefits of renting – you can more easily move house when you change jobs.

• **Offset some of the emissions** of your car by planting trees to help combat the greenhouse effect.

• **Share a ride** wherever possible. Organize a carpool with workmates. You can make a carpool fun by turning one trip a week into a regular breakfast date. If you're a parent, organize a carpool to school with the parents of your child's classmates – or walk them.

• **Working from home** is worth investigating. Although you may miss the social aspects of the office environment, there are some fringe benefits to the home office. At home you can have a bad hair day, work in your pyjamas with an avocado facemask or play old Duran Duran CDs and no one will know.

Making space for cars

A side effect of using private cars for transportation is the sheer amount of land it takes up. Roads, driveways, parking lots and other car-related infrastructure take up at least a third of the average city's land space, according to the Worldwatch Institute. That's a lot of real estate. Inner-city land values are now so high that it's not unusual for someone to add a downtown car-parking spot to their real estate portfolio! "The Green Guide to David Suzuki's Nature Challenge" observes that Europe's pedestrian-friendly cities have less than 10% of their land devoted to transportation, while car-loving North American cities devote up to 50% or more urban land to roads and parking. Write to your local municipal or provincial government and encourage it to set aside more green space, foot paths and bike trails to foster lower reliance on cars.

FOR A GREENER GARAGE:

WALK or use public transportation.

DRIVE smoothly and efficiently.

CONVERT your car to natural gas.

BUY a fuel-efficient car.

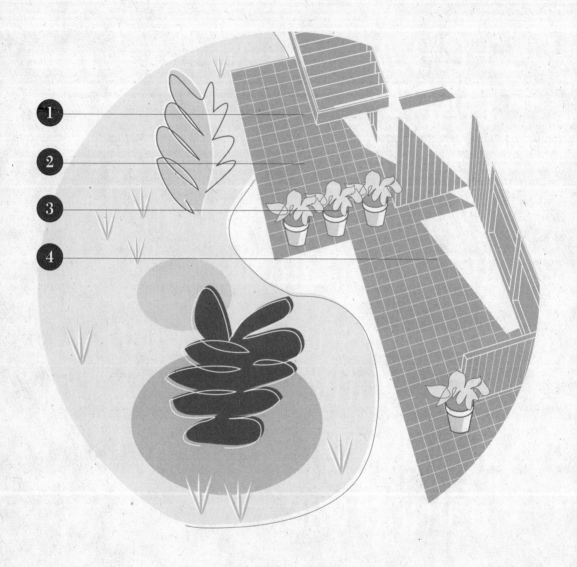

1   Shade
2   Eco-paving
3   Pest-deterring plants
4   Entertaining area

>> The green garden

Where would a green house be without some actual greenery? You have to admit that a garden, from a few potted plants on a windowsill to several acres, can be beautiful and can bring you a lot of enjoyment and satisfaction.

You don't have to be a black belt in feng shui to know that it's more pleasant and relaxing to look out of your window and see trees, shrubs and flowers than traffic, concrete and factories.

Plants and gardens put us back in touch with nature and help us to understand its processes. They help to clean the air and can even delicately perfume it. If well designed and cared for, a garden can provide an attractive space for outdoor entertaining and is like an extra room. If you have children, a child-friendly garden can turn this outdoor room into an extra playroom, a place where their imaginations can run wild, giving you some peace and quiet back inside.

If you don't have a garden but want to exercise your green thumb, there are other ways to do it. Many suburbs have community gardens and allotments where fruit and vegetables are grown as a co-operative community project. There are also hundreds of "friends of" groups (for example, Friends of Cold Creek), conservation authorities and other tree-planting and conservation organizations that you can get involved with.

Lifestyle and aesthetics aside, a garden gives you an opportunity to compost your waste, grow your own food and support local biodiversity. All this helps the broader environment. However, there are some things that you may do in your garden that can also damage the environment, through ignorant gardening.

Considerations for a green garden

The first thing to do is to look at the pros and cons of what you have in your garden, what you're doing with it and how it all affects the health of the planet. Consider the following helpful and harmful actions and see which apply in your own garden.

How a garden can help the environment

• Trees and other plants combat the greenhouse effect and slow the effects of global warming.

• Plants soak up carbon dioxide and exhale oxygen for us to breathe.

• Trees and shrubs provide shade, keeping houses cool during hot weather. They also provide shelter, breaking powerful winds.

• Plants improve water quality by acting as a filter to unwanted nutrients and pesticides.

• Native trees, plants and flowers can help conserve the diversity of local native wildlife by providing it with food and shelter.

• Garden furniture, compost bins and landscaping products can be made from recycled materials. Buying these products supports the recycling industries and leaves raw materials in the ground for future generations.

• A garden compost heap or worm farm can help to reduce the amount of food and garden waste being sent to landfill by turning it into plant food, which can be used to enrich the soil and keep your garden healthy.

• Vegetation reduces stormwater run-off. Too much stormwater run-off can cause small-scale flooding and can wash pollution into nearby waterways and the sea.

• In areas prone to the overpumping of groundwater, filling space with vegetation instead of paving can help to prevent land subsidence. An unsealed garden bed with plants allows rainwater to seep into the soil, recharging groundwater and the water table, which supports the land above it and the structures on it.

• Plants can enrich the soil by converting nitrogen into nitrates.

• Vegetation helps rainwater seep into the soil, recharging groundwater supplies.

• Vegetable gardens can provide you with food. Buying locally grown produce is better for the environment,

Waste not

did you know...

Canadians produce more than 21 million tonnes of garbage annually. Around 30% of the waste our households produce is organic material, much of which could be put into compost bins or worm farms and recycled into plant food.

Minimizing mower pollution

You wouldn't normally associate gardening with causing air pollution. However, the small engines in lawn mowers, weed trimmers and leaf blowers contribute to urban smog. Older, gasoline-powered mowers are the worst offenders. The exhaust from these pieces of equipment contains high levels of carbon monoxide, VOCs and nitrous oxides. Thousands of litres of gasoline are also spilled in Canadian gardens each year while refilling outdoor equipment. Consider retiring your old, noisy, polluting mower and replacing it with a newer, less polluting gas or push mower. The Clean Air Foundation runs an old mower scrappage program through Home Depot outlets around Canada. For more info visit www.cleanairfoundation.org/mow_down.

and your own backyard is about as local as you can get.

• Trees can prevent erosion, landslides and soil salinization.

How a garden can harm the environment

• Gardens with plants that need more water than rainfall provides can use up a lot of fresh water.

• Pesticides can harm other non-target wildlife. Many are toxic to humans and some contain known carcinogens.

• Pesticides and artificial fertilizer can be washed into stormwater drains and carried to nearby waterways or beaches. These chemicals can harm aquatic life.

In fact, run-off from suburban gardens is a significant cause of water pollution problems.

• Exotic (i.e., introduced non-native) plants that are unsuited to the local environment tend to require more pesticides and fertilizer.

• Introduced plant species can escape from the garden and infest nearby parks and woodlands.

• Decking, fences and other landscaping materials can be made from unsustainable plastics or rainforest timbers. Some timber products can also be treated with unsustainable and harmful chemicals, harming wildlife and potentially posing a health risk for your family.

Understanding your ecosystem

The range of plants that you can grow easily will depend on the local climate and weather patterns, the soil composition and quality, the water supply and any particular local environmental sensitivities. Each portion of the earth's surface has its own natural ecosystem. This will include certain types of vegetation that are suited to the local conditions. Planting indigenous plants (natives specifically from your local area) is an easy way to choose species that will do well in your local environment. Plants that aren't suited to the natural landscape are high maintenance and the land itself can suffer.

The main things that will influence the kind of garden and plants that you can grow are:

Climate

Your local climate will nurture some kinds of plants and kill others. Exotics from warmer climates will struggle with our winters, many needing to be lifted before the cold sets in. Overwintering can be a lot of hard work. Rainfall patterns and leaching also influence the mineral, nutrient and salt content of the soil. Dry summers and droughts, common in some areas, can also damage and kill plants.

Soil

Soil is the backbone of a healthy garden. Soil isn't just plain dirt; it's the growing medium for all of your garden plants and will do well if nurtured.

The composition of soil can vary dramatically from one region to another. It can also have varying acidity, alkalinity and nutrient content. Since soil is basically made up of ground-up rock and decomposed organic matter or humus, your local soil will depend on the composition of the "parent" rock and the range of plants and animals that have lived in the area. Different plants are suited to different soil types. Find out about the composition of the soil in your garden by asking your municipal government

about soil in the area or by using a home test kit, available from hardware stores and nurseries.

Water

The next thing to consider is the supply and flow of water. You'll probably already know a little about your local snow and rainfall patterns. Choose plants that will require little additional watering in summer. Also consider mulch and groundcovers that will help to reduce water loss in summer months. Look at any slopes within your garden. The relative heights of garden beds will affect the drainage of the soil. The root systems of some plants prefer well-drained soils. Keep this in mind when planning your garden.

Problem plants

Make sure you're aware of plants that can cause problems. Some areas have problems with seeds that escape from suburban backyards only to germinate where they're not wanted. Some municipalities have lists of plants that they consider pests or that are proscribed by provincial or local laws. Find out about poisonous or allergy-causing plants that may pose a risk to children, pets and native wildlife. Some very common and popular garden plants fall into this group.

Ecosystem types

Gardens in Canada fall into three broad plant habitat themes, reflecting the natural ecosystems of their areas. Regardless of what you try to force your garden to do, your region's plant habitat type will determine what your garden is trying to be, with or without your help. Woodland gardens happily support tall, mature trees with an understorey of shade-loving plants and wildflowers. Prairie and meadow gardens are suited to areas with nutrient-poor soil, lots of sunshine and hot, dry summers. Drought-prone regions can generally support well-planned wildflower meadow gardens. Wetland gardens love moisture, with plants that prefer moist, boggy soil. Choose wetland plants if your yard is prone to periodic flooding.

The final thing to consider before you start planning and planting your garden is what you want to get out of it. Think about:
• the views from various rooms in the house
• the direction of any strong winds and where they hit the house
• shade to help keep your home cool in summer
• shade for outdoor living and entertaining areas
• shade for pets and play areas
• positions of vegetable gardens and fruit trees
• an area for compost heaps or worm farms
• areas that can be made more private with trees and shrubs.

Plant size
Whenever you plant a tree or shrub, take into account the full width and height it will grow to. Make sure trees won't grow to obstruct overhead power lines.

Natives versus exotics

Gardening in Canada has gone through several trends since European settlement. Early settlers tried to recreate traditional English and European gardens to remind them of home. Some people embraced native plants, once they became more

Keep up with the neighbours

When you first move into an area, go for a walk around your neighbourhood and have a look at the gardens. This will give you an idea of the kinds of plants that thrive in your area.

familiar. In the 1970s, the native wildflower garden became a bit of a trend. The wild native garden is starting to become popular again, but it isn't the only way to use natives. Many gardeners have assumed that native plants should be allowed to grow unrestrained, as they do in the wild. However, native plants, like any other plants, can be pruned, shaped and trained to fit into a more formal garden. In fact, most popular garden styles can be adapted to incorporate native plants. As a general rule, out of all plants, indigenous plants can bring the most benefit and least harm to your local environment.

The benefits of native plants

• Native trees provide the right habitat (i.e., homes and food sources) for the wildlife of your area.
• Native trees and shrubs are better suited to the weather and soil of your area and have a better chance of thriving.
• Native plants tend to be less susceptible to local pests and plant diseases. This will reduce your need for pesticides.
• Native plants often need less additional watering.
• Planting a tree that's native to your local area can enhance and protect the gene base of native trees in your area.

Your local municipal government, nursery, naturalists' club or conservation authority can give you more information on the indigenous trees, shrubs and grasses of your area.

Flora for fauna

Our ever-expanding suburban sprawl has destroyed large tracts of natural vegetation that provided habitat for native animals and birds. We can give a little back by using our gardens to provide some backyard habitat for our local wildlife.

Already, the efforts of conservation projects are restoring species that are threatened through loss of habitat. For example, the Douglas College Institute of Urban Ecology's Green Links project is involving households and individuals in creating habitat "islands" and migration corridors of native vegetation in Greater Vancouver. The aim of the project is to connect isolated patches of green space in urban areas with parks and even backyards. These links provide a wildlife corridor, conserving the region's biodiversity by allowing animal populations to move between parks and interbreed. Vancouver residents interested in getting involved can visit www.douglas.bc.ca/iue for more information.

You can create some urban habitat for wildlife by making your garden wildlife-friendly.
• Plant native trees and shrubs to attract and feed native birds and butterflies. You need caterpillars to get butterflies, so don't forget to plant food trees for caterpillars too. The Canadian Biodiversity Institute School Grounds Transformation project's website has plant lists of suggested native species and the wildlife they attract. Visit

Gardens in wildfire zones

Wildfires are a frightening but normal part of nature. With global warming and an increase in the frequency of drought conditions, we're unfortunately seeing wildfires more often.

If you live in an area of high wildfire risk, you need to maintain your garden in a way that will minimize the potential damage that fire can do.

>> Plant native, fire-resistant species in your garden whenever possible.

>> Space trees and shrubs 3 or more metres apart.

>> For trees taller than 5 metres, remove branches within 2 metres of the ground to keep ground fires from spreading to treetops.

>> Make sure the ground around the house is cleared of materials that can act as fuels, such as dry grass, dead leaves, branches and thick undergrowth. Trim branches well clear of the house.

>> Make sure your roof, eaves and gutters are cleared of twigs and leaf litter during high-risk periods.

>> Prepare firebreak areas. For example, a well-watered lawn can act as a firebreak.

>> Remove flammable items from around the house, such as woodpiles, garden furniture made from wood or other flammable materials, paper-recycling piles, any crates or cardboard boxes, and hanging baskets made from plant fibres.

>> Make sure that you have garden hoses long enough to reach all sides of the house.

>> Get a backup water supply, such as a rainwater tank with a pump.

>> Consider installing garden and rooftop sprinkler systems.

>> Make sure any propane or gas stores are kept well away from the house.

>> Do not have wooden fencing connected to the house.

www.biodiversityonline.ca for more information.

• Get a cat-proof birdbath to provide a safe water source for birds. Either hang the bath from a tree or put it on a high pedestal and regularly change the water.

• Create shelter and nesting sites for birds by placing bird houses in trees. Surround the trees with shrubs to create a protective thicket. Birds in the garden live off seeds and small insects. They will help to keep the numbers of unwanted insects down.

• Plant nectar-producing species such as milkweed and spirea to attract butterflies, insects and small birds.

• Garden ponds can be turned into frog habitats. Plant shrubs that attract insects, which provide food for the frogs. You may wish to include small native fish in the pond to prevent mosquitoes breeding in the pond, particularly if you live in an area that has had outbreaks of the mosquito-borne disease West Nile virus.

The range of wildlife that you can attract to your garden will depend on the area you live in. Consequently, this will affect the kind of plants that you can use to create backyard habitats. Many groups and initiatives are making this information available. For more information and specific advice on what you can plant, and other information on biodiversity, go to the Canadian Wildlife Federation website at www.cwf-fcf.org.

Backyard bullies

People have often admired the romantic beauty of English ivy, the bright colour of the purple loosestrife or the delicate beauty and perfume of the lily of the valley. But put them in the wrong place at the wrong time and these beauties become garden thugs – backyard bullies that start out as the new kid on the block and end up terrorizing the natives.

Together with many other countries around the world, Canada is facing problems caused by introduced plant species. Many of these introductions start out innocently. In their own native ecosystems they exist in a delicate balance with other species. When you take them to a new environment where they are free from their natural controls, such as

>>

Problem plants

Environment Canada's report *Invasive Species of Natural Habitats in Canada* lists principal invasive plants wrecking havoc in the countryside. Here are a few and what they do:

Wetland species:

>> Eurasian watermilfoil *(Myriophyllum spicatum)* – displaces virtually all species in wetlands and streams where it takes root

>> European frog-bit *(Hydrocharis morsus-ranae)* – shades out sunlight needed by underwater vegetation; removes oxygen from the water

>> Flowering-rush *(Butomus umbrellatus)* – displaces native plants

>> Glossy buckthorn *(Rhamnus frangula)* – shades out sunlight

>> Purple loosestrife *(Lythrun salicaria)* – destroys habitat; competes with native plants

>> Reed canary grass *(Phalaris arundinacea)* – displaces native species; forms sterile mats

Upland species:

>> Common buckthorn *(Rhamnus cathartica)* – destroys habitat; excludes native seedlings

>> Garlic mustard *(Alliaria petiolata)* – forms dense stands, replacing native vegetation; implicated in endangering native wood poppy and American ginseng

>> Glossy buckthorn *(Rhamnus frangula)* – blocks sunlight from other plants

>> Leafy spurge *(Euphorbia esula)* – competes with native grasses; destroys grazing lands; is poisonous to livestock

predators or the limitations of climate, they can go feral, literally. Once established, they compete with other plants for water, soil and sunlight. As well as threatening crops and pastures, they can choke out native plants, destroying the food sources and habitat that native plants provide for local animals. Some clog up rivers and waterways; others affect human health and poison animals.

Keep in mind that even Canadian native plants can be invasive in parts of Canada beyond their original range. For example, the Manitoba maple is native to the prairies but considered alien (non-native) in southern Ontario.

There are several thousand weeds (or unwanted plants) in Canada. It has been estimated that there are 700 alien plant species (27% of the total flora) in Ontario alone. Many of these are backyard bullies, escapees from our suburban gardens. Garden escapees growing wild in Canada include flowering rush, English ivy, purple loosestrife, European birch, forget-me-not and tatarian honeysuckle.

You may not be aware of it, but your garden could be helping the spread of backyard bullies, particularly if you live in a rural area or on the suburban fringe. You may contain the plants within your yard, but the wind can carry seeds of problem plants over great distances. Birds and other animals also eat the seeds or fruit of problem plants and spread the seeds by leaving them in their droppings.

If you live in such an area, call your municipality and ask about any problematic plants, particularly any popular garden plants that may be considered weeds in your area. The Canadian Wildlife Federation also has a searchable database of Canada's invasive species, both plant and animal.

What is a weed? Don't look for a universal list of species of plants that are classified as weeds because you won't find one. Strictly speaking, any unwanted plant is a weed. Any plant in the wrong place at the wrong time can become a weed.

Controlling weeds

For the good of your health as well as that of the environment, resist the urge to nuke weeds close to home with herbicides. Herbicides can kill non-target plants as well as the weeds, they can leach into the soil and into groundwater, they can make your garden an unhealthy environment for you and your pets and they will leave a residue on any food that you grow in your garden.

Organic weed control can be time-consuming and hard work, especially if your garden wasn't designed with weed control in mind. However, it's well worth doing. Here are things that you can do to remove existing weeds and prevent new weed growth.

Clip them. Remove the seed heads using gardening scissors or shears.

Dig them out. Remove weeds by digging them out with a garden fork. Be careful not to damage the root systems of plants that you want to keep.

Chop them. Use a sharp blade, spade or hoe to remove the top of the weed at ground level without disturbing the soil.

Smother them. Cover weeds with weed matting, mulch or newspaper to block out the sunlight. After a few weeks without sunlight for photosynthesis, the weeds will die.

Solar cook them. Cover the weeds with black plastic, particularly in hot weather. Heat will build up under the plastic and this heat will kill the weeds and their seeds.

Burn them. This method also uses heat to kill the tops of weeds and their seeds, but with steam or boiling water.

Pull them out. Pulling weeds is the best, most selective way to remove unwanted weeds that have grown among plants that you want to keep. Be careful not to redistribute their seeds.

Give them competition. Grow other plants and groundcovers, hand-pulling the tiny weed seedlings as they appear. Once the plants you want are established, they will block the sun from new weeds and will starve the weeds of water and nutrients.

Block them out. Other materials can be used in landscaping that will block out sunlight from weeds as effectively as other plants and groundcovers. Consider paving or pebble gardens that will still allow rainwater to seep into the ground.

The no-dig garden

So you're a lazy gardener – you want to start a small garden but can't be bothered doing the hard preparation and groundwork. Or perhaps the earth in your garden is more like clay or is too compacted or just poor quality. No problem! You can build a no-dig garden.

No-dig gardens are raised, boxed garden beds built directly on top of the surface of the ground. They're easy to build and save the time and effort of digging into and preparing hard earth. They're a good way to make a raised garden bed and are well suited to vegetable gardens. Because they're built on top of the soil with new organic matter, they can provide a fertile garden bed in a garden with otherwise poor soil.

Purple loosestrife on the loose

Purple loosestrife, also known as "the beautiful killer" or "the marsh monster," has often been innocently recommended as a beautiful flowering plant that is also hardy and easy to grow. The trouble with purple loosestrife is that it is *too* easy to grow – quickly dominating its habitat and allowing no other species to grow. Purple loosestrife plants produce a huge number of lightweight seeds, which can be carried great distances by wind. These seeds have nearly a 100% germination rate and remain viable even after years buried in the soil or submerged in water. Purple loosestrife is very difficult to kill once it's established and can regenerate from the smallest piece of root tissue left in the soil after weeding. It is one of the few species of national significance, considered a problem from coast to coast.

If you have some in your garden, carefully remove it to ensure that you have the entire root system. Put it into a thick, black garbage bag and seal it well to prevent it from spreading near landfill sites. Wherever permitted, plant material should be burned.

Don't let people convince you that special garden varieties or cultivars of purple loosestrife, like Modern Pink or Dropmore Purple, are safe. There are many native flowering plants with pink, purple and white flowers, such as the spiked gayfeather. Plant these instead.

Early in spring, once the ground has dried following winter thaws, is the ideal time to start a no-dig garden. First, place some edging around the proposed garden bed area. The edging can be bricks or rocks or timber. Many people use old timber railway sleepers. Spread out a thick layer (around 1.5 cm) of overlapping sheets of newspaper. Soak it with a hose. Then put down a 5–7 cm layer of alfalfa hay. If you have some, put down an additional layer of old leaves, twigs and pieces of seaweed. Soak with a hose. Spread a thin layer of animal manure (chicken, horse, cow or sheep) over the alfalfa/twig layer. Next add a 5 cm layer of straw. Finally, add a 3–4 cm layer of compost.

Plant seedlings directly into the compost layer and water them well. Water regularly while the seedlings establish themselves. Over time the hay, straw, manure, paper and compost will break down into a dark, rich and well-aerated soil.

Water in the garden

Each Canadian uses an average of 343 litres of water inside the home every day. Residential water use increases by around 50% in the summer, largely due to lawn and garden watering and car washing. Buckets and buckets of water are wasted on sprinkler systems turned on and forgotten, on hosing down pathways instead of sweeping

Sprinklers
If you really want to use a sprinkler for lawns, measure how much water you're using. Put an empty takeout container on the lawn to catch some of the water. When the water level in the container reaches around 2 cm, your lawn has had an adequate soak.

them, and on watering plants too thirsty for the local conditions. A lot of the water used on the garden is of better quality than it needs to be – it's fit for human consumption, but plants, soil and stormwater drains are the things that actually consume it.

Just as there are 3 Rs for saving water inside the home (see page 14), there are also 3 Rs for water in the garden:

Reduce your water consumption by following some water-saving tips.

Replant your garden with water-wise plants and groundcovers instead of thirsty exotics and lawns.

Collect and use **rainwater** instead of tap water.

Water-wise gardening tips

There are specific things you can do to save water while maintaining a lawn and garden, but you can also help by changing your habits with some everyday garden jobs.

• Use mulch in the garden to reduce evaporation. Better still, buy mulch that's made from recycled materials.

How to spot a water-wise plant

There are some plants that are naturally able to survive dry conditions. They may be proficient at storing water or reducing water loss, or able to access water deep in the soil. There are a few telltale signs of a water-efficient plant that can help you to make choices for your garden without needing to be a horticulturalist.

>> **Small leaves** mean smaller surface area, which reduces water loss. Most water-efficient plants have small, tough leaves or needles.

>> **Tough surfaces** on the outer layers of leaves or a waxy surface often indicates water-efficient plants.

>> **Light leaf colours** reflect sunlight rather than absorbing it. Look for light green, blue-green or grey-green foliage. Thirstier plants tend to have soft, dark green leaves.

>> **Hairy leaves** act as windbreaks, reducing water loss through transpiration. Some plants have fine hairs around their pores.

>> **Backbone** in a plant means it has a tougher internal structure and is likely to be more water efficient. Thirsty plants will wilt more easily.

>> **Deep root systems** mean that a plant is likely to make better use of soil moisture.

• Sweep pathways with a broom rather than hosing them down.

• Install a well-designed water-efficient watering system. Look at products such as drip systems, tap timers and micro-irrigation systems.

• Water late in the day in summer. Watering during the heat of the day will only cause more evaporation. Splashes of water on leaves heated by the sun can also scald delicate plants.

• Avoid watering on dry, windy days to reduce the amount of water lost to evaporation.

• Use a trigger nozzle on your hose.

• Use a sprinkler or another watering system that delivers water in large droplets instead of a fine mist to minimize evaporation.

• Water deeply every few days, instead of daily light watering. This encourages the roots of lawn and plants to grow deeper as well as ensuring that more water permeates to the soil.

• Water in several short sessions, separated by intervals of a few minutes, rather than one long session to allow the water to permeate the soil more deeply, with minimal run-off.

• Use lots of compost in your garden. Compost helps to retain water in the soil, particularly in the root zone, where it's most needed.

Lawns

• Reduce the amount of lawn area in your garden. Lawns generally require more water than other parts of the garden. Consider replacing lawns with decking or plant groundcovers.

• Choose the right lawn. Ask your local nursery about water-efficient grasses.

• Don't trim your grass to a length shorter than 2 cm. Trimming the grass too closely exposes the lawn to the sun, increasing the loss of water to evaporation and taking away some of the protective foliage. Longer grass puts down deeper roots and needs less water.

• Consider buying a mulching mower. Mulching mowers, as the name suggests, help to mulch the lawn, reducing the amount of watering it needs.

• Water by hand, using a hose. You're less likely to overwater by forgetting to turn off the sprinkler.

• Know when to stop. Water the lawn, but don't drown it.

Plants

• Water potted plants by hand using a hose or watering can.

• Reduce water loss from potted plants by reducing the amount of exposed earth or potting mix. Plant groundcovers, such as wintergreen, in large pots around trees. In smaller pots, cover the exposed earth with a layer of small pebbles or tumbled crushed glass.

• Group plants with similar watering needs together in your garden.

• Set up or plant windbreaks to protect delicate seedlings and to prevent the increased water evaporation caused by wind. Make sure you choose drought-tolerant plants for windbreaks.

How rain barrels help the environment

>> Using rainwater reduces the amount of tap (mains) water used. Fresh drinking-quality water supplies are ultimately limited.

>> Rain barrels allow you to water your garden during times of water restrictions.

>> Collecting rainwater and keeping it within your property reduces the load on your local stormwater drainage systems, which is where the run-off from your roof would otherwise flow.

>> Reducing our consumption of mains water keeps our demands for fresh drinking water within the capacity of our exisiting reservoirs and catchments. If our demands exceed this capacity, new dams will have to be built, which will have an environmental impact in particular areas.

• Choose water-efficient native plants over thirsty exotic plants.

Rain barrels

Why do we fail to make the connection between the water we pay for and the free stuff that falls from the sky? The reason we do this in the cities is that it's easier to just turn on the tap and use mains water than to think about installing a rain barrel. In the country, where not everyone is connected to mains water, rain barrels are more popular.

Rain barrels used to be common before our urban water systems were developed. With recent droughts and greater environmental awareness, the rain barrel is making a comeback. Depending on the level of rainfall in your area and the size of your garden, using a rain barrel can take a huge load off your household's water demands, but there are some issues you need to be aware of. Rainwater can also pick up some pollutants from roof, gutter and pipe materials, bird and animal droppings, leaf litter collected on the roof, local pollution and dust. The quality of the water collected in rain barrels can depend on the level of pollution in your local area. Some industrial areas have a problem with acid rain. However, most rainwater is of good enough quality for use on the garden. Rain barrels, like any still water body, can also breed mosquitoes. For these reasons you shouldn't use rainwater collected in barrels for drinking. Most health authorities and government bodies will allow rain barrels for garden use only.

Rain barrels are available from municipalities, water retailers, hardware stores and specialist alternative-technology stores. Prices start from around $60 for a 170 litre (45 gallon) barrel, $120 for a 341 litre (75 gallon) barrel and more for larger sizes. Larger barrels (up to 1000 litres) are available but harder to find. Some municipal governments offer rebates or subsidies on rain-barrel purchases.

Tips for collecting rainwater

• Empty your rain barrel and disconnect it from the downspout over winter. When water freezes, it expands. If this happens inside your barrel, it could produce cracks.

• Have your roof checked to see what it's made of and painted with to make sure it's safe. Some roofs are coated with paint containing lead or petrochemical coatings, which may be toxic.

• Cover all openings with mosquito-proof mesh.

• Put a tablespoon of olive oil in the water to produce a thin film over the water, discouraging mosquitoes from breeding in the barrel.

• Fit gutters and downpipes with traps to catch leaf litter and twigs.

• Make sure the barrel has an overflow outlet that is connected to stormwater drains or a subsoil irrigation system.

• The barrel should have air vents (covered with mosquito mesh) to prevent the water from becoming stagnant.

• Periodically clean out the inside of the barrel.

Well water

Cool, clean groundwater from underground rivers, or "aquifers," is one of nature's buried treasures. A well allows people to tap this treasure in places without adequate surface water or connection to water mains.

However, wells are a responsibility as well as a resource. Private well owners need to make sure that their well is maintained, kept safe and free from contamination.

• Surface spills of fuels (gasoline, fuel oil or diesel), solvents, paints and pesticides can seriously contaminate groundwater. Rain and melting snow carry these chemicals through the earth and into the water table. Spills near your well may make the water unfit for human consumption. The contamination can spread through an aquifer, carried by flowing contaminated water. Never bury these liquids to dispose of them.

• Clean up accidental spills with absorbent materials such as sand, old newspaper or kitty litter and take the materials to a household hazardous-waste depository (contact your municipal government for details). Never hose down spills.

• Make sure any underground fuel storage tanks or septic systems are in

sound working order. Cracks can allow fuel or effluent to leak and potentially contaminate the aquifer. Locate aboveground storage tanks at least 15–30 metres away from the well, as required by law.

• Keep pet and livestock wastes well away from your well.

• Use sand instead of salt to melt snow on paths and driveways.

• Inspect your well regularly and keep it in good running order.

• Test the quality of your well water regularly. Respond to any quality problems promptly. Also test water after plumbing work or well repairs have been done or after any local floods.

• Don't surround your well with garden. Instead, plant the area with a low groundcover that doesn't need fertilizer or pesticides.

• If you detect a bacterial contamination, don't drink untreated water. Sterilize water for drinking by boiling it vigorously for at least one minute. Store cooled, boiled water in the fridge in clean food-grade containers. Note that boiling can concentrate other contaminants such as metals, minerals, nitrates and other chemicals. Alternatively, use bottled water for drinking.

• Unused and unsealed wells can pose a health and safety risk to animals and people, especially children. An unmaintained well or one that has just been filled with sand or gravel can provide a shortcut for contaminants to enter the aquifer. Regulations require a licensed well contractor to seal unused wells. Hire a contractor and

have the job done safely and properly.

For more information, visit the Well Aware program at www.wellaware.ca.

Keeping run-off clean

What we do in our gardens can have an effect beyond the boundaries of our properties. Rain and melting snow wash pesticides, fertilizers, spilled motor oil, lawn clippings and other materials from our yards into the gutter and into stormwater drains. This soupy storm water ends up in lakes, streams and the ocean. Water seeping through the soil can also carry chemical contaminants and bacteria from animal wastes into groundwater. This contamination can flow many kilometres through aquifers – underground rivers of water that flow through porous rock. This can make the drinking water for people who rely on wells unfit for human consumption. It can also harm water ecosystems, cause algae blooms and kill fish and other aquatic life. Some of these chemicals can enter and accumulate in the food chain. For these reasons, it's vitally important that we reduce the potential for water pollution from our gardens.

Reduce your use of pesticides and synthetic fertilizers and practise organic gardening as outlined in this chapter. It's better for your health and that of your household and neighbourhood. Don't dispose of liquid wastes, such as leftover house paint or solvents, by pouring them in the gutter. Your municipality can advise you of local depositories for these and other hazardous materials. If your car is dripping lubricant oil, have the leak fixed promptly. A huge amount of the motor oil that ends up in our waterways is leaked oil washed off urban roads and driveways. Also reduce your use of road salt in winter by using sand instead. Remember to sweep paths and driveways instead of hosing them down. This saves water as well as preventing unnecessary run-off.

Recycling in the garden

Recycling doesn't just belong in the kitchen – there's a whole range of materials that can be composted or mulched and used in the garden. This puts nutrients back into the soil, and helps the environment by reducing the amount of waste needing to be collected and sent to landfill.

Green waste or organic waste comprises any garden waste, food scraps and wood wastes that can be composted. This organic matter makes up around 30% of the waste we produce in our homes. You can recycle your organic waste, such as food scraps and garden clippings, by composting or using a worm farm at home. An added bonus is that many worm farms and compost bins are themselves made from recycled plastic. Buying these recycled plastic

Reuse in the garden

Don't waste your waste. Instead, reuse it in the garden. Here are some ideas for common waste items that can be used in the garden.

>> Plant seeds and seedlings in milk cartons with some large drainage holes punched in the bottom. The carton will protect the young seedling from the weather and pests, but the cartons will biodegrade as the plant grows.

>> Shredded newspaper can be used as mulch over the summer months. The newspaper will reduce evaporation and lessen the amount of watering needed by your plants.

>> Shredded newspaper is also great for composting, particularly if you find you need to balance a high content of "green" food scraps with some dry "brown" materials. Don't forget that tea bags, coffee grounds, eggshells and hair can be put into compost bins.

>> Old car mats are great for kneeling on while working in the garden.

>> Plastic 2 litre milk bottles make great poop scoopers in the garden for pet owners. Cut off the bottom of the bottle at an angle in order to make a scoop with a handle on it. The leftover plastic can act as a scraper to bring the poop into the scoop.

>> Baby-food jars are ideal for storing garden seeds.

>> Orange bags can be used as nets to keep pests off fruit and vegetables.

>> An old favourite – stockings can be used to tie plants to garden stakes.

products helps to close the loop by putting the end products of recycling to good use.

Recycling organic matter through composting is particularly important if you want a healthy garden in an area with otherwise poor soil. Green waste can be turned into compost, which enriches and improves soil. Drier, brown organic waste, such as dry leaves and twigs, can also be used as mulch, protecting the root bed from the elements and reducing moisture loss from the soil. Mulch can prevent water run-off, ensuring that rain and irrigated water seep deep into the garden bed.

Compost

In areas of natural vegetation, soil is slowly but constantly renewed through the natural breakdown of rock through erosion and the decomposition of organic matter. This organic matter includes leaf litter, dead bugs and other animals, fallen branches and overripe fruit. Bacteria in the soil and other little creatures such as earthworms break this organic matter down into rich, brown humus. Humus is the organic component of the soil, the part that makes it healthy and fertile. The minerals come from broken-down rock. Composting systems take the natural process of biological decomposition and concentrate it in a garden-based humus-making factory. By concentrating the rotting organic matter in one place, the heat produced by decomposition builds up, which speeds up the process. Compost bins allow food scraps and garden clippings

to be turned quickly into plant food that nourishes the soil and helps the garden bloom.

Compost systems generally consist of a well-ventilated bin with an open bottom and a lid that helps keep small animals from scavenging in the bin. You can also make an unenclosed compost heap in a corner of the garden, but using a bin makes it much easier to control and maintain and to keep out pests.

Steps to home composting

1. Setting up. Compost bins are available from hardware and gardening stores. Prices range from $30 to $60 for a basic bin, though some municipalities offer subsidized compost bins at a lower price. Look for compost bins that are made from recycled plastic. You can also get compost bins on support frames that allow the bin to be rotated by turning a handle. Choose a shady spot for your compost bin because too much sunlight can dry out the heap and slow down decomposition. It needs to be well ventilated, so don't position it too closely to trees, fences or walls. Try to locate it within easy access of your kitchen – but it's not the most attractive garden feature so you may want to put it out of sight. You'll appreciate a compost bin that's close to the back door in winter, when you won't want to venture too far into the snow and cold.

2. Build the layers. Gradually fill your compost bin with alternating layers of food scraps, garden clippings and shredded paper. An occasional layer of soil also helps. A compost heap benefits from a mix of green components, such as veggie scraps and fresh lawn clippings, and brown components, such as dry leaves and shredded newspaper. Blood-and-bone or dolomite can also be added to the heap to enrich the compost. You can also add small amounts of poultry or pigeon manure to give the compost extra nutrients. Do not add meat, dairy products, fish, bones, bread, rice or oily food (some municipalities will take these in municipal composting programs). Do not add clippings from diseased plants or those containing seeds. Do not add dog, cat or human manure as it can spread disease.

3. Maintenance. Keep your compost moist and well ventilated. Occasionally turn and mix the layers with a garden fork. You can also add compost worms (available from gardening centres) to compost to help break the organic matter down faster.

4. Use the compost. It takes around four months for the bulk of the organic matter to break down. When the compost is dark and crumbly, it's ready to use. Some compost bins have doors at the base so that you can remove deeper, older compost that may be ready while the top of the heap is still breaking down. You may wish to have two compost bins, filling one bin first then putting fresh material into the

Compost trouble-shooting

PROBLEM	SOLUTION
The compost smells bad.	The pile may be too wet, have too much green content or not be well ventilated enough. Mix in some dry ingredients, make sure it's well ventilated, and wear a mask and turn the compost with a garden fork.
The compost attracts small animals and flies.	Small vinegar flies are a sign of a functioning compost heap. However, bluebottles and rodents and other animals are a sign that you've added the wrong ingredients. Cover each addition of food with a good layer of soil. Set rodent traps around the bin.
The compost is taking too long to break down.	Compost systems need air, moisture and warmth to break down. Check that the pile is damp and well ventilated and that there's a balance of green and brown waste.

A good thick layer of mulch – over 7.5 cm – can reduce the evaporation of water from the soil by up to 70%.

second bin while the contents of the first bin break down. Dig the compost into your garden beds or spread it over the top of established beds as mulch. Remember to wear gardening gloves when handling the compost.

Winter composting

Cold winter winds and snow can put off even the most enthusiastic composter. With colder temperatures, the composting action will slow and the heap may even freeze solid. However, once the warm weather returns, your compost heap will spring into action again. Freezing temperatures can actually help the decomposition, as the freezing process breaks down the fibres in plant materials, making them decompose faster once the heap thaws. When you return to gardening activities, you'll probably want to use some completed compost, so it's worth persevering. Here are a few tips to help:
• Store food scraps in a container with a lid under the sink and empty it into the compost bin once a week instead of making daily trips outside.
• Consider insulating your compost pile or bin with hay bales or fallen leaves.
• When outdoor composting is too hard, consider indoor composting with a worm farm.

>>

Safety tip

Compost, potting mix and fertilizer products can contain a number of substances that can harm your health. They can contain spores, fungi and other allergens, bacteria and synthetic chemicals, many of which can irritate the skin, particularly if you have scratches and small cuts on your hands as often happens when gardening. These substances can also easily become airborne when handled. Once airborne, they can irritate the eyes and enter the lungs, sometimes causing illness. For these reasons it is important to always wear gloves and a face mask when handling compost, fertilizer and potting mix. Always open new bags of these products outside and take care with how you handle them, to minimize the amount that is dispersed into the air.

Mulch

Mulch is like an insulating blanket for your garden beds. It provides a barrier between the top of the soil and the elements. Mulch reduces the loss of water through evaporation, prevents weeds from springing up, keeps the soil a stable temperature and protects the topsoil from erosion by wind and water.

As well as being functional and helpful to the environment, mulch can also be decorative. Pebbles, for example, are becoming a popular form of mulch.

Types of mulch

• **Compost** is not the most attractive of all mulches, but is one of the most nutritious. It is a good form of mulch for vegetable gardens, rather than more ornamental gardens.

• **Newspaper** makes a cheap and effective form of mulch that eventually breaks down into the soil. Modern inks are often soy-based and no longer contain heavy metals that would otherwise contaminate the soil.

• **Commercial mulch products** are readily available. Most are made from paper, wood and plant waste. They will help reduce water loss and nourish the soil as they break down. Look for those made from recycled materials.

• **Straw and hay** are low-cost mulch options. They are good for vegetable gardens. Straw from legumes, such as pea straw and alfalfa, adds beneficial nitrogen to the soil as it breaks down.

• **Leaf litter and twigs** can be gathered from your own garden and make a cheaper mulch. They can also be quite attractive, depending on the source. Pine-needle litter is particularly effective. From an aesthetic point of view, it is well suited to woodland-style gardens. Pine needles will also help to nourish the soil as they break down.

• **Pebbles and gravel** are a great way to cut down moisture loss in more simply styled, minimalist gardens. They go well with succulent plants and are

You don't have to break your back digging compost into the soil. Spread compost on the surface of your garden beds. Earthworms will do the job of carrying the nutrients deeper into the garden bed for you.

Worm trivia

>> There are many different types of worms. Reds, Tigers and African Night Crawlers are just a few.

>> Each worm will consume its own weight in organic waste every day.

>> Compost worms are hermaphrodites; each worm is both male and female. Mature worms can fertilize or be fertilized.

>> Each egg capsule contains between 1 and 20 young (4 on average), and these young worms hatch in about 21 days.

>> Worms take about 60 to 90 days to mature. Given the right conditions, the worm farm can double in numbers every two months.

>> Worms regulate their own population.

>> Worm castings hold up to nine times their weight in water and their Ph level is neutral so they will help in releasing the maximum available nutrients and minerals into the soil. This helps to make the water-soluble nutrients in worm castings accessible for plants and their root systems.

>> Worm castings contain many times the available potassium, nitrogen and phosphorus of average garden soil.

>> Worm castings contain other micro-organisms that will enhance plant growth and will not harm even the most delicate plants. There is never any chance of overfertilizing or burning your plants.

Worms like to eat:
>> most fruit and vegetable scraps
>> soaked and shredded pizza boxes, cardboard, paper and newspaper
>> leaves
>> dirt
>> hair
>> eggshells
>> cooked potato

Worms don't like:
>> onion
>> citrus fruit
>> raw potato
>> anything you shouldn't put into a compost bin (e.g., meat, dairy)

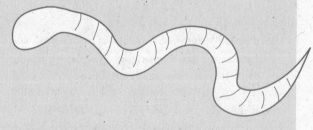

great for covering the dirt in potted plants. They can be expensive but do not break down into the soil. Remember that if you change your mind later, they will be a pain in the neck to remove. It's worth laying some porous weed mat or mesh underneath to help with removing them, just in case. Look for artificial "river" pebbles instead of natural pebbles and stones, as these may have been taken unsustainably from natural river and stream habitats.

• **Crushed glass** is a recycled product used in a similar way to pebbles. The crushed glass is tumbled to remove any sharp edges. It is available in a range of colours and can look fantastic in a well-designed garden.

Worm farming

Earthworms are fantastic things for gardens. They do a great job of aerating and enriching the soil. Worms are proficient at munching through copious amounts of organic waste and are great helpers in reducing the amount of household waste sent to landfill. Worm castings are a good natural fertilizer and soil conditioner. In its passage through the worm, the mineral subsoil undergoes changes that make the minerals available for plants. The castings contain 5 times the nitrate, 7 times the available phosphorus, 11 times the potassium, 3 times the exchangeable magnesium, and 1.5 times the calcium that occurs in the top 15 cm of uneaten soil.

However, worms don't need a garden to chomp through food scraps. They can be kept in a worm farm – a food-scrap garbage disposal unit of sorts. Worm farms do not even require a yard to be kept in, so they are a good alternative for apartments or small units. They're a great way to compost kitchen scraps, and the worm castings are good for keeping indoor plants healthy. Worms happily munch through huge amounts of food scraps. In fact, 1 kg of worms can eat and recycle 1 kg of food every day.

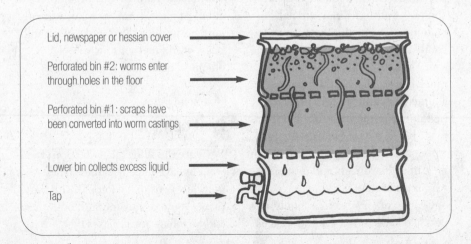

Lid, newspaper or hessian cover

Perforated bin #2: worms enter through holes in the floor

Perforated bin #1: scraps have been converted into worm castings

Lower bin collects excess liquid

Tap

Worm farms have simple structures. They consist of a series of perforated layers, stacked one on top of the other, allowing a comfortable amount of room for the worms in between. Food scraps are put into the upper layer. Worms wriggle up into this layer to eat the food, leaving their castings in lower layers. Liquid worm waste trickles down to collect in the bottom, non-perforated layer.

Worm farms, like compost bins, are available from hardware and garden stores. They generally cost around $50–$100. Alternatively, you can make your own worm farm. Live worms are sold separately. Red worms, or "red wrigglers," are the best. Believe it or not, worm farming can become a hobby.

Going organic in the garden

Organic gardens work with nature, rather than against it. Organic gardening involves growing plants without using artificial fertilizers and pesticides. Instead, it uses natural compost, worm castings, animal manure, green manure or a combination of these to fertilize the soil. These natural fertilizers do a much better job than their synthetic counterparts and are less likely to pollute stormwater run-off. There are many benefits to organic gardening:

• You save the money otherwise spent on artificial fertilizers and pesticides.
• Your garden is a healthier environment for you, your family, any pets and local native wildlife species.

• The biodiversity of your garden's ecosystem is protected, right down to the beneficial micro-cultures in soil.
• Any fruit and vegetables that you might grow are healthier and often more nutritious than those bought at the supermarket.
• Organic gardens often need less watering.
• Because nature is in balance in organic gardens, once established they need very little work to maintain.
• Any run-off from your garden into stormwater drains is free from chemical pollution from pesticides and fertilizers. Polluted stormwater in our waterways and oceans can harm aquatic life.

Converting your garden to an organic garden is easier than you would think. We've already looked at garden recycling, which provides much of the nutrients your garden needs. Make your own compost or worm castings as outlined to fertilize your soil. In the meantime, if you want to add fertilizer while your compost or worm farm matures, buy organic compost mixes from your hardware or garden supplies store, and use natural pest control methods instead of chemical pesticides.

Pest control

Pests are the things that you don't want to have in your garden. They may be weeds that compete with the plants you're trying to grow, bugs that eat the foliage, or diseases that damage the plants. The trouble with pesticides, apart from being a health hazard, is that they're not always very selective. They can kill the plants, bugs and other organisms that you want to keep, along with those that you're trying to get rid of. When you interfere with nature, the balance between species is upset, and before you know it your garden has more problems rather than fewer. Natural pest control methods enlist the help of nature and can be very effective. After all, arsenic occurs naturally in apricot kernels, so nature has the potential to be quite ferocious. Natural pest control makes the survival of the fittest work in favour of you and your garden.

The basics of pest control in the garden

Natural pest control and other non-chemical methods can control a range of garden pests and creepy crawlies. As with indoor pests, there are some basic greener methods of pest control:

Enlist predatory allies by encouraging the beneficial bugs and animals that eat the pests. This method lets the predators do the job of keeping pest numbers down for you.

Make pests unwelcome. They will tend to leave your property if you don't allow them to establish cozy, protected nests. Be a home wrecker by carefully destroying any nests you find (as long as it's safe to do so) or by limiting the places where they might build homes, such as woodpiles or junk heaps.

Companion planting works by putting plants that are like living insect repellent wherever there are plants that pests love. By planting them together, you can keep the pests away from the plant you want to protect.

Get some chemical help. Some natural substances are non-toxic to humans but poisonous to pests. Others simply repel them. Strategically place repellents around the garden to keep pests away or, if all else fails, use a non-toxic insecticide, such as pyrethrum.

Put up barriers. Block the access of pests or birds by putting up physical barriers such as nets or wire-covered frames.

Green manure

Green manure is a way of fertilizing and conditioning a patch of soil by growing a nitrogen-fixing crop on it, such as alfalfa, then digging it back into the soil. It puts nitrogen into the soil, brings up nutrients and trace elements from deeper in the soil, and adds texture to the soil.

Green manure crops are often used in crop rotation to rejuvenate the soil. The same principle can be applied to home gardens with poor soil.

A single ladybug can eat 400 aphids in one week. One toad can eat over 1000 earwigs in a summer.

Use brute force. Another option is to kill pests using old-fashioned traps, a trusty fly swatter or boiling water.

Garden pest control – critter by critter

Ants aren't much of a problem by themselves, but they're great buddies with aphids. They love a sweet substance produced by aphids, so they protect them and carry them from plant to plant. Sprinkle the ground with bone meal to keep ants away and plant vulnerable seedlings in sawn-off milk cartons to protect them. Geraniums, southernwood and pennyroyal plants deter ants, so plant them near aphid-prone plants such as roses and near the doorways and windows of your house.

Aphids can be removed by splashing soapy water onto the affected plant, followed by cold clean water. Collect the soapy wash water from your washing machine to do the job. Protect plants troubled by aphids by companion planting them with orange nasturtiums, catnip, catmint and garlic. Encourage ladybugs, as they eat a whole range of garden pests, including aphids. A single ladybug can eat 400 aphids in one week.

Birds can be a gardener's friend or foe. While they can make a mess of seedlings, you should encourage them, as they eat a lot of common garden pests. Make your garden bird-friendly so that you can enlist their help in pest control and enjoy their songs and

Make your own bug spray

Mince 5 cloves of garlic and around 18 hot chili peppers. Mix in around a litre of water and allow to stand for a week or so. Strain the spicy water and put it into a labelled spray bottle.

Use this spicy spray to kill ants, spiders, slugs, caterpillars and other pests. However, make sure you wash your hands well after making and using it and be careful not to get any spray in your eyes or the eyes of pets. It can sting you as well as the pests.

company. Protect fruit and vegetables with mesh orange bags and hang unwanted computer CDs in any fruit trees to deter the birds from the fruit.

Caterpillars could be the kinds that turn into the butterflies you may be trying to encourage. To get rid of others, sprinkle finely ground pepper onto dampened plants that are threatened by caterpillars.

Flies can be deterred by basil, tansy, pyrethrum and eau-de-cologne mint plants. Strategically place pots of these plants and citronella candles around the house near doors, windows and barbecue areas. However, keep

Mosquitoes and West Nile virus

Mosquito bites in Canada were, until recently, just a minor annoyance. But in recent years, West Nile virus has appeared in Canada. This insect-borne disease can infect humans with varying severity. Some people infected with the virus have mild symptoms or no symptoms at all. A very small percentage can become seriously ill. A small number of people have died. It is very important to reduce your risk of contracting the disease by taking steps to keep mosquito numbers down and avoid getting bitten. Here are some suggested measures.

To avoid mosquito bites:
• Use insect repellents when outdoors.
• Limit how much skin you expose when outdoors by wearing long pants and long-sleeved tops.
• Choose light-coloured clothing, as mosquitoes tend to be attracted to dark colours.
• Make sure your doors and windows have well-fitted mesh screens, free of holes. Don't leave unscreened doors or windows open.
• Burn citronella candles when entertaining outdoors in summer.

To reduce mosquito breeding sites:
• Twice weekly, drain any still pools of water that may have gathered in flowerpot saucers, recycling bins, garbage cans, bin lids and any other containers.
• Twice weekly, change the water in pet bowls, wading pools and birdbaths.
• Make sure any rain barrels have screens over any openings.
• Make garden ponds mosquito-safe by keeping native fish in them or incorporating an aerator, fountain or other water feature that will keep the surface of the water moving and therefore inhospitable to mosquito larvae.

Health Canada has a website for the West Nile virus. The West Nile Monitor part of the site has information on where outbreaks have occurred so that people can be aware of whether or not their local region is at risk. See www.hc-sc.gc.ca/english/westnile.

tansy in small pots, as it can be an invasive plant.

Mosquitoes can be controlled by taking away the pools of water they breed in. Don't allow such pools of water to collect outside. Keep mosquitoes outdoors by placing pots of tansy or southern-wood near windowsills and doorways.

Slugs and snails have delicate bodies and don't like moving over rough ground. Sprinkling lime or wood ash around garden beds will deter them. They also don't like crawling over bark, so bark can be a good slug-resistant groundcover or mulch. Birds also eat them. Slugs and snails are killed by salt, so if deterrents or predators don't solve your slug problem, sprinkle salt on your paths and around garden beds. Alternatively, you can set traps for them by leaving out small saucers or partially buried containers of beer. Snails and slugs love beer and will be attracted to it. Once they fall into the pool of beer they'll drown, but at least they'll die happy.

Garden decor

A gorgeous garden consists of more than just plants. Decking, garden furniture, water features, barbecue areas and play areas for kids can turn a garden into an outdoor room, a place that you'll want to spend time in.

However, some garden hardware is definitely greener than others. Like everything else, it's important that your fencing, garden furniture and other landscaping structures are made from sustainable materials that provide a healthy environment for both you and the planet. Take into account the following to make your garden more than green to look at.

Use the good wood. It's easy to think that anything made from wood is good because it comes from a tree and we all love trees. However, sometimes using wood is bad for the environment, depending on where the wood is from and how it has been treated. As with indoor furniture, choose fencing and outdoor furniture that is made from ancient-forest-friendly timber. Rainforest timbers may look beautiful in outdoor furniture, but they look more beautiful in their parent rainforest trees, complete with resident wildlife. You can also find second-hand outdoor furniture at garage sales and second-hand stores.

Take care with wood treatments (or mistreatments). Many outdoor wood products, including decking, furniture and play equipment, are treated with chromated copper arsenate (CCA), a highly toxic compound. This is sometimes labelled as "tanalized" or "pressure-treated" timber. CCA is a preservative, but it has also been linked to various forms of cancer. Traces of

CCA are left on the skin when the wood is handled and can also leach from wood into surrounding soil. Although studies show that this is not an immediate health threat, we still don't fully understand the cumulative effects of the many chemicals we are exposed to today. The potential for harm from CCA dramatically increases when wood treated with it is burned, so you should never burn CCA-treated timber or other treated timbers with unknown histories. It is much safer to choose wood products that are either untreated or treated with preservatives that have a low toxicity and are arsenic-free.

You can protect wood where it meets the soil by encasing it in a metal shoe or concrete. Never treat wood posts with used motor oil, as is sometimes suggested. Used motor oil contains a cocktail of chemical nasties that can contaminate soil, groundwater, other waterways and the air. It should be safely disposed of or recycled as outlined in the Garage chapter.

Choose greener deck washes and finishes. Timber decks are traditionally sealed with flammable, petrochemically derived stains and varnishes. These sealants are not sustainable and emit air-polluting gases, which can trigger allergies. Instead, apply a deck sealant formulated from plant oils to a well-cleaned and sanded deck. Good preparation of the decking wood will ensure that the sealant will apply better and last longer.

Consider wood alternatives. You may wish to avoid wood altogether. Synthetic wood products made from recycled plastics or recycled plastic and wood composites are now available, though they can be harder to find. They are manufactured to need no further painting, preservatives or stains, are weather- and rot-resistant and are often easier to maintain. They also make use of a waste product that would otherwise be sent to landfill.

Green walls and rooftop gardens

Many people would consider ivy-covered walls and rooftop gardens purely an aesthetic choice. However, this kind of vegetation helps to control pollution caused by stormwater run-off, by soaking up precipitation. It also reduces the need for heating, and consequently greenhouse gas emissions, by providing extra insulation and protection from wind. A study commissioned by the Canada Mortgage and Housing Corporation found that a 16 cm thick blanket of plants can increase the R-value (level of insulation) of a wall by as much as 30%.

Landscape to save energy. Remember that what you have outside in the garden will affect the amount of light and heat that comes into your house. Use this to your advantage. Plant deciduous trees or grow deciduous vines on a pergola on the south face of your house. The bare branches will allow warmth and light in during winter and provide shade in the summer, reducing your need for additional heating and cooling. The transpiration of water from plants draws heat energy from the surroundings and so has a cooling effect – like a living air conditioner. Alternatively, you can put up removable sailcloths or shadecloth to shade south-facing windows in summer and take them down in winter.

Go for greener grounds. Concrete may seem like a good low-maintenance idea, but it's not. Aside from being ugly, it prevents seepage of rainwater into the ground, absorbs and reflects heat and smothers all living things underneath it. Instead, use groundcover, bark or paving that allows rainwater to seep through it.

Buy recycled. A huge number of landscaping products are the fruits of your recycling labour. Compost bins, retaining walls, garden furniture, garden boxes, edging, pots and even birdbaths made from recycled materials are all available. You can also use reclaimed bricks and pavers for paving. The fact that they're aged and a bit battered is the very thing that gives them their character.

Use a greener grill. Even the humble barbecue can have a small but noticeable environmental impact. Charcoal-burning barbeques produce more air pollution and are less

Solar-heated swimming

There are around 600 000 swimming pools in Canada. The average pool in Canada, if heated, uses the same amount of energy to heat it in the summer months as many homes use in a year. It's well worth using solar energy to heat your pool, both for the sake of the planet and for your energy bills. Solar thermal pool-heating systems have purchase and installation costs similar to natural gas and electric heat pump heaters. However, once you've bought a solar pool heater it provides free heating with minimal maintenance costs. Gas and heat pump pool heaters cost hundreds of dollars to run and maintain each year. A solar pool heater quickly pays for itself through reduced running costs when compared with other pool heaters, so it's worth going solar if you want to heat your pool.

   For more information about solar energy, including pool heating, visit the Canadian Solar Industries Association website at www.cansia.ca.

efficient than gas models. Go for gas instead.

Use light from the sun, day and night.
Solar-powered garden lights with their own solar panels are ideal for providing outdoor lighting, as they do not require electrical connections. There is a wide range of solar garden lights available from hardware stores and some nurseries. Although they are relatively expensive to buy (starting at around $40 for a good-quality path light), they provide free, clean light.

Pets

Your four-legged friends might not always appreciate your efforts to green up their life. After all, stopping a cat from chasing wild birds could be seen as spoiling its fun. However, other creatures, great and small, will benefit from your efforts.

Making your pets wildlife-friendly
Domestic pets, strays and feral animals claim the lives of thousands of wild animals each year. It's not their fault; they're only doing what comes naturally. However, you can even up the odds and give the wild animals a sporting chance.
• Feed your animals regularly. If they're hungry, they're more likely to try to make a meal of other animals.
• Keep cats indoors at night.
• Put a bell on your cat's collar to give birds and small animals an audible warning.

• Have your cat or dog neutered. This will mean fewer unwanted litters. Neutered animals are also less inclined to wander and hunt.
• Never dump unwanted cats or kittens. Strays are forced to kill wildlife for food to survive.
• Make sure any pet birds you obtain come from reputable sources. The illegal capture and trade of exotic birds is threatening some species.

Eco-friendly pet products
You can be a green pet owner and a green consumer by choosing environmentally preferred pet products and avoiding those that are less than green.
• Buy biodegradable kitty litter. You can even get kitty litter that's made from wheat, corn or recycled newspapers.
• Buy more baking soda! Put a box out of reach in your dog's kennel or liberally sprinkle some between a pet basket and its lining. Baking soda absorbs smells.
• Buy herbal flea rinses instead of chemical rinses. Alternatively, look for flea collars that contain citronella and cedar oils or extracts from pyrethrum flowers, and add brewer's yeast and garlic to your pet's food to deter fleas.
• Particularly avoid flea rinses that contain the organophosphate chemicals chlorpyrifos or diazinon. These are highly toxic chemicals that often end up in waterways, harming aquatic life and sometimes the people and animals that have used

them. They're banned in the US and will hopefully soon be banned elsewhere.

• Remember the first line of attack when controlling fleas – stop the infestation from happening in the first place. Put some herbal flea deterrents, such as citronella, eucalyptus, pennyroyal or citrus peel oils, on your pet's bed or basket. Also do regular flea combing so that you can spot the problem early, while there are just a few fleas to deal with.

• As for food, try to prepare fresh food for your pets instead of overpackaged processed food. It's better for the pet and better for the environment. You can even get some organic pet food products.

• Consider buying a worm farm for dog poop. That way you can turn unwanted dog poop into worm waste, which is good for the garden. Have one worm farm for food scraps and a separate one for dog poop. If you put the lot into one worm farm, the worms will go for the food scraps first, leaving the poop to rot and go smelly.

• Don't put cat or dog waste in your compost.

• If you do buy canned pet food, remember that the cans themselves are recyclable wherever normal food cans are collected.

FOR A GREENER GARDEN:

CHOOSE indigenous plants.

THINK local when planting.

CONTROL weeds the green way.

RECYCLE garden waste.

2

Lifestyle >>

Greening up at home is a great start, but there are lots of other things to do with the way we live our lives that need careful evaluation in terms of environmental impact. Shopping is an area where responsible decisions can be easily made, and the same with grooming. There are also particular situations that happen only every now and again: buying or renovating a house and having a baby. These can be life-changing choices, and offer new opportunities to make a difference to the health of the planet.

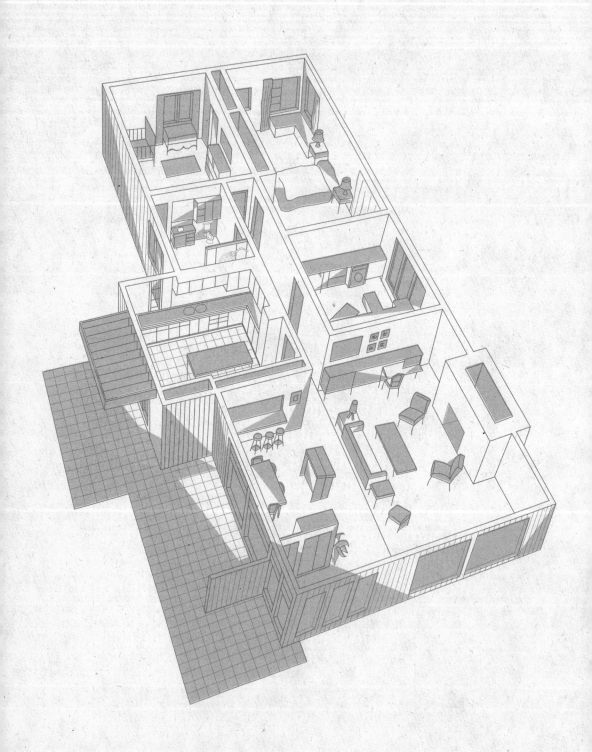

>> Green building and renovating

Buying a home can be the single biggest financial commitment that a person will make. Changing homes, whether renting, buying or building, is also one of your greatest opportunities to reduce the impact that your life has on the environment.

If you show some care for the planet when planning or choosing and adapting your house, you will be repaid with a comfortable, warm place to relax, with lower energy and water bills, and with a cleaner, healthier environment to live in.

Tens of thousands of new houses are built each year in addition to or replacing the millions of existing dwellings. If you're one of the thousands who are building a new house, then you have a unique chance to build a greener, more energy-efficient one that will take a lesser toll on the environment throughout its life. Simple design features built into a house from the outset, such as good insulation, can make more of a difference to our energy use than the combined benefits of smaller energy-saving tips. The Natural Resources Canada (NRCan) R-2000 initiative has a training and licensing program for builders, helping them and their customers to achieve healthier, more energy-efficient and water-wise new homes. It would be great if we could gradually see eco-homes become more common and the energy-efficient "green house" become the normal way to build, rather than the exception.

This chapter is a snapshot of what to look for and what to ask your builder or architect to consider. You will need to seek expert advice because individual sites, settings and climate zones have particular considerations, and different local laws and regulations will have some influence over what you can build in your area and how easy it is to get planning approvals. Remember that there are many design features, sustainable materials and new technologies that are readily available. If you understand the issues, you will know what questions to ask.

What makes a house green?

There are new green houses that we tend not to notice because they don't always stand out and they don't fit the hippie stereotype. In fact, a green house can look exactly like any other house.

Key factors in greener buildings are:
- energy efficiency
- water efficiency
- material use

Energy efficiency is about how well your house uses energy. It involves the appliances, heating, cooling, ventilation and lighting systems of your home. The design of the house and the use it makes of natural light and heat (passive solar heating), natural ventilation and insulation will also determine how much extra heating, cooling and lighting it will need.

Water efficiency involves water supplies (from water mains, wells and rainwater), how water is used in the home and how wastewater is disposed of.

Material use considers the sources of the materials used to build your house and whether or not they are sustainable, how they are made or processed before being used in the house, and their effect on how healthy and efficient the house is to live in.

The EnerGuide for Houses program aims to make Canadian homes more energy-efficient. Like the other EnerGuide programs, EnerGuide for Houses gives new or existing houses a rating – a standard measure of a given house's energy performance or energy efficiency. The rating is a number between 0 and 100, from low to high efficiency. For example, older unrenovated houses are likely to have a rating of under 50; older houses that have had energy-efficiency upgrades may have a rating of around 65 to 70; and energy-efficient new houses are likely to have a rating of over 75. Aim for a house that has an EnerGuide efficiency rating of 75–80 or more.

Building a new house
EnerGuide for new houses

The decisions that have the greatest effect on your ongoing energy bills are made before the first brick is laid. EnerGuide advisers can work out a proposed home's energy-efficiency rating from the plans and blueprints and, if needed, can suggest changes to your building plan that will improve its energy efficiency and save you money year after year. New houses generally have a new-house EnerGuide label that states the design's rating. Some larger home builders who construct entire developments offer energy-efficiency upgrade packages for standard house models. In other words, you can choose a house design and pay extra for a set of construction features that increase the house's base rating to a higher, more efficient one. It's an upfront investment of money, but one that brings returns through saved energy. If you're an owner/builder or are having a unique home designed by an architect, you can call in the services of an approved EnerGuide adviser to rate your plans and suggest improvements. The EnerGuide program has a database of approved EnerGuide advisers in each province (see Further Information, page 290). Remember that a high rating is also a selling point for houses. In the future, with energy prices expected to rise, this may be the difference between a good and a bad resale figure.

R-2000 standard

If all of this green building information sounds appealing but you'd rather not have to work it out for yourself, then choose a R-2000-standard home or builder. R-2000 is a system for building and certifying new homes to a higher environmental standard, well above the base requirements of the building code. The R-2000 program is a joint effort between NRCan and Canada's home construction industry. The R-2000 standard is awarded to homes that meet or exceed certain requirements for energy efficiency, reduced environmental impact and the provision of a healthy indoor living environment. Any home design can be built to the R-2000 standard.

Location

Choosing where you're going to live will immediately affect your ongoing greenhouse gas contribution.

Transportation accounts for nearly half of the greenhouse impact of the average Canadian. The bulk of these greenhouse gases come from the exhaust pipes of cars, so look for a site near a train station or other public transportation route so that you don't have to drive. If you live close enough, you could even walk or ride a bike to work in good weather.

Also look at the services in the area. An established community with shops, schools and other facilities and services will reduce the amount of time you need to spend in your car.

Planning and design

Before you think about the specific design, think about what you need and want in your house. Consider the amount of space you'll need now and in the future. Don't forget to plan for outdoor needs as well: allow space for things like a clothes line, rain barrel, outdoor entertaining area, barbecue and garbage bins.

Remember that you have to pay for every square metre of the building of your home. Once finished, each extra square metre is another to keep clean and possibly another to heat or cool. Try to avoid designs that need a lot of hallways for access. Instead, have areas of open-plan living, adequately closed off from the rest of the house to prevent drafts and heat loss.

Orientation

Once you've chosen your land, it's time to decide how your dream home will sit on the land and which way the rooms will face. Harnessing the light and energy of the sun will save you a lot of money. The south face of houses in Canada (and the northern hemisphere in general) gets direct sunlight through most of the day. This sunlight can be used to help heat and light your home. Ideally, your block and the placement of the house on it should allow clear access to the south (often called solar access). It should not be overshadowed in winter by other buildings, tall trees or fences to the south.

What goes where?

The location of each room also makes a difference. Consider the following tips.
• Locate rooms in which you spend a lot of time during the day to the southern side of the house. This includes living and family rooms.
• Put bedrooms to the north of the house. This side tends to be the coolest.
• The west of the house gets hot in the afternoon. Put service rooms such as the laundry, bathroom and garage and storage rooms on this side.
• "Zone" rooms with similar uses and heating or cooling needs close together to make the distribution of heating and cooling easier to control and more energy efficient. In a single-storey house, the three main zones are the living zone, the sleeping zone and the wet areas (kitchen, bathroom and laundry room).

• Place your wet areas as close together as possible to reduce the length of pipes needed. This will also reduce energy costs by shortening the distance that hot water has to travel.
• If need be, place the bedrooms away from the front of the house to keep these sleeping areas away from traffic noise and pollution and to provide privacy.

Building materials

The choice of building materials is complicated and best done in consultation with your architect or builder. It requires expert knowledge and will depend upon the design of the house, the local climate and the condition of the land you're building on. From an environmental point of view, the main considerations are:

Material properties

Different building materials have different properties that make them suited to particular climates and uses. For example, a humid climate will need materials that are moisture-resistant, while coastal areas will need materials that resist corrosion. In climates with cool winters, use heavy building materials inside that have a high thermal mass to help capture and store the sun's daytime warmth.

Durability

As a general rule, the longer a building lasts, the less impact it has on the environment. Materials chosen should be durable, or easily replaceable, should they have a shorter lifespan than the building as a whole. Often, higher-quality materials will cost more, but they will save you money in the long term by needing less maintenance, not needing premature replacement and improving the house's resale value.

Renewable or recyclable resources

Plant-based materials are renewable in that they can, in theory, be replaced by growing more, but our supply of resources such as metals is limited. It's important to make sure that, whenever possible, non-renewable materials can be easily recycled at the end of the building's lifespan.

Forest-friendly timbers

Some natural building materials, particularly forest timber, are harvested from areas of natural vegetation. This destroys habitat, harms wildlife and has an impact on biodiversity. Always question the source of any timber that is used in your home and ask for alternatives, such as recycled or FSC-certified timber.

Energy efficiency

Materials have varying degrees of energy efficiency too. For example, materials that have a high thermal mass (concrete, mud brick, rammed earth, stone and slate) are slow to heat and take a while to cool down. They help to regulate the temperature of

Choosing the good wood

Canada's extensive forests are a wonderful natural resource, prized by logging operations, Canada's Aboriginal population, conservationists and resident flora and fauna alike. There are a number of different ways to harvest timber, from highly destructive clearcut logging (see Hot Topics, page 260) to ecologically sustainable harvesting.

When you are building or renovating, you have the opportunity to choose forest-friendly timbers and support eco-forestry operations. Look for timber and wood products that are certified in line with the Forest Stewardship Council (FSC) standards. FSC is an international non-profit organization working towards the environmental, social and economic management of the world's forests. Choosing FSC certified wood products gives you the confidence that your wood has come from forests managed to a triple bottom line standard.

Other "good woods" include wood reclaimed from demolished buildings, wood from community and First Nation forest operations, wood from sustainably managed plantations and recycled plastic "lumber."

For more information, visit www.fsccanada.org and www.certifiedwood.org.

your home by capturing and storing the sun's heat during the day and releasing it at night.

Indoor air quality

Synthetic building materials, finishes and paints can all give off high levels of polluting gases, including volatile organic compounds (VOCs). These pollutants pose a significant health risk and can bring about symptoms such as headache, fatigue, respiratory problems, dizziness, and eye, nose, throat and skin irritation. Where possible, limit your use of carpets (particularly those made from synthetic fibres), synthetic adhesives, paints, varnishes (particularly those containing polyurethane) and other finishes, as well as particle board and MDF. It can be very difficult to build a new house totally free from materials that give off these gases, so make sure that you ventilate the house thoroughly for the first year, particularly the first six months.

Waste and recycling

Some materials and building methods generate a high amount of waste, while others can actually use recycled waste. A quarter to a third of Canada's total waste stream comes from the building sector. Wherever possible, choose building or landscaping materials that are made from recycled materials. Ask your builder about his or her waste minimization practices, and consider incorporating waste minimization and recycling clauses and incentives into the contract. You can also use building materials and features that have been salvaged from demolished buildings. Reclaimed bricks, for example, can add a lot of character to a home or garden and are sometimes cheaper than new materials. Keep an eye out for unusual or interesting pieces that can bring interest and individuality to your home.

Windows and shading

Windows can be made into better insulators by adding additional layers of glazing. Double-glazed windows are common in Canada, but a third and even a fourth layer of glazing can be added. Windows can also be further insulated with thick curtains and well-fitting pelmets.

Another recent development is the low-emissivity (low-E) coating – a thin transparent layer of metal oxide over the glass that allows visible light through but reflects back infrared heat radiation. This helps the window to keep heat out in summer and reflect heat back into the house in winter. It also has the added benefit of reducing incoming UV light and so protects furniture and drapes from fading. The space between panes in multiple glazing can also be filled with argon gas, as inert gas that is more insulating than air. Gas filling in combination with a low-E coating is particularly effective at improving the insulating level of windows.

Size and placement of windows and how they are shaded will depend on their orientation and the room they're placed in. The materials the window and its frame are made of and how well they are fitted will also influence how well the windows perform.

Tips for windows

• If there is good solar access, use large windows for south-facing living areas. Keep windows on the north face of the house smaller.

• Put small windows on the east and west faces of the house, with good summer shading. The east gets direct sunlight in the morning hours, while the west gets hot, direct sun in the afternoon.

• Position windows that can open and close in places that allow for cross-ventilation in living areas.

• Use multiple layers of glazing for windows that are high up and hard to get at, such as skylights. These windows may be hard to put curtains on or may not be intended to have curtains for aesthetic reasons.

• For the framing material, metal frames (usually aluminum) without a thermal break allow heat loss and gain. If you choose metal frames, make sure that they have some form of insulating treatment. Wooden frames insulate well but need more maintenance than aluminum. PVC frames are low-maintenance and insulate well but are made from non-renewable resources and contribute to pollution in their production. PVC in general should be avoided.

• Always seal gaps between the window frame and the wall to reduce air leaks, drafts and heat loss.

• Fit windows that can be opened with screens to keep insects out and to remove the temptation to use bug spray.

• Depending on your local climate, consider getting storm windows and doors, particularly on the faces of the house that take the brunt of the force of strong winds.

• Use window coverings that will make your house more efficient. For more information, see the window-dressing tips in Green Living Room, page 49.

Tips for shading

• Make sure that your roof has eaves that overhang the south face of the house. During winter, the path of the sun is low enough in the sky to allow light and radiant heat into the room. However, in the summer, when the sun is higher, the eaves will block the sun and help to shade the room.

ENERGY STAR windows

The ENERGY STAR initiative for windows and glass sliding doors separates Canada into four climate zones (Zone A includes Vancouver and Victoria; Zone B includes Toronto, Quebec and Calgary; Zone C includes Edmonton, Winnipeg and Whitehorse; and Zone D includes Yellowknife and Churchill).

The ENERGY STAR symbol appears on labels and product literature of qualified products along with the zones for which the standard applies. Visit the ENERGY STAR website (energystar.gc.ca) to see a map of the climate zones. Once you know your zone, choose products that are qualified for that zone.

• External blinds can effectively prevent much of the summer heat coming through the windows. Particularly consider them if you don't have much shade on the west side of the house.

• Deciduous plants can provide shade in the summer and lose their leaves and allow the light through in the winter. Consider planting these to the south of your house or near windows on the east and west faces of the house.

Insulation

Insulation is essential for keeping your home a comfortable temperature throughout all seasons, and may be needed in the roof, ceiling, external walls, basement and floor. You may also wish to consider acoustic insulation to block out noise pollution, particularly if you live near a busy road or rail line. Soft furnishings, such as rugs, curtains and wall hangings, can also provide some insulation.

Some people try to skimp on insulation, especially when the building budget is tight. This is a false saving as you pay more in heating and cooling bills over the time you live in the house, not to mention the suffering from being too hot or too cold. Particularly consider insulation for external walls, basements and floors when you're building because it is harder to install in existing constructions.

Insulation is made and sold in specific thermal resistance (RSI) or Imperial measurement (R) values. Both are accurate measures of the

insulation's resistance to heat flow. For each measure, the higher the value, the more insulating the material is. The NRCan Office of Energy Efficiency recommends certain levels of insulation by R or RSI value for walls, basement walls, ceilings, solid roof decks and floors in different climate zones in Canada. These have been published in the Government of Canada's *Model National Energy Codes for Buildings and Houses,* which can be ordered through the Office of Energy Efficiency. An overview of suggested R and RSI values for different parts of British Columbia is also included in BC Hydro's Power Smart HELP sheet "Insulating for Energy Efficiency," available at www.bchydro.com/powersmart/tips.

If your house is built on a concrete slab, the edge of the slab should also be insulated, as a single square metre of exposed slab can lose as much heat as several square metres of uninsulated wall. This is particularly important in homes with in-slab heating systems, which can lose even more heat and waste huge amounts of energy.

Draftproofing and ventilation

Venting stale air without losing heat can be a fine balancing act, so it's important to get both right. Draftproofing is an important consideration when you're building, otherwise a lot of the energy you use for heating is wasted. It is easier to make a house airtight during the building process than to try to seal drafts later.

With air and heat kept in, you also have to make sure that stale air is expelled and replaced with fresh air from outside. Canada's building codes specify minimum ventilation requirements of around eight complete air changes per day. Ventilation systems can be ducted to the whole house and can incorporate bathroom and kitchen fans. More information on ventilation is included in the Bedroom chapter, on pages 112–3.

Flooring

When choosing a floor covering, you need to consider the durability of the flooring material, how easy it is to clean and maintain, how it affects your health, how sustainable the material is and the special needs of particular rooms for flooring. Some materials are better suited to some rooms than others.

Floorboards are easier to clean than carpet and discourage dust mites. They can also be better for the quality of indoor air compared with gas-emitting or dust mite–ridden carpet, provided they're not finished with a synthetic varnish. If you're looking at timber floorboards, consider the option of using recycled FSC-certified or plantation-grown timber.

Carpets are often preferred in bedrooms because they're softer on bare feet and help to keep out drafts. However, they can provide the right conditions for dust mites, so carpets shouldn't be used if you have family members with respiratory problems.

Synthetic carpets, like other synthetic materials, produce gas pollutants, and even pure wool carpet often has a synthetic underlay or chemical treatment that can contribute to poor indoor air quality. Consider washable rugs as an alternative.

Natural fibres, including sisal, coir and jute, make sustainable and low-allergy floor coverings.

Cork is a natural, sustainable material harvested every nine years from the bark of the cork-oak tree. It grows without the need for chemicals, fertilizers or irrigation. Cork is also non-polluting, biodegradable and recyclable. If you decide to use cork flooring, avoid tiles that are PVC-finished. Consider buying them unvarnished and finish them yourself with a water-based varnish or beeswax polish.

Bamboo is an incredibly fast-growing plant – a renewable and quick-to-produce green alternative to timber floorboards. Bamboo floorboards function similarly to hardwood floorboards. Bamboo flooring is cost-effective and readily available in tongue and groove strips. It can be bought both unfinished and polyurethane-finished. Floorworks and Silkroad bamboo brands are EcoLogo-certified alternative floor coverings.

Resilient flooring is soft, rubbery-feeling flooring that comes as tiles or roles of sheet flooring. It is generally made from vinyl, rubber, cork or linoleum. Resilient flooring comes in a wide range of designs, finishes and prices. It is often used because it is fairly easy to install and maintain and is relatively cheap to replace. However, it can be thin, can be easily damaged and can show irregularities in the surface over which it is laid. Care must be taken when choosing the adhesives that stick the flooring to the subfloor as some adhesives give off high levels of VOCs. Look for water-based adhesives where possible. Resilient flooring products made from the natural materials cork, rubber and linoleum are renewable and sustainable. Vinyl and other PVC products are generally polluting in their manufacture.

Slate, stone, ceramic and terracotta tiles and exposed concrete are popular flooring materials, particularly in the wet areas of the house. Because they are made from mineral resources mined from the earth's crust, they are not renewable, but the main environmental impacts from these materials are the damage done to local ecosystems when they're extracted. Materials that have to be fired in a kiln, such as ceramic tiles, also have a high energy cost.

For these reasons, stone and ceramic flooring products are a good choice environmentally when they're recycled or salvaged stocks, sourced from a local supply. Other benefits are that they are generally easy to clean

without the need for harsh cleaning agents and they also provide better indoor air quality than carpets, as long as they haven't been finished with fume-emitting varnishes or sealants.

Green fittings

Nowadays there's a lot more to a house than four walls and a roof. Most houses also come with heating and cooling systems, a hot water service, cooking appliances, toilets, baths and showers, and a range of tap fittings. All of these can be chosen to reduce your ongoing use of energy and water. Here's a snapshot of what to consider.

Heating and cooling systems

Particularly consider whether or not you would like an in-floor heating system, such as hydronic or electric slab heating. These have to be built into the floor and generally cannot be fitted later without taking up the floor. For more information about choosing a heating and cooling system, see Green Living Room, pages 46–60.

Hot water service

Locate the hot water service as close as you can to the kitchen to reduce the amount of cold water sitting in lengths of pipe that gets wasted while waiting for the hot water to come through. If you're considering a solar hot water system, make sure you factor this into the roof and plumbing design for the house. For more information on choosing a hot water service, see Green Bathroom, pages 76–82.

How hard is it to build green?

Fortunately, the government now wants us to build more energy-efficient houses and more builders and developers are seeing the competitive edge that greener, more energy-efficient homes have, and are developing project homes with higher energy ratings.

Look out for display homes and house plans that are designed with energy or the environment in mind, particularly those produced by R-2000 licensed builders or those who have a policy of using EcoLogo-certified materials where possible. Don't assume that the designs on offer are set in concrete. You'll find that developers are often willing to modify standard plans at little or no additional cost. You can also pay a little extra to incorporate environmental features such as additional insulation. Don't be afraid to ask. Even if they say no, your interest in environmental concerns will often be registered and they may consider designing greener alternatives in the future. Change often begins with enlightened people asking for it.

Buying an existing home

When you're looking at existing houses to buy, remember that renovations can turn a moderate house into a greener house, but all renovations come at a cost, both in time and money.

Here's a green checklist for what to look for in an existing house.

• Are the living areas on the south side? Are the bedrooms on the north side? Are the service rooms on the west or north sides?
• Is the house well zoned to make heating and cooling easier?
• How well is the house insulated? Can more be added if need be?
• Does the placement of windows allow for quick cross-ventilation?
• What are the floors covered with? Are the coverings in good condition?
• How much natural light is there in the living areas?
• Is the house drafty? Are there cracks or gaps in the walls or floors?
• What is the current heating system? How efficient is it?
• What appliances are included in the goods and chattels?
• Have any toxic materials been used inside, such as lead-containing paint?
• Are the windows single-pane or double- or triple-glazed? Are there storm windows and doors?
• Overall, how energy-efficient is the house and how much electricity and gas does it typically use? You can ask to see past energy bills to get an indication of what it costs to run, taking into account the previous number of occupants and their particular living habits and appliances. You can also ask if the house has recently had an inspection and assessment from an EnerGuide adviser. If it has, ask to see the EnerGuide report.

Green renovations

Renovation is a way to bring new life to an old home. Many of the green ideas for building a new home can be applied to an existing house. The added dimension is that there are solid structures to change, move or demolish. While your aims may include helping the environment, this process can instead harm it. A few simple green renovating tips will help you to change your house into your dream home without producing an unhealthy home environment or needlessly harming the planet.

Bringing in a home inspector

A professional home inspector can give the house you live in or one you're considering buying a building checkup. It is your responsibility to know or find out what state your house is in.

You can find professional home inspectors in the Yellow Pages, in house and building trade magazines or through the Canadian Association of Home and Property Inspectors (CAHPI) (see Further Information, page 290). Ask prospective inspectors if they are members of the CAHPI or similar professional groups and if they have the appropriate liability insurance.

Similarly, you can have an EnerGuide for Houses evaluation. The EnerGuide for Houses evaluation service focuses on how a home can be improved so that energy use and costs are reduced while improving comfort. Advisers are independent inspectors certified to conduct the EnerGuide evaluation. Details of home inspection organizations certified to perform EnerGuide for Houses evaluations are available on the EnerGuide for Houses website at oee.nrcan.gc.ca/energuide/houses.

It's definitely worth having a home inspection, particularly prior to renovating or if your energy bills seem unreasonably high. Inspections generally cost under $500 and take around two to three hours. EnerGuide for Houses evaluations generally cost under $325, with government or industry bodies in many areas subsidizing evaluation costs. However, if an inspection leads to modifications to your home that reduce your energy use, the inspection costs will be more than repaid. This will give you real value for your renovating dollar.

Home energy-efficiency retrofit grants

Another benefit of having an EnerGuide evaluation is that you may be able to have the costs of subsequent improvements paid back in part by a government grant. The Government of Canada offers grants to homeowners who have had an EnerGuide for Houses evaluation and who complete retrofits based on their EnerGuide report's recommendations. The amount of the grant depends on the difference between the pre-retrofit and post-retrofit EnerGuide for Houses energy rating of the house – in other words, the amount of improvement in the energy efficiency of the house as a result of the retrofit. Grants can range from $100 to over $3000.

Some energy authorities also offer grants or subsidies to help people buy more energy-efficient systems or retrofit their houses. Contact your energy provider and ask if any are available to you.

Green renovating tips

Sanding should be done with a sander with a vacuum attachment. Wear a mask to protect your lungs. Take particular care if you're sanding wood that has been treated, as the fine wood-dust particles will also contain potentially harmful chemicals.

Paint stripping should be done with water-based, low-allergy paint strippers. Avoid conventional paint strippers, particularly those that contain dichloromethane (DCM), which is believed to be carcinogenic.

Vermiculite insulation containing asbestos was commonly used in Canada until the mid-eighties. If your house contains vermiculite (a mica-like mineral) insulation and was built before 1990, it is likely to contain cancer-causing asbestos. Health Canada advises that if the fibres are enclosed or tightly bound in a product, there are no significant health risks. Asbestos becomes a problem when its fibres are airborne, so renovations that disturb insulation containing asbestos can lead to asbestos exposure. If you have vermiculite insulation and wish to have it removed, under no circumstances should you attempt it yourself. Dust masks for the face offer no protection. Have it removed by a professional. They are generally listed in phone directories under "Asbestos abatement/removal." If you suspect that you have vermiculite insulation in your walls but don't plan any immediate renovations, make sure that all cracks or holes in the walls are sealed as a safety precaution. For more information, visit the Health Canada website at www.hc-sc.gc.ca.

Paint containing lead may be found in older houses. Homes built before 1960 are likely to contain lead paint. Those built between 1960 and 1980 generally don't have lead paint on the interiors but may have it on exterior surfaces. Homes built after 1992 are no cause for concern. Lead is a highly toxic element. Exposure to even the tiniest amounts of lead in dust or debris from renovations can cause health problems. Some painting or building contractors have equipment that can sense lead on painted surfaces. Alternatively, you can send paint chips to certified labs that specialize in paint testing. Such labs are certified by the Standards Council of Canada or the Canadian Association for Environmental Analytical

Laboratories. Contact the lab first for its guidance on safely getting and sending the paint chip sample. If your home does have paint containing lead, get professional advice before removing or disturbing it. Health Canada has information on lead paints and useful links for related information: www.hc-sc.gc.ca.

Wallpapering can cause fungal growth. Mix borax into wallpaper paste to prevent this instead of using a fungicide.

Painting can be made less wasteful by getting your estimates right. Choose plant-based paints and finishes, as they're made from sustainable materials rather than petrochemicals. They also produce far fewer indoor air-polluting fumes.

Don't paint. Consider opting for natural, unpainted finishes where possible. Some porous materials such as cork and wood can be adequately sealed and preserved with natural oils or beeswax.

Recycle. Carefully remove any slate or ceramic tiles, aiming to keep as many intact as possible. Recycled tiles can often be sold second-hand or reused in landscaping or other areas of the house. If you feel like getting crafty, keep broken tiles for making mosaics.

Clean up safely. Never pour unused paint, solvents or water from washing brushes into stormwater drains. Unwanted paint and solvents should be disposed of in an environmentally responsible manner. Many municipalities have chemical collection days.

Always remember to clean up thoroughly after any renovating. Over the following days, vacuum frequently and air the house to allow any potentially harmful fumes to dissipate. That way you can enjoy your greener, new-look home without risk to your health.

FOR GREENER BUILDING AND RENOVATING:

THINK about where to live.

DESIGN for energy efficiency.

MAXIMIZE free heat and light.

CHOOSE sustainable materials.

>> Green shopping

Being a green consumer, like being a bargain hunter, is a shopping art form. Just as a bargain hunter outsmarts retailers who would have her pay full price, a green consumer outsmarts manufacturers who are trying to convince her that she needs something entirely unnecessary and wasteful, or that an environmentally harmful product is actually kind to dolphins.

A good green consumer can see through the "greenwash" and make smarter product choices. These choices are often better for your budget and for your health as well as better for the environment.

If you become a green consumer, you'll be helping the environment in a number of ways. You're helping the planet by buying and using a greener product instead of a more harmful alternative.

The greener product may:
• have taken fewer resources to be produced,
• be more environmentally friendly in its use,
• be reusable or recyclable, or

• be more easily and safely disposed of at the end of its useful life.

When you buy any product, you're exhibiting consumer behaviour. Marketers and product developers take careful note of the choices we make when we're shopping, choices that reflect our values, ideals and tastes. When you buy green products, you show the people who make them that the environment is important to you. As consumer behaviour gets greener, manufacturers will respond by making more of their products better for the environment. To see the influence of green consumerism you only have to go to the supermarket and see how the range of free-range and organic products has increased over recent years.

The flip side of buying green is boycotting products with a bad environmental record. When carefully planned and well targeted, consumer boycotts can be effective ways of getting environmentally harmful products off the shelves or of influencing manufacturers to change the way products are made. For example, consumer concern over the safety of PVC plastics led many brands, including The Body Shop, Ikea and Sony, to start eliminating PVC from their products. Even McDonald's made the decision in 1999 to remove PVC from all Happy Meal toys. Similarly, a Friends of the Earth campaign against the use of unsustainably sourced rainforest timber became a consumer boycott, which eventually resulted in a series of major home hardware chains agreeing to stop selling mahogany.

Some products assist the environment by helping to raise funds for environment groups. When you consider fundraising products, make sure that the product actually is a better environmental alternative or at least is environmentally benign. Some marketers may use donations to environmental causes as a form of "greenwashing" to make a bad product appear environmentally friendly.

Finally, when you buy a green product, you're rewarding a business that is doing the right thing environmentally. With the sale of every product, a percentage of the price is profit for the manufacturer. Wouldn't you rather see your money and purchases bring profits to environmentally responsible companies, instead of to offenders?

The basics of being a green consumer

Being a green consumer means taking the time to do a little research into what's on the market and how environmentally responsible the different options are. It's about thinking about your purchases and the available alternatives and then weighing up your needs and wants against the well-being of the planet.

So what actually makes a product green? To understand how products can improve environmentally, it's important to first understand that each product has a life cycle. The design stage uses few resources but determines how environmentally responsible the product is through the rest of its life cycle. Good design is like preventative medicine. It stops problems from developing in the first place or limits their development. In the manufacture stage, raw materials are processed to make a new product. These raw materials can come from virgin sources or from recycled materials (often called "secondary raw materials"), or a combination of the two. Processing uses energy and water and produces wastes and by-products, some of which can be used elsewhere. Others can contribute to pollution and need to be disposed of responsibly. Finished products are transported to warehouses and shops, using energy. We buy the products and use them. This may also involve using energy and water and may produce more pollution. Finally, when we no longer want them, they are either disposed of or recycled.

The main way in which we, as consumers, can easily make a difference to a product's environmental impact is by choosing not to buy products that pollute and that use energy and water resources inefficiently. We can also make a difference at the disposal stage by buying products that cause limited disposal problems and/or are recyclable.

Additionally, we can indirectly influence the design and manufacture stages. If we choose products that have been designed to have a lower impact on the environment and that have been manufactured in a less harmful manner, then manufacturers will be encouraged to improve the environmental performance of their designs and their own operations.

To buy or not to buy

Imagine if everybody bought a new car every time their car broke down. In our consumerist society it's easy to forget that many items can be repaired. Maintaining your purchases and having them repaired by a specialist can extend their life. It can also save you a lot of money compared with the cost of buying replacements.

Product life cycle

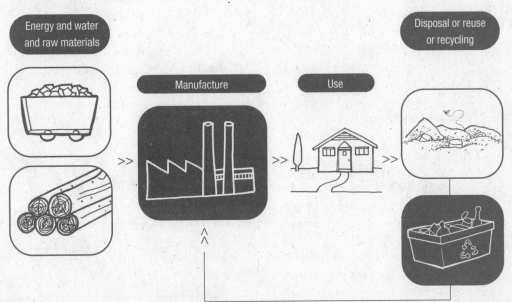

Energy and water and raw materials

Manufacture

Use

Disposal or reuse or recycling

Before you go out and buy a new product, ask yourself a few questions.

Can this item be fixed?

If you're replacing a broken product, find out if you can fix it or get a repairer to fix it before throwing it out. When you're buying new products, see if you can pay a little more for an extended warranty. That way, you can let the manufacturer worry about fixing it instead if it breaks down.

Do I really need it?

Be honest with yourself when asking this question. Most of us will remember countless occasions when we've gone to great lengths to justify why we really needed a new toy, game, CD, dress, shoes, more shoes, gorgeous house thing, another pair of shoes, car or even house. If it helps, think about the last product you bought that you really thought you needed and see whether it did make a difference to your life. More often than not, you'll find that the attraction to the product was greater before you bought it.

Can I borrow it?

Consider borrowing items that you won't get a lot of use from. For example, see whether you can borrow a dress for the odd special occasion, or a particular tool for a one-off task.

Can I rent it?

There are some things that you'd like to borrow but that none of your friends seem to have. Renting is another good way to have something for the short term that you won't get your money's worth from by buying in the long term. For example, you may wish to hire an electric sander to polish old floorboards when renovating.

Can I buy it second-hand or reconditioned?

There are a number of perfectly good products that can be bought second-hand. Some are reconditioned and even given a limited guarantee. Vacuum cleaners, for example, are often sold second-hand. IBM also sells certified used PCs at cheaper prices.

Good bag, bad bag

Before we look at actual shopping, there's a by-product of shopping that's become a popular pet hate. We hate seeing them blowing around the streets, we hate the harm they do to wildlife, and we hate the fact that they'll still be here doing a poor job of biodegrading long after we've gone. Yet somehow, despite this, Canadians still manage to take home an estimated 55 million plastic bags every week.

There has been some discussion in the media about how to reduce our use of plastic bags and the litter they make. Some people think that the government should be doing more, or that supermarkets should use alternatives or provide biodegradable bags. It's even been suggested that plastic supermarket bags should carry a deposit that is refunded when people return them for recycling. It's easy to forget that plastic bags are only a problem because people insist on using them.

In 2002, the Irish government imposed a 15 euro-cent levy (around 24 cents Canadian) on every plastic shopping bag taken from stores. Five months after the scheme was introduced, plastic bag use had dropped by around 90%. This was not because everyone on the Emerald Isle suddenly became a greenie. It was more due to the fact that people didn't like being hit in the pocket. It took a financial disincentive to effectively reduce plastic bag use in Ireland.

The take-home message from this is that you can actually do without plastic bags. Take old bags into the supermarket and reuse them. Better still, take your own alternatives to the supermarket, such as backpacks, cloth bags or baskets. Alternatively, use the biodegradable paper bags that some supermarkets offer or use their unwanted cardboard boxes. Remember to take any supermarket bags that you do have back to the supermarket for recycling. Many supermarkets in Canada now have special recycling bins for these plastic bags, which then get turned into new plastic products.

When you come across plastic bags and other plastic products that are said to be biodegradable, ask what they are made from. Some "degradable" plastics are actually made from tiny pieces of petroleum-derived plastic held together by biodegradable plant-based binding materials. A plastic bag of this sort may appear to break down, but in truth it simply disintegrates into smaller pieces or plastic dust, which still takes tens to hundreds of years to fully break down. Truly biodegradable plastic bags made from sustainable materials, such as tapioca or cornstarch, are now available, though not yet widely used. These bags are nevertheless a disposable product, so reusable bags are still environmentally better.

Reading between the lines

Environmental claims on labels and in product advertising aren't always what they seem. Sometimes you have to read between the lines and ask more questions. For example, in the eighties we suddenly became aware of the importance of the ozone layer and the hole in it, brought about by gases in aerosol cans of hairspray. Most consumers got the vague message that chlorofluoro-carbons (CFCs) were bad. Now we're seeing a barrage of products proudly boasting that they're CFC-free. But these labels are misleading and very annoying when products that have never used CFCs in the first place call themselves CFC-free in an effort to look greener.

Environmental information on labels and in advertising is useful when it is specific and accurate. Statements such as "environmentally friendly," "earth-conscious," "ozone-friendly," "green" and "recyclable" don't give you much useful information and don't mean much. For example, just about any material can be said to be "recyclable" but in reality some of these materials are rarely recycled, either because there is little use for the product or because the material is difficult to collect.

Another difficulty with eco-labelling is that different people consider different aspects of the environment to be more important than others. For example, consider a product that's made from non-renewable and non-biodegradable materials but that uses very little energy in its manufacture and use. Is this product better or worse for the environment than an alternative that needs huge amounts of energy to be produced and used but is made from renewable, plant-based materials? This makes it hard to produce an overall green stamp of approval. This is why environmental claims need to specify how they are better for the planet.

There is now an international environmental labelling standard, developed under the ISO14000 international standards for environmental management. This standard (called ISO14021) aims to make claims more trustworthy and easier for consumers to understand and has been adopted as a National Standard of Canada (referred to as CAN/CSA-ISO 14021-00). Under this standard, certain claims are banned and manufacturers are provided with guidelines for what they can say about their products. However, compliance with this standard is voluntary. Currently, there are many products on supermarket shelves that make environmental claims but do not adhere to these standards.

Favour products that you can recycle over those that you can't. Ask about manufacturer repair, servicing or take-back programs, particularly with electronic goods, that ensure that the producer takes some of the long-term responsibility for the use and disposal of their products.

The Environmental Choice Program

The Environmental Choice Program is Environment Canada's eco-labelling initiative, which helps consumers identify products and services that are less harmful to the environment. By providing the customer with such information, manufacturers are given an incentive to improve the eco-credentials of their business in order to gain a competitive edge. The program uses the EcoLogo as an easily recognizable symbol that a company or product is certified.

Look for the EcoLogo on cleaning products, office goods, appliances, automotive products, building materials, green electricity products, machinery, mutual funds, paints and surface coatings, paper products, plastic products and printing services.

What to look for on labels and in advertising

There are some specific and reliable standards and claims that appear on product labels and that are stated in advertising. They will help you to identify products that are more environmentally responsible. Ignore general, fluffy-sounding statements such as "manufactured with care for the environment." There are a few claims to look out for.

Food products

• **Free-range** – Look for free-range eggs and poultry products.

• **GE-free**, **not genetically modified** or **certified organic** – Look for canola, corn/maize, soy and cottonseed oil food products that state that they are free from genetically modified food content. You can also avoid GM foods by buying organic food.

• **Certified organic** – Look for "certified organic" labels, particularly those that state the certifying body. The word "organic" on its own is commonly used to mean a number of different things, so it doesn't necessarily mean that a food product has been made from organically grown or raised foods.

Paper products

• **xx% recycled** – Look for this statement of recycled content on tissue, paper and cardboard products. Occasionally, recycled products will state on their labels that they are made from varying proportions of pre-consumer or post-consumer waste. Pre-consumer waste includes materials such as paper offcuts or printing rejects. Post-consumer waste is material that has left the factory as a product, been used by consumers and then been recycled. If there is a range of choices available, look for products with recycled content that comes predominantly from post-consumer waste.

• **Made from FSC-certified wood or pulp** – Look for this statement on wood, tissue, paper and cardboard products.

• **Unbleached** or **oxygen bleached** – Look for these chlorine-free products.

Packaging

• **Recyclable** – Check whether this statement applies to the product itself or just the packaging. There is often advice on how it should be recycled. Ultimately, a product is only easily recycled if there are recycling collections for it in your local area. Call your municipality for advice.

• **Recycling symbols on plastics** – Plastics often have recycling symbols that feature a chasing-arrow loop or Mobius shape with a number in the middle. These numbers are part of the plastics identification system and indicate the type of plastic used. The symbol does not necessarily mean that the plastic can be recycled. As a general rule, many municipalities commonly recycle plastics 1, 2 and 3.

Cleaning products

• **Phosphate-free** – Look for laundry detergents that are completely phosphate-free.

• **Petrochemical-free**, **chlorine-free**, **CFC-free** and **biodegradable** – All of these are important environmental considerations in cleaning products.

• **Biodegradability standards** – Look for products that have been tested for biodegradability. Many use the Organisation for Economic Co-operation and Development (OECD) guidelines for biodegradability, as these are recognized worldwide. There are five test methods – 301A to 301E – for the OECD standard for "readily biodegradable." The 301D protocol tests whether or not individual ingredients are readily biodegradable and is the most stringent of all the tests. Look for products that have been deemed "readily biodegradable" and in particular for active ingredients that have been tested. This will sometimes be stated on product ingredient lists with the relevant test number in brackets.

Electrical goods

• **Energy rating labels** – Look for the EnerGuide energy rating labels on appliances, heating and cooling equipment and water heaters. Choose products with better energy-efficiency ratings.

• **ENERGY STAR** – Look for the ENERGY STAR symbol on electrical and electronic products. This indicates that the product has certain energy-saving functions.

The ENERGY STAR initiative for Canada covers many product categories, including Office Equipment; Heating, Cooling and Ventilation; Windows and Glass Doors; Lighting and Signage; Commercial and Industrial Products; and Consumer Electronics.

Avoiding chemical cocktails

Advances in science, particularly chemistry, have produced an incredible range of compounds that are new to the biological world. They've also isolated and concentrated naturally occurring substances that previously had existed in trace amounts. Many of these substances are benign or non-reactive. However, there are chemicals that are available on supermarket shelves that are bad for our health and the health of the planet, particularly if not handled with caution. Many should be avoided altogether.

Think before you buy. Don't limit your consideration to just your own or your family's health. Remember that the health of plants, animals and the broader environment may be at risk during the production of the product (before you buy it) and after you've disposed of it. You may be able to wash chemicals down the drain and out of your house, but think about the aquatic life in our waterways that then gets stuck with polluted water.

Tips for avoiding chemical nasties

- Don't buy laundry products that contain phosphates.
- Don't buy chlorine bleaches.
- Limit your use of antibacterial cleaners.
- Find less toxic alternatives to fertilizers, anti-flea rinses and pesticides that contain harmful chemicals.
- Consider buying organic products.
- Avoid synthetic fragrances and air fresheners.

 More information on the products listed above can be found in Green Kitchen, pages 20 and 40–1, Green Bathroom, pages 74–5, and Green Laundry Room, pages 91–102.

Green shopping hit list

IN
reusable
natural
renewable
cloth bags
quality

OUT
disposable
synthetic
non-renewable
plastic bags
quantity

Buy right, recycle right

Your grocery choices determine the amount of packaging you buy and therefore determine some of the waste that you will need to dispose of. There are four ways that you can "buy right" to reduce waste and support recycling:

- Aim for less packaging.
- Make sure that the products you buy have recyclable packaging that can be recycled in your area.
- Buy products that have recycled content in their packaging.
- Buy products made from recycled materials.

 These strategies are discussed in more detail in Green Kitchen. See pages 30–3 for packaging and pages 33–9 for recycling.

Asthmatics beware!

If you're an asthmatic or have sensitivities to fragrances, remember that it can be dangerous to set foot in department stores whenever there's a major fragrance promotion on. The key danger times are:

>> Christmas
>> Valentine's Day
>> Mother's Day and Father's Day

The surprising results of our recycling efforts

Paper
Paper products that may contain
recycled content include:
    newspapers
    cereal boxes
    writing paper
    fast-food bags
    cardboard containers
    wrapping paper
    tissues and towels
    animal bedding
    mulch
    insulation

Plastic
Plastic products that can be made
from recycled materials include:
    soft-drink bottles
    detergent bottles
    picnic tables
    office products
    bags
    bicycle racks
    carpeting
    highlighters
    markers
    benches
    thermometers
    brooms
    T-shirts
    jackets
    compost bins and worm farms
    garbage bins
    landscaping materials
    decking and boardwalks

Glass
Products that can be made from
recycled glass include:
    glass containers
    abrasives
    tiles
    insulation materials
    decorative tumbled-glass gravel

Steel
Products that contain recycled steel
are:
    automobiles
    refrigerators
    bicycles
    nails
    steel cans

Construction materials
Construction materials that are made
from recycled products include:
    concrete
    bricks
    drainpipes
    fence posts and fencing
    thermal insulation

Rubber
Products that are made from recycled
rubber include:
    bulletin boards
    floor tiles and mats
    playground equipment
    traffic calming devices
    asphalt modifier

FOR GREENER SHOPPING:

ASK yourself if you really need it.

BUY wisely to reduce waste.

READ the labels before you buy.

CUT DOWN on plastic bags.

>> Green grooming

Is it possible to be green and gorgeous? Most of us make some effort to look our best. The question is, at what price, both for our wallets and for the environment?

There's more to being green than just protesting and planting trees. The good news is that you can make a huge difference to the well-being of the planet without cramping your style. Being green in the new millennium can be fun and funky, without being feral.

The first step to being green and gorgeous is to look after your health from the inside. We've all heard it before – good diet and exercise will do much more for the way you look than a truckload of beauty products with miracle ingredients. The truth is, we think a miracle cure is easier than changing our diets, trying to fit in exercise routines and avoiding pollution. We try to drink the two litres of water a day recommended by supermodels and nutritionists, but it's not always convenient. Besides which, we might not want to give up smoking, coffee, chocolate or junk food.

Get real! If you're not going to change a poor diet and lifestyle to one that's healthier, accept the fact that it's going to limit how naturally good you

look. The best way to produce the appearance of healthy skin is actually to have really healthy skin. No manufactured product such as foundation or concealer can do as good a job. Similarly, clothes don't make you look fat; fat makes you look fat! If you're ruining your inner environment and putting on an unhealthy amount of weight by eating too much meat and junk food, do something about it.

Once you've exhausted the possibilities of enhancing your natural beauty by looking after your health, it's time to call in the beauty reinforcements. There is much debate about how effective commercial beauty potions really are. On the one hand, some materials are very difficult for the skin to absorb, so putting them in a jar of pleasantly perfumed cream won't do much for your complexion. On the other hand, some substances can be effectively absorbed through the skin, as is shown by the creams used in hormone replacement therapy and nicotine patches.

Somewhere between a simple cleansing and moisturizing routine and the application of cleanser, toner, moisturizer, day cream, night cream, eye cream, lip conditioner, neck firmer, pore-refining masques and age-defying concentrate, we've crossed the line into gross overconsumption. As green consumers, can we afford to spend money and the planet's resources on a range of unnecessary items that don't really work anyway? The key is to know when to stop. By all means choose greener grooming products, but keep your beauty ritual under control.

Some occasions call for a bit of extra effort or polish, through the use of makeup that can accentuate favourite features and disguise others. Beware of being a slave to fashion. It will cost you a fortune and take a heavier toll on the planet, just like when you're buying clothes. Apply the "less is more" rule. Choose a small range of basic versatile makeup colours that won't date quickly, instead of those that will be out of fashion long before the product is finished.

Greener grooming products

So what makes a bottle of toner or a tube of lipstick "green"? Unfortunately, there's no black and white answer. There are no accepted standards for what constitutes an eco-friendly cosmetic, but there are ways in which cosmetics can be better or worse. Information on these issues can be hard to extract from the average manufacturer, but some cosmetic brands have embraced care for the planet and are miles ahead of conventional cosmetics.

The beauty business is a mega money-making business. According to the Canadian Cosmetic, Toiletry and Fragrance Association, the Canadian beauty industry alone is worth $5.3 billion retail annually. Out there on the department store floor, at the pharmacy, the specialty shop or beautician, it's a jungle of special extracts, age-defying promises, scientific research, pretty packaging and images of gorgeous supermodels, all competing for our attention. Cutting through the hype to find the information you need can be a nightmare. If you also want to factor the environment into your decision, it gets even harder.

This chapter gives you the information you need to make choices that reflect your values when looking for cosmetics and toiletries.

When weighing up the planetary pros and cons of cosmetics, ask the following questions:.
• What does the product claim to do?
• Do I believe these claims?
• Do I really need it in the first place?
• What is in the product?
• Where does it come from and how was it made?
• How environmentally friendly is its production?
• How is it tested? Is it tested on animals?
• How is it packaged?
Information that comes with the product, on its label or in its

advertising, can answer some of these questions. However, in some cases it can hide the answers. Beauty is big business, and the green consumer is becoming increasingly important to marketers. Learn to tell the genuine article from the greenwashed product.

What's in a name?

If we were to read (1'R,6'S)-(-)-1-(2',2',6'-Trimethyl-cyclohexyl)-but-2-en-1-one on a jar or in advertising, we wouldn't go near the substance, let alone put it on our skin. Yet this is the chemical name for one of the oils that gives roses their fragrance. Everything is chemical. Even water is also known as H_2O.

There are no blanket rules, no guarantees and no "best products" for what's better for the environment or what's better for an individual person's skin. "Natural" isn't always best and "synthetic" isn't always bad.

Don't be blinded by science

There tends to be two approaches to the words used in cosmetics marketing. There's the caring-sharing, warm, fuzzy approach, where marketers avoid long chemical names and opt instead for using general terms about the benefits or the ingredients. You can spot these products by the use of words such as "pure," "organic," "natural," "simple" or "vital." Then there's the "blind them with science" approach that uses long chemical names, technical references and statistics. The average shopper doesn't understand scientific names, but these complicated names and scientific statements give us the comforting impression that this

Eco-brand: Lush

Lush is a brand of handmade cosmetics from the UK with a literally fresh approach to beauty.

>> Lush limits the use of preservatives by using combinations of ingredients to stabilize the products so that they have a naturally longer shelf life. The company also makes its products from fresh plant ingredients and refrigerates them if necessary. Once you've made your purchase, you keep these products fresh at home in your own fridge. Products are clearly marked with when they were made and when they should be used by.

>> Lush does not use any animal products and does not use animal testing.

>> Lush uses simple and minimal packaging. Some products, such as soaps or bath bombs, come unwrapped.

For more information, go to www.lushcanada.com or www.lush.co.uk.

Flower-farming geese

The Gloucestershire lavender fields in the UK, which supply Cotswold lavender, are weeded by geese – a traditional French farming method.

did you know...

product or substance is the very latest technological advancement in skin care and therefore must work!

The classic example of this is the nineties craze for alpha-hydroxy acids (AHAs). For months it was the phrase on every cosmetic consultant's matte-lipstick-covered lips, yet very few had much idea of what they were talking about. Few people realized that AHAs have been used in skincare products for years. When you're looking at beauty products, don't be blinded by science or afraid of it. If the manufacturers really wanted you to understand the specifics of their scientific statements, they would put them into simpler terms. If you want to know more about a product's claims, don't be afraid to ask the consultant. Most cosmetic companies also have customer service and enquiry hotlines, so use them to clarify any marketing claims, particularly those that claim the product is better for the environment.

It's only natural!

When people talk about products being chemical-free, they usually mean that the ingredients are not synthetically derived. Similarly, don't be misled by the word "natural." There are very few restrictions on the use of this word in product labelling. Just about anything can truthfully be said to be derived from natural sources. All ingredients for manufacturing occur in nature first but are mined, tapped, collected or harvested. They are then physically or chemically altered to produce products often with no resemblance to their original source.

The flip side of this is that nature is not always kind. Just because something is natural doesn't mean that it is good for you. Many plants and animals protect themselves with chemical defence systems rather than physical strength or a protective shell. Myriad naturally occurring substances are harmful to humans. Arsenic, for example, occurs naturally in apricot kernels. Just because something grows on a tree doesn't mean that you should put it through the food processor and slap the goop on your face!

There are instances where synthetic ingredients are greener (i.e., less harmful to the environment) than naturally derived ingredients. Many compounds originally found in animals, such as the fragrance from the musk deer, can be manufactured synthetically, without the need to hunt and kill possibly endangered species.

How to read cosmetics labels

The Guidelines for Cosmetic Advertising and Labelling Claims were first developed in 1998 as a joint effort between Advertising Standards Canada (ASC), the Canadian Cosmetic, Toiletry and Fragrance Association (CCTFA) and the Cosmetics Division of Health Canada (HC). These guidelines are regularly reviewed and updated. The primary goals of the organizations that regulate the cosmetic industry are to make sure that any products on the market are safe to use and that their ingredients lists are accurate and not misleading. However, there are currently only guidelines on what can or can't be

said in the advertising of cosmetic products or on their labels, rather than standards, which are regulated minimum requirements and are enforceable. These guidelines focus on claims about what the products can do rather than how they are produced or what they are made from. The words "natural" and "organic" can be and have been used to mean a range of different things, in a number of different contexts. Because of this, there is no restriction on the use of these words in advertising. With organic produce, farmed either for food or for use in other products, it is more important to look for "certified organic" products than the word "organic" on its own.

The same rules apply to reading cosmetic labels as reading between the lines on product labels. See pages 203–6. Ignore statements like "earth friendly" or "eco-conscious," unless they're backed up with specific

Eco-brand: Aveda

Aveda estimates that lipstick wearers inadvertently eat 1.5–4 tubes of lipstick in a lifetime, so it comes as no surprise that its lipsticks are made with plant oils and waxes, mineral pigments, plant pigments and essential oils instead of petroleum-derived oils and waxes and synthetic fragrances and colours.

The Uruku product range is designed around a red seed pigment from the urukum palm tree. The refillable lipstick case is 30% natural flax fibres, the base is 65% post-consumer recycled aluminum, the box it comes in is made from 100% post-consumer recycled newsprint, and even the tester units are made from recycled salvaged timber. Aveda stores worldwide celebrate Earth Month each April. Behind the scenes, Aveda's manufacturing facility in Minnesota has achieved ISO14001 certification.

Beautiful hemp

Hemp is a member of the controversial cannabis family. However, industrial hemp has negligible amounts of THC, the hallucinogenic component that made marijuana famous. Hemp is a lot softer on the environment than most other fibre crops, particularly cotton. It produces useful fibre and oil.

The oil from hemp seeds has high levels of beneficial oils, is a great moisturizer and is perfect for really dry skin. It's an excellent plant oil for cosmetics and toiletries and an alternative to using animal fats in soap-making.

The Body Shop has a range of hemp-oil products, including a great hand cream. Look for hemp-oil soaps and toiletries in health food stores and environmental retailers.

information on exactly how the product helps the environment.

Also be wary of product claims, particularly about results that are too specific. For example, a statement like "30% younger-looking skin" tries to put a scientific and credible-sounding number on something that can't be quantified. Youth, beauty and freshness are concepts that can't be accurately measured, so how can you assign a percentage to them? Percentages and statistics are another way of trying to impress us with science.

Cosmetic ingredients: the usual suspects

The US and many member countries of the European Union require ingredients to be listed on cosmetic products. In the past, this hasn't been legally required for products marketed in Canada. However, in 2004 Health Canada proposed changes to the Cosmetics Regulations requiring mandatory ingredient disclosure on all cosmetics sold in the country. After a public consultation and review process, the proposed changes will be finalized before becoming law. Cosmetic companies will then have a couple of years to comply, although many already list their ingredients voluntarily. Ingredient lists are important because they allow consumers to make a more informed choice if they are so inclined. They also help allergy suffers to avoid problem products and shop with greater confidence.

Here's a list of the common groups of cosmetic ingredients, what they do and what to look for.

Emollients

Emollients moisturize, lubricate and soften the skin, prevent and ease dryness and help to protect the skin. Natural emollients tend to allow the skin to breathe better than synthetic emollients.

Look for products that contain plant oils (such as almond, avocado, coconut, grapeseed, sunflower, olive, wheatgerm and jojoba oils), cocoa butter, vegetable glycerine, lecithin and squalene (derived from plant sources). Lanolin, a wool by-product, is also an effective emollient, depending on how you feel about animal products. Avoid products that contain silicones, such as dimethicone and cyclomethicone (which can cause allergic reactions), mineral oil and petrolatum (petroleum jelly).

Emulsifiers

Emulsifiers bind the oil-based and water-based ingredients in cosmetics, holding the product together as a suspension or emulsion. Many greener grooming products avoid using emulsifiers altogether by allowing the ingredients to separate but instructing the user to shake well before use.

Look for products that contain lecithin (an emulsifier as well as a moisturizer), beeswax (provided you're not allergic to it) and polysorbates. Polysorbates can dry the scalp, so look for polysorbate haircare products with moisturizing ingredients to compensate. Many other emulsifiers can be made from either plant or petrochemical ingredients, so it's hard to list emulsifiers to avoid. Wherever possible, use products that are entirely plant-derived.

Humectants

Humectants are moisturizers that attract water. They help the skin to maintain moisture.

Look for vegetable glycerine or glycerol, lecithin, plant-derived glycols, sorbitol and amino acids.

Avoid petrochemical glycols (diethylene glycol, ethylene glycol and propylene glycol), some of which are potentially harmful to health. Avoid urea if you have sensitive skin. Urea is often used with formaldehyde, which is a suspected carcinogen and should also be avoided. Collagen, elastin and ceramide are heavily marketed humectants that are sourced from animals. There is no evidence that collagen and elastin (natural proteins that help keep skin looking youthful) applied to the surface of the skin can penetrate to the deep layers of the skin where they can replace those lost through the natural aging process.

Preservatives

Preservatives extend a cosmetic product's life and help to prevent the growth of bacteria, but they can also cause allergic reactions. Remember that the decaying process is part of nature and no cosmetics should last forever. The real benefits of preservatives are not for the consumer but for the manufacturer, by reducing the cost of products deteriorating on the shelf before being sold.

Look for products that contain citrus seed, grapefruit seed, rosemary and/or olive extracts; benzoic acid (which comes from many plant sources and is antifungal but can also irritate sensitive skins); and the antioxidant vitamins A, C and E (which slow down the process that makes creams go rancid). Vitamin C is also called ascorbic acid and vitamin E is also called tocopherol. These ingredients help to naturally extend the shelf life of cosmetic products.

Avoid other preservatives in general. Particularly avoid formaldehyde, also known as methanal, formalin and formol.

Solvents

Solvents take solid or gaseous ingredients and carry them in a liquid form. They're also used in the extraction of some materials.

Look for products that contain water, plant glycerol and plant-derived ethanol. Avoid methanol, acetone, turpentine, toluene, benzene and benzaldehyde.

Surfactants

Surfactants, or "surface active agents," weaken the surface tension of water, making it penetrate the skin more easily. In creams they act as emulsifiers, while in cleansers they act as detergents.

Look for plant-derived saponins or glycosides (made from chickweed, yucca, saponaria and soapwort plants). These substances help to make a bubbly lather. Also look for amino acids and surfactants made from soy.

Avoid surfactants made from mineral oil and, in particular, avoid cocamide diethanolamine, diethanolamine and triethanolamine (often abbreviated to DEA and TEA), which may contain carcinogenic nitrosamines.

Thickening and stabilizing agents

As the name suggests, these add body to creams and lotions.

Look for products that contain carrageen and vegetable gums and waxes. Avoid mineral oil and other petroleum products.

General things to look for

• Look for ingredients that are plant-based, rather than derived

Ethically grown grooming

Some of the more enlightened cosmetics companies are joining with conservation groups and local communities in projects that provide ingredients while protecting the local economy and landscape.

>> The Body Shop's Community Trade program buys natural ingredients, sustainably grown in a number of projects worldwide. For example, it buys brazil-nut oil for hair treatments from Brazilian Kayapo villages.

>> Aveda buys pigment for lipstick from the Brazilian Yawanawa tribe. This means that the Brazilian rainforests in these areas won't be lost to provide grazing land for beef cattle. Instead, the local communities can be productive and make money and still preserve the forests.

from petrochemicals or mineral oil. Petroleum products are not sustainable, pollute the environment in their extraction and use, and can also cause allergies.

• Look for products from cosmetics companies that have their own plantations or that have a policy of buying from reputable and sustainable sources.

• Avoid products with a long list of synthetic chemical ingredients.

• Look for products with ingredients that are organically grown. Again, look for "certified organic" statements.

Animal welfare issues

Some pretty nasty things have been done to or with animals to produce cosmetics for humans. Cosmetic companies are constantly developing new products to keep ahead of their competition in the highly lucrative beauty market. In an effort to fulfill legal health and safety requirements, the products have to be tested, often on guinea pigs and other animals. These test animals often live in constant pain and in pitiful conditions. Animal testing and use of animal ingredients in cosmetics are particularly controversial because these products are non-essential, luxury items. Animal rights advocates understandably question whether these animals should be made to suffer and die for the sake of human vanity, particularly when there are alternatives.

Animal testing

The truth is that virtually all the ingredients in cosmetics and toiletries have at some time been tested on animals but, until recently, most of us were unaware of the suffering this entailed. Fortunately, a few companies concerned with animal welfare issues offered us alternative products that were not tested on animals and supported the development of alternative testing methods. Yet for some reason, certain cosmetic and pharmaceutical companies still deem it necessary to test new, and retest existing, ingredients and products despite the growing number of alternatives. Three main types of test are performed; these are listed and explained below. Be warned that these tests are not at all nice, so you may find reading about them distressing. You may wish to skip ahead to the heading "Are these tests reliable or necessary?"

At the end of all these tests, all animals are killed.

To measure toxicity

Generally the LD50 test is used. The substance in question is fed in gradually increasing quantities to a group of animals (usually rats or mice, occasionally rabbits, guinea pigs or dogs) until 50% of them die. The remaining half, in varying states of ill health, such as suffering cramps, convulsions, vomiting, or ulcers, are killed at the conclusion of the test.

Where a product has a suspected low toxicity, a limit test or fixed-dose test is done instead of trying to force-feed test animals enormous amounts of the product. One dose is fed of up to 10 g of product per kilogram of animal body weight. The product is considered harmless if there is no measurable effect.

To measure eye irritancy

The product is dripped or sprayed into the eyes of conscious rabbits. Rabbits are used because their tear ducts are unable to flush such substances away. The process may continue for some days. The eyes are checked for redness, discharge, swelling, cloudiness and ulceration.

To measure skin irritancy

A patch of skin on the animal (usually a rabbit or guinea pig) is shaved. The product is applied to the patch and held to the skin with gauze and tape for a few hours. Sometimes the skin is lightly scratched to make it more sensitive. The skin is checked for redness, inflammation, swelling, weeping and scabs.

Are these tests reliable or necessary?

One of the biggest issues surrounding all animal testing is how relevant it is to human situations. There are major differences between the skin and eyes of humans and animals. Even within a species, individuals have different sensitivities. Humans are a perfect example: some are lactose-intolerant, some are violently allergic to peanuts, and some seem to be immune to everything. Animals have a similar variation, so large sample groups, generally 100 to 120, are needed for each test to account statistically for individual variation.

Sensitivity is also affected by seemingly unrelated factors. The age and sex of the animals, their living environment and how recently they've eaten can all influence the results of LD50 testing.

Results of tests on the same product have also been known to differ between laboratories. Can such tests, without a means to standardize the testing or provide a control group, be considered meaningful or relevant?

Cosmetic companies and government regulatory agencies have already tested a broad range of cosmetics and cosmetic ingredients. Unfortunately, some cosmetic houses like to keep the exact results and test information secret to maintain a competitive edge. It has been suggested that a shared database that recorded the results of animal tests worldwide could prevent the unnecessary repetition of some of these tests.

What alternatives are there?

• **Eytex** – This vegetable protein gel behaves similarly to the tissue of the cornea in the presence of an irritant. Like the cornea, it appears cloudy when "irritated." The cloudiness can be measured accurately.

• **Tissue-culture testing** – A number of different human and animal cells can be maintained and even grown in a laboratory in culture dishes. Some examples are chick amniotic membrane (from the inner skin of eggshells), human corneas (from eye banks) that are no longer suitable for transplantation, human afterbirth and reconstructed human skin (multi-layered skin produced in a lab, originally pioneered and used for skin grafts).

• **Computer modelling** – A computer database could be set up of known substances, their toxicity/irritancy and their chemical structure and behaviour. New substances could then be compared to products with similar chemical structure and could be assumed to have similar toxicity/ irritancy.

• **Human volunteers** – Human volunteers are often used when a new product has been manufactured from ingredients that are relatively common and known not to be irritating, or when alternative tests have already been successfully used. Because the end-users are fellow human beings, human tests are the most reliable of all.

What can I do?

Vote with your dollar! If major corporations won't listen to the voice of ethics, they will listen when money talks, so if you are concerned for animal welfare, then choose "cruelty-free" products. As customers, we can show our refusal to support animal testing by not buying any of the products made by companies that conduct tests on animals, commission external animal testing, or buy ingredients from suppliers that use animal tests. If we buy cruelty-free cosmetics and toiletries instead, and if ethical manufacturers are seen to prosper, then those companies that still do support animal testing are bound to follow suit.

Find out about a brand's testing policy before buying it. Make sure that the manufacturer extends its policy to its suppliers. For example, The Body Shop will not buy any ingredient tested on animals by its suppliers for cosmetic purposes after December 31, 1990. It requires suppliers to submit a biannual declaration on every ingredient supplied, and its supplier-monitoring systems are independently audited against the international quality assurance standard ISO 9002. Other cosmetic companies, including Avon, have said that consumer behaviour, boycotts and demonstrations were major influences in their decision to stop animal testing.

One final note: the words "natural," "herbal" and "organic" on packaging and in advertising do not in any way relate to whether the product is cruelty-free or not. Be wary of cruelty-free claims. Some companies that make such claims actually commission other laboratories to do it for them. The Coalition for Consumer

Vegetable-oil soap
Many soaps are made from animal fat, or tallow. Look for vegetable soaps made from natural plant oils, such as olive oil and palm oil.

Hemp-oil soap is an environmental favourite because hemp is a sustainable plant crop and hemp oil is highly moisturizing.

Information on Cosmetics (CCIC) is made up of eight US animal welfare groups, one European group and our own Animal Alliance of Canada to provide a single international standard to make cruelty-free shopping easier. The result is the Leaping Bunny logo. The CCIC produces and updates a comprehensive shopping guide of brands that don't use animal testing or ingredients from suppliers that use animal testing. Companies that use the logo are independently audited. The program applies to personal care products, cosmetics and household products. Before you shop for these items, visit the Leaping Bunny Logo website and view its shopping guide: www.leapingbunny.org.

Animal ingredients

"Cruelty-free" in the language of the beauty and toiletries industries refers only to animal testing and not to the use of animal ingredients. Many animal ingredients are by-products from other industries. It can be argued from an environmental point of view that these products make use of animal by-products that would otherwise contribute to the amount of waste going to landfill. More worrying are animal-derived cosmetics ingredients for which the animal was specifically killed. If the use of animal by-products concerns you, here is a list of common animal by-products used in cosmetics manufacture, which you can check against a product's ingredients list.

• **Ambergris** is taken from the intestinal tract of the sperm whale and used as a fixative in perfumes. Whale ingredients, including ambergris and spermaceti, are no longer used in Australia, Europe and North America. However, some countries still allow them, so certain products from such countries may contain them.

- **Castoreum** is taken from the beaver's dried sex glands and used as a fixative in perfumes.
- **Collagen** is a protein found in connective tissue, skin and bones, which forms gelatin on boiling. There are claims that it can counteract the effects of aging and overexposure in human skin, but there is much debate among medical experts over its effectiveness. Its molecules are believed to be too large to enter the skin.
- **Elastin** is used to improve the elasticity of skin. It is often made from animal sources.
- **Glycerine** (also glycerol or glycerin) is a thick, sweet, syrupy liquid used as a

Home-grown green grooming

The beauty industry has well and truly gone global. Just as it can be hard to find the eco-alternative among the myriad grooming and personal care products on store shelves, it is even harder to find one that's Canadian. Here are a few local eco-brands to look out for:

Deserving Thyme
Deserving Thyme produces a range of aromatherapy, skincare, massage, body care, soap and essential oil products. The products are made by Canadians with fellow Canadians in mind – with emphasis on both "natural" and "fun." The products are plant-based with therapeutic-grade essential oils and no artificial colour or fragrances. Animal testing? As if! Look for them in stores, spas and even upmarket hotels.
   More info: www.deservingthyme.com.

Caqti
Caqti is a range of natural haircare products, including shampoos, conditioners, treatments and styling. Its logo is a stylized saguaro cactus – "the giant of the desert" – as a reminder of how fragile our ecosystems are. Caqti products contain no animal ingredients, aren't animal-tested, and are plant-based, biodegradable and non-polluting. They are available only through salons.
   More info: www.caqti.com.

Mountain Sky
Mountain Sky is based in the Selkirk Mountains in British Columbia where it makes a range of soaps, shampoo bars and massage bars that look and smell good enough to eat. Mountain Sky products are made with plant oils, essential-oil fragrances, natural colours and food-based exfoliants and are not tested on animals. They are available by mail order or through selected retail outlets.
   More info: www.mountainskysoap.com.

solvent, emollient or lubricant in skin creams. It can be derived from animal fat as a by-product of soap manufacture, produced synthetically from propylene alcohol, or produced naturally from the coconut palm or other vegetable oils. Currently, manufacturers do not have to list whether the glycerine used is animal-derived or plant-derived. Fortunately, it is usually plant-derived.

• **Hyaluronic acid** is derived from the combs of roosters and is used in skincare products.

• **Mink oil** is a by-product of the mink fur industry and used in shampoos and conditioners and as an emollient in moisturizers.

• **Musk** is a dried secretion from glands of the northern Asian hornless deer. It is used in perfumes, although most manufacturers now use a synthetic version.

• **Estrogen** is a hormone used in skin care. Estrogen can be made synthetically, but animal estrogen is cheaper to produce.

• **Spermaceti** is a wax made from sperm-whale tissue and is used in some creams and shampoos. Also see Ambergris.

• **Stearic acid** is a fatty acid used in a large number of cosmetics to give pearliness to lotions. It can be obtained from both plant and animal sources. Legally, the ingredients do not have to state the source, but some manufacturers now state whether it is obtained from palm oil or tallow.

• **Tallow** is an animal fat obtained by boiling the organs and tissues of sheep and cattle. It is used in soap, lipstick, shampoos and shaving creams.

Sun-safe skin

Sunscreen is more important for the good of your health than for the pursuit of beauty. Protecting our skin from the harsh rays of the sun is vital. Overexposure can cause painful sunburn, premature aging, depression of the immune system and, worst, skin cancer. Skin cancer (melanoma) is Canada's most commonly occurring form of cancer.

It's important to note that using sunscreen is only one of many lines of defence we can use to reduce the harmful effects of sun exposure. Other tips for reducing your exposure to the harmful wavelengths of sunlight are:

• In summer, try to spend time in the shade, rather than in direct sunlight. Put sail or shadecloths over outdoor entertaining, barbecue and children's play areas. Plant shade trees or build covered pergolas over these areas if they are exposed.

• Cover exposed skin with a lightweight shirt, T-shirt or other loose clothing when outdoors.

• Protect your head, neck and shoulders by wearing a hat with a broad brim. A headscarf or baseball cap can protect your scalp but leave your ears and neck exposed. If you're not planning to wear a hat and your hairstyle has a part, consider trying a different style to cover the exposed

area, or put a little sunscreen on your scalp on the part line.
• Don't forget that reflected light at the beach or in the snow can add to the level of sun exposure. Even in winter you can get an unsafe level of exposure, thanks to snow.
• Protect your eyes with sunglasses.
• Remember that you can still be exposed to harmful UV rays on days with light cloud cover.
• In summer, avoid going outside from 11 a.m.–4 p.m., when UV levels are at their highest.
• Apply sunscreen to your skin 20 minutes before going outdoors.
• To help protect local ecosystems, avoid wearing sunscreen when swimming in freshwater lakes and streams.

Choosing a sunscreen

Sunscreens can have inorganic or organic active ingredients, or a combination of the two. Look for products that have inorganic active ingredients (usually zinc oxide or titanium dioxide) in a plant-based medium or carrier cream rather than in a petroleum-based cream or mineral oil.

Inorganic UV-screening agents act by reflecting and scattering UV radiation. Inorganic screening agents (sometimes called non-chemical sunscreens) are less likely to irritate sensitive skins. From a cosmetic point of view, micro-fine titanium dioxide products tend to look less milky on the skin than those that contain zinc oxide or zinc cream.

Organic UV-screening chemicals work by absorbing UV light and dissipating it as heat. Some of these organic UV-screening chemicals are suspected hormone-mimicking chemicals and are therefore a potential health risk. Watch out for benzophenone-3 (Bp-3), homosalate (HMS), 4-methyl-benzylidene camphor (4-MBC), octyl-methoxycinnamate (OMC), and octyl-dimethyl-PABA (OD-PABA). For more information on these potential endocrine disruptors, see page 33. Health Canada hasn't advised discontinuing use of these chemicals. However, the Danish EPA has recommended that sunscreen products containing 4-methyl-benzylidene camphor (4-MBC) shouldn't be used on children under 12 years of age.

Sunscreens with little or no petrochemical content tend to be better for sensitive skin and are less likely to trigger skin allergies. These plant-oil ingredients are renewable, unlike mineral oils and creams, which are derived from petroleum. Sunscreen products based on plant oils include the Dr. Hauschka suncare range. Other brands of alternative suncare products are often found in health food stores.

Packaging

Packaging in the beauty market is designed to do three things:
1. Contain and preserve the product.
2. Make the product look desirable and attractive.

3. Make the product look like reasonable value for the often-ridiculous amount of money we pay.

Some level of packaging is necessary to help products stay fresh and last longer. Some companies are able to do this in a more environmentally responsible way by designing and using better packaging. For example, the Aesop range of skincare and haircare products is packaged in simple brown glass bottles and jars. The brown glass uses fewer resources to be produced than coloured or decorative glass or plastics. It also blocks out some of the light that can affect certain ingredients.

The cosmetics, perfume and beauty industry is an area where over-packaging is rife. Lotions and potions are bottled, put in boxes, wrapped in cellophane, then wrapped again in wrapping paper. Some products even come in little plastic single-serve ampules. A pump-pack could just as easily deliver a measured dose of the lotion, but the size of the pump-pack would give away the tiny amount of actual liquid you're getting for your money.

Gift-box specials can be the worst overpackaging offenders. Perfume gift sets often come in boxes that are five times the size of the product. Again, they're presented this way so that you feel like you're getting good value. Instead, if you want to buy a gift set, choose the products and put it together yourself. Alternatively, look for sets that come in a reusable toiletries bag or purse instead of a box that you'll throw out.

What you can do
• Look for products with less packaging.
• Look for products in reusable, refillable or recyclable bottles.

Eco-brand: The Body Shop

The Body Shop is a great example of a cosmetic company that is working on reducing the waste generated by its products.

>> Products **reduce** the amount of waste generated by using minimal packaging and offering many products in larger, "bulk" containers.

>> Some products are designed so that you can **reuse** the packaging. The Body Shop offers a refill service on some products, and its gift boxes are designed to be reusable.

>> The Body Shop **recycles** by making sure that all of its packaging can be recycled and by providing recycling bins in each shop. The Body Shop also uses recycled paper for its brochures and product literature.

For more information, go to www.thebodyshop.com.

• Look for makeup compacts that are refillable.
• When you find a product that you like, buy it in larger sizes.
• Use the product sparingly, so that it lasts longer. For example, many people use much more shampoo and conditioner than is needed or recommended.

DIY green grooming

The lowest-impact, greenest beauty products are the ones that you can make for yourself. While they may not look as pretty in your bathroom cupboard or smell as nice as commercial products, they're a lot cheaper and are worth trying. Here are some natural skincare and haircare ideas for you to try at home.

Cleansing
• Soak oatmeal in water and use the water for washing your face.
• Buttermilk can be used to gently cleanse the face. Saturate some cottonwool or the corner of a washcloth with it and apply to your face. Rinse or tissue off. Buttermilk is lightly astringent and restores the acid mantle of the skin.
• Many plant oils such as almond oil can be used as cleansers to melt away a day's buildup of makeup, dirt and pollution. Wash off with a washcloth and warm water.

Exfoliation
• Baking soda is a great exfoliator, particularly for acne-prone skin. It

softens the skin and is antiseptic. Put a teaspoonful in your hand and make it into a paste with just water or a little bit of cleanser. Gently run it over your face and wash off.

Facemasks
• Mix a lightly beaten egg white with a little lemon juice to make a facemask for oily, spotty skin. Smooth it over the skin, allow it to dry, and wash off with warm water.
• Raw honey mixed with natural yoghurt makes a nourishing and soothing facemask. Apply it to damp skin, leave for up to 30 minutes, gently massage it into the skin and then rinse off.
• Make a gentle honey and oatmeal mask by putting two heaped tablespoons of oatmeal into a small pot with 200 ml of water and boiling gently for five minutes. You can also dangle a chamomile tea bag into the brew while it's simmering. Stir in a teaspoon of honey and allow the mixture to cool. When cooled sufficiently, apply the mixture to your face and leave for 10 minutes. Rinse off and follow up with a moisturizer.

Toning
• Witch hazel is an astringent, making it a good freshener and toner for oily skin. It is cheap and available from supermarkets and pharmacies. It is also useful as an underarm deodorant.
• Make your own almond-milk toning lotion to tone and soften all skin types. Mix 4 tablespoons of almond meal

with 300 ml distilled water in a blender for a few minutes. Strain through cheesecloth in a funnel into a bottle.

Moisturizing
• Almond and apricot oils are light enough to be used on some skins as a facial moisturizer.

Hair colouring
• Steep rosemary leaves in water and use the water as a hair rinse to enhance the colour of dark brown hair. Chamomile flowers can be similarly used for blond hair. Diluted lemon juice can be used to highlight brown hair.

Body and bath
• Almond, jojoba and even olive oils are great moisturizers for the skin. Rub a little into your skin, especially your legs, knees and heels. Almond oil is light and easily absorbed into the skin.
• Wheatgerm oil is a particularly good moisturizing oil and can help to improve the skin's elasticity. For this reason it is great to rub into expanding pregnant bellies (mix in a few drops of lavender and neroli oil). It is also rich in vitamin E.
• Aromatherapy oils can be used instead of perfume. Mix your own blends, using your favourites. However, some oils shouldn't be applied directly to the skin or used during pregnancy. Instead, dab a little onto your clothes or onto a tissue or handkerchief worn underneath your clothing. Aromatherapy oils can also be added to your bath.
• Make a bath bag (like a tea bag) for your bath using a thin muslin bag. Fill it with a combination of your favourite herbs and petals, such as rose petals, lavender, rosemary, mint and citrus peel. Hang the bag from the tap and allow the water to run through it. Fresh mint leaves with citrus peel make for a refreshing bath, while rosemary and lavender are relaxing.
• Add some baking soda to your bath to soften your skin.
• A bucket of warm water with a knob of grated ginger and a few drops of tea-tree and peppermint oils makes a great foot soak.

Miscellaneous
• Soothe puffy eyes with slices of cucumber or cold, wet tea bags.
• Aloe vera soothes irritated skin and helps to heal sunburn. Cut the leaf and use the clear gel inside.
• Floral waters are inexpensive, natural alternatives to perfumes and fresheners. Many pharmacies sell rosewater in plain glass bottles. They are a refreshing mist for hot days and can be sprayed on drying bed linens to leave a light scent.

FOR GREENER GROOMING:

CARE about your health.

CHOOSE plant-based ingredients.

AVOID products tested on animals.

MAKE your own skincare products.

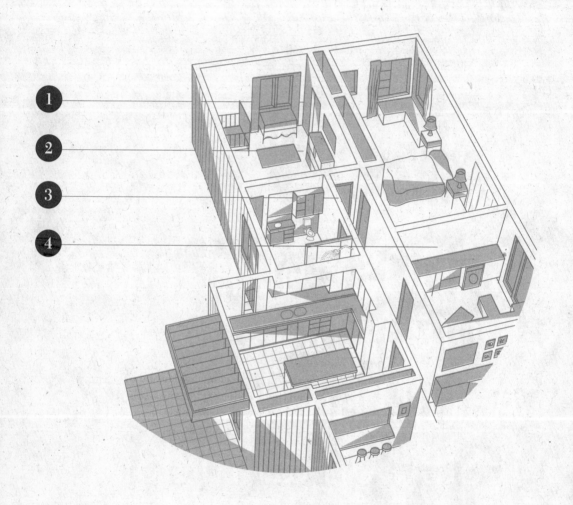

1 Green paint
2 Green diapers
3 Green baby-cleaning
4 Green laundry

>> How to have a green baby

If you're reading this section, you're probably either pregnant or you've already had a baby. You may also be particularly concerned about the future of the planet for the sake of the child you're bringing into it.

It's not easy being a mom, but with some planning and awareness of your choices, it's not any harder to be a green mother. This section looks at some of the alternatives available to new moms (or Mr. Moms, for that matter) and offers some simple tips for reducing your impact on the environment while raising your child.

Leading up to and during your pregnancy, your biggest environmental concern is the baby's own local environment – your body! This is a time to clean up your body to ensure ideal surroundings for your child during gestation.

In the months prior to conception and during pregnancy, it is important to avoid exposure to toxic metals (lead, mercury, cadmium and aluminum), chemicals and radiation (X-rays, for example).

During pregnancy, the baby's cells are rapidly growing and dividing and are highly sensitive to certain chemicals. Your intake of clean air and water and of food that is free from chemicals and synthetic hormones is important for the normal development of your child. At particular stages during pregnancy, exposure to chemicals and bacteria can cause serious problems for the development of the fetus. The exact times of these stages are not predictable, so it is best to err on the conservative side and avoid exposure to chemicals for the duration of your pregnancy.

Tips for a low-toxin pregnancy

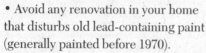

• Avoid any renovation in your home that disturbs old lead-containing paint (generally painted before 1970).

• Reduce your exposure to aluminum by not using aluminum pots or cookware, and don't use deodorant or antiperspirant containing aluminum.

• Have any dental work done well in advance of pregnancy and look into the possibility of replacing any amalgam fillings you may have with non-amalgam alternatives.

• If you're decorating the new nursery, use plant-based paints with low fumes. Avoid using solvents and fume-emitting adhesives. Better still, talk someone else into doing the hard smelly work. Milk your "delicate" situation for all it's worth!

• Avoid hair-colouring products during pregnancy. Most have health warnings on them advising against use by pregnant women.

• Eat organic food wherever possible. At the very least buy organic broccoli and grapes in place of non-organic broccoli and grapes. Broccoli and grape crops tend to make high use of pesticides. They also have a large edible surface area, which increases the amount of pesticide residue you finally eat.

• Limit your consumption of tuna, fish that dwell on the sea floor and shellfish.

• Eat free-range, organic chicken and eggs. Non-organic chickens are often fed synthetic hormones and antibiotics to improve their growth and avoid diseases. Exposure to synthetic hormones can confuse the development of the reproductive organs, while the antibiotics in the chicken and eggs can depress both the mother's and child's immune systems.

• Use the green cleaners outlined in the Kitchen, Laundry and Bathroom chapters.

• Quit smoking (if you are a smoker) and avoid smoky environments.

Soothing stretched skin

did you know...

Genes are more of a factor in whether or not you get stretchmarks than any amount of moisturizing product. However, rubbing moisturizer onto the skin over your expanding belly is a wonderful and pleasurable way of pampering yourself and connecting with your growing baby. If you find massage oil too messy, try shea-butter massage bars from Lush or Mountain Sky. The warmth of skin melts the solid shea butter onto the skin. Ask your partner to rub some onto your belly each night. It's a great way to gently involve the expectant dad in your progressing pregnancy.

Cigarette smoke is a cocktail of toxic, unhealthy chemicals that are particularly dangerous to both children and pregnant women. Smoking is linked with low-birth-weight babies and increases the risk of sudden infant death syndrome (SIDS).

Green food preparation

For newborns, the best food environmentally, and the healthiest, is breast milk. It has all the nutrients the newborn needs and is easy to make – you can do it in your sleep! It must also be said that not all women can breastfeed and they shouldn't feel guilty or inadequate. Problems with milk supply, inverted or cracked nipples, having to return to work and many other factors can make a mother unable to breastfeed.

Breast milk is particularly important in the development of a baby's immune system. Children who were breastfed as babies for at least their first six months tend to have lower incidences of allergies and asthma. They also tend to be healthier, as breast milk carries immunity from the mother to the infant.

A common misconception is that women's nipples are not sterile and are therefore dirty, making breastfeeding unhealthy for the child. Breasts do *not* have to be sterilized. A simple wash with soap in your normal shower is all they need.

Breast shields
If you're breastfeeding, use reusable cotton breast shields instead of disposable ones to prevent the telltale signs of leaking breasts. Most disposable shields are made of cotton and cellulose (a wood fibre) so they can sometimes be irritating, particularly on cracked nipples.

>>

Organic food for babies

BabyOrganic.com is a home-based company that delivers organic baby formula to homes in Canada and the US. Three sisters with eight children between them run the company. The sisters started the business after experiencing difficulty getting infant formula that was organic, as close to natural as possible and not highly processed. After finding a brand and recognizing that, like many organic products, it wasn't widely available, they set up their delivery service to make it easier for other mothers to go organic. More info: www.babyorganic.com.

Sterilization of bottles and bottle nipples, however, is an issue. Even breastfeeding mothers will generally start introducing solid foods into a baby's diet at around 4–6 months and may want to sterilize plates, bowls and utensils.

There are two basic methods of sterilization. Heat, whether by dry heat, boiling or steam, uses a physical method to kill bacteria. Chemical sterilization uses a chlorine solution (usually sodium hypochlorite) that is toxic to the bacteria to kill them. Sodium hypochlorite for sterilizing infant feeding equipment is sold as water-soluble tablets or as bottles of concentrated solution. This method can't be used with metal objects, as they tend to corrode in the chlorine solution.

It is always better to avoid using chemicals. Chemical sterilization leaves chlorine and dioxin residues, even when rinsed with water. Any concern over the energy used in heat sterilization is far outweighed by the greater concern with dioxins and the health problems they are suspected of contributing to.

To sterilize using heat, the items should be subjected to 95°C heat for around two minutes. Immersing the items in boiling water, or using a steam-sterilizing machine or a microwave sterilization kit, can do this. However, take care with boiling and microwave sterilizing; both can melt some plastic objects.

As your child gets older, feed him or her healthy food and drink. Use filtered tap water or bottled water for drinking. Try to prepare fresh, organic foods. There is a growing number of brands of prepared organic baby food, such as Baby's Only Organic and Earth's Best Organics, which are available from most supermarkets. Heinz also makes a range of organic baby-food products in addition to its conventional range.

Fresh organic is also becoming more readily available. Many of the large supermarket chains now stock a range of organic produce, pasta and other wheat products.

Recycling rules apply to those tiny jars, bottles and food tins. Rinse them in old washing water and put them in your recycling bin. As with all food preparation, fruit and vegetable scraps can also be composted.

Baby-food jars are great for reusing around the home. They're particularly good for storing small bits and pieces, like spare buttons, paper clips and hairpins. If you're stewing food for a baby, why not use a double boiler and use the steam to sterilize the containers in the top half while the food is cooking?

Doing the laundry

It's amazing how one tiny little person can produce the same amount of dirty laundry as four adults. This then escalates when solid food is introduced – the adult usually ends up wearing more food than the infant actually eats.

Wash with pure soap flakes or a laundry powder that has a low

>>

Dioxins

You may be wondering what dioxins are and what all the fuss is about. "Dioxin" is the common name of a family of chemicals called chlorinated dibenzodioxins. There are around 75 variations, but at least 12 are dangerously toxic. They are by-products of the chlorine bleaching process. Small amounts or residues can be found in chlorine-bleached paper products, including disposable diapers, tissues, sanitary pads, filter paper and toilet paper. Dioxins are also emitted in car exhaust fumes, from steel mills and when PVC plastic is burned. They do not break down in the environment.

High doses can cause severe facial acne, lowered immune resistance and liver damage. They are suspected of causing birth defects and increased cancer risk. Dioxins readily dissolve in fatty animal tissue. Effluent discharged from paper mills into waterways brings dioxins to fish and other marine life, harming their health. Humans and other animals eat the fish and the dioxins accumulate in the food chain. While high doses of dioxins are avoidable, scientists are particularly concerned with the suspected effects of low-level, long-term exposure to dioxins, both through the food chain and from residues in bleached products. This is why it's best to reduce our use of chlorine-bleached products.

environmental impact and is phosphate-free. Low-environmental-impact products with no phosphates, optical brighteners or petrochemicals tend to be kinder to the sensitive skin of babies and provoke fewer allergic reactions. For more information about phosphates and optical brighteners, see Green Laundry, pages 91–2.

If you're worried about the sanitation of clothing, washing in water heated to 65°–95°C will kill most of the bugs. Also, sunlight has a sanitizing and bleaching effect, so if the weather is warm, sun-dry your laundry. If you really feel that you must use a diaper soak, again use one without phosphates, and use non-chlorine bleach.

Choose safe toys

The first place a baby puts a toy is in his or her mouth. Canada has strict laws about the kinds of materials and paints that can be used to make toys for infants. However, the laws (and how tightly they're adhered to) will not necessarily be the same overseas.

Wooden toys and artefacts brought back from overseas holidays, particularly those bought from roadside markets, should generally not be given to babies to play with. You may be giving the baby an item painted with toxic paint. Remember that many of these souvenirs are made to be looked at. They are probably not designed to be safely munched by a teething infant.

Also be careful with plastic toys, particularly those made from PVC (polyvinyl chloride or vinyl). PVC is one of the worst plastics environmentally, largely because it is produced using chlorine and is very common. Basic PVC is hard, brittle and difficult to use, so stabilizers and plasticizers are added to it to produce finished vinyl products. It is these additives that are cause for concern.

Alarmingly, two common stabilizers are lead and cadmium. Lead poisoning is a well-known public health concern. Cadmium can be more toxic than lead, can cause kidney damage and is linked to cancer. Plasticizers are used in soft vinyl toys like the old favourite rubber ducky. Studies have shown that when children put these soft vinyl toys in their mouths, they can ingest plasticizers called phthalates. Phthalates have been linked to kidney damage as well as to problems with the liver and reproductive organs.

Greenpeace International has launched the Toxic Toys campaign to raise the awareness of these health risks and to place pressure on governments internationally. The aim of Greenpeace and its allied groups is to have governments around the world ban children's products containing lead and other potentially dangerous additives.

Good old-fashioned wooden toys are still available. The Swedish furniture manufacturer Ikea prides itself on the fact that its toys do not need batteries, they're painted with non-toxic paints and the wood is from sustainable sources.

In the bath

See if there are ways that you can reuse your baby's bathwater (for example, car, floor and window cleaning).

Pure soap and water will often do just as good a job on the change table as baby lotions. Use simple vegetable-based soaps and shampoos and other plant-based formulations instead of petrochemicals or soaps made from animal fats. Soaps derived from animal fats tend to need more preservative, which can provoke allergies. In fragrances, look for natural essential oils, which will also irritate less than synthetic fragrances.

Be careful when choosing and using baby shampoos. Some "no-tears" formulas work by adding an antihistamine or similar anti-irritant, which just masks the irritation rather than preventing it. If you're not sure, it's best to just try to keep the soap out of junior's eyes.

cycles: the material, energy and water resources used to make them, their production methods, the effect of their use and finally their disposal or reuse. Results are clouded by the fact that disposable diaper manufacturers or environmental pressure groups have funded many of the studies.

Unfortunately, there is no easy black and white answer in this debate because each method has its own environmental benefits and impacts. However, there are better ways to use each type of diaper. The latest studies conclude that, if both are used in the best way environmentally, cloth diapers do appear to be preferable to disposables, but only by a narrow margin. This is certainly one environmental choice that you shouldn't sweat over. To follow is an overview of each method, and its pros and cons.

The great diaper debate

Cloth versus disposable – what is the answer? It's the question on every mother's (and sometimes father's) lips, especially when you consider that the average baby has gone through around 6000 (sometimes up to 8000) diaper changes by the time he or she is toilet-trained.

Dozens of studies have been done around the world to try to weigh up the environmental impact of both cloth diapers and disposables. Most have looked at all stages of their life

King James's diapers

did you know...

In 1567, when James VI (who was later James I of England) was crowned King of Scotland, he was just 13 months old. If he had been wearing modern disposable diapers, disposed of in landfills as they are nowadays, some still would not have completely biodegraded.

Disposable diapers

Tips for using disposable diapers

Flush the poop before throwing away the diaper. This keeps the excrement out of landfill and reduces the greenhouse gases produced as it decomposes.

As a compromise, limit your use of disposable diapers to occasions when convenience really counts, such as going out or going on a holiday.

The fact that disposables keep wetness away from the baby's bottom is not an excuse to be lazy! Leaving a wet diaper on a baby provides a nice warm and moist environment for bacteria to happily grow. Change disposable diapers regularly to prevent diaper rash and the proliferation of bacteria.

>> Advantages of disposable diapers

Reduced water and detergent use – Disposable diapers do not need the detergent and water use of washing that cloth diapers need. Laundry detergent use is particularly a problem when it contains phosphates, which are bad for the health of our country's waterways. If water supply is a big issue in your area, then disposable diapers may be your only real choice.

Convenience – Washing stained and smelly fabric is not high on the list of the nation's favourite hobbies. Disposables are light, not bulky, and easy to take with you away from the home.

Reduced wetness – Keeping excessive moisture away from a baby's skin can give the baby a better night's sleep. The baby is less likely to be woken up by the discomfort of a wet bottom. This may be a particular issue if you have a baby with difficult sleeping patterns.

Reduced diaper rash – On the health front, most disposables are designed to keep moisture away from the baby's skin, which can help to prevent diaper rash.

>> Disadvantages of disposable diapers

Waste disposal problem – Disposable diapers are a significant contributor to landfill, being the third largest single item in the municipal waste stream after newspapers and food and beverage containers. Sending waste to landfill is not a long-term solution to any waste disposal problem. It just leaves a problem for future generations to solve. Disposables end up in landfill, and it's not just their bulk that's the problem. Their contents, particularly when it rains, can leak into the earth along with other landfill leachate and contaminate groundwater. This is becoming less of a problem as landfill sites are increasingly better managed.

Poor biodegradability – Disposable diapers can take 200–500 years to decompose. However, some diaper manufacturers are developing new products made from more biodegradable materials.

Dioxins – Chlorine bleach is used in the production of disposables to give them their whiteness. Dioxins are a by-product of this process and are hazardous for people and the environment. Dioxins are of particular concern because they accumulate in human tissue.

Cost – Buying disposable diapers adds a significant chunk to your weekly grocery bill.

Land use – Disposables require land use and irrigation to produce the trees for the pulp filling. It takes around 200 kg of fluff pulp to supply a baby with diapers for two and a half years, compared with 10 kg of cotton for a supply of reusable cloth diapers.

Petroleum-derived product – Disposables are made partly from plastics, which are an oil-derived product. The planet's oil resources are limited and not replaceable. Two and a half years worth of disposables uses 130 kg of materials other than fluff pulp. Most of this is plastics.

Possible health risk – There is some evidence to suggest that there is a link between disposable diapers and male infertility. Wearing disposable diapers tends to raise the temperature of the boys' testes. Studies have shown that temperature is important for the normal development of testes and a good sperm count. However, there are other suspected factors in the rising incidence of male infertility, such as sitting for long periods, tight underwear, exposure to synthetic hormones in the environment and inadequate nutrition.

Cloth diapers

>> Advantages

Cost – Buying a one-time supply of cloth diapers is a lot cheaper than buying disposables each week. Even using a diaper service is usually a similar price to buying disposables.

Reusable – Aside from the obvious day-to-day reuse, cloth diapers can have a life after toilet-training. They can be kept for future babies or used as rags around the home.

Less waste – The contribution of cloth diapers to Canada's landfills is negligible compared with disposable diapers. Using cloth diapers for one baby prevents sending around 6000 used disposables to landfill.

Biodegradable – Once the diaper is no longer useful, it is biodegradable.

Made from cotton – Cotton is good for sensitive skins that may otherwise react to the elastic and plastic in disposables. As a product of agriculture, cotton is also renewable, compared with plastic, which is made from petroleum.

>> Disadvantages

Water, detergent and energy use – Cloth diapers require water, energy to heat the water, detergent and your time and effort to clean them.

Made from cotton – The use of cotton is both an advantage and a disadvantage environmentally. Cotton is a crop that has substantial environmental impacts. Non-organic cotton farming generally uses a very high level of pesticides and fertilizers. Such farming methods are harmful to the land and surrounding waterways and can kill plant and animal life. However, organic cotton diapers are available from environmental and baby-product retailers over the Internet or by mail order.

Poor fit – Folded cloth diapers don't fit as snugly as disposables and can be more likely to leak. They can also be difficult to put on a wiggly baby.

Dioxins – The cotton may be bleached to make it white, before being made into diapers.

>> Wiping bottoms

Cleaning those tiny bottoms uses more toilet paper, particularly during toilet training. Why not preserve timber and support the recycling industries by buying unbleached toilet paper made from recycled paper? Every household buys toilet paper. It's an easy opportunity to buy recycled-content products and support Canada's recyclers.

Cotton: good or bad?

The arguments against cloth diapers often cite the negative environmental effects of cotton growth and manufacture. Let's put this into perspective.

It takes 10 kg at the most to make enough cloth diapers for one child. If you want to justify the use of disposables on the grounds of producing 10 kg less cotton, you first have to think about other areas where you may be using cotton, and switch to organic cotton wherever possible. Organic cotton infant clothing is available through some environmental stores and specialty retailers and by mail or Internet order. Organic cotton infant mattresses and bedding are also available. For example, the Canadian company Willow Natural Home makes crib-size organic cotton bedding.

Tips for using cloth diapers

A wide range of more convenient cloth diapers is available from retail baby-goods stores or over the Internet. These include specially made, shaped diapers, usually with elasticized legs and sometimes Velcro fastenings. These cloth diapers are designed to fit like disposable diapers and they take out the hassle of having to fold flat diapers. However, they can take longer to dry after washing.

You can easily reduce the environmental impacts of washing diapers by following the tips in the Laundry section of this book. For example, using a front-loading washing machine will immediately make a huge difference to the water use for diaper washing.

Diaper wash service

The diaper method with the lowest environmental impact is using cloth diapers through a diaper service. Diaper services collect used diapers, wash them and deliver clean diapers. They use less water and energy by washing them on a large scale. However, you must choose your diaper service with care.

When you're shopping around for a service, ask about any environmental auditing or accreditation they may have had done. Make sure you use a service that uses detergents that are phosphate-free. Also, ask whether they use chlorine in the rinse water. Chlorine bleaching can leave dioxin residues in the diapers.

For those on a tight budget, diaper services are a similar cost to that of disposables, sometimes cheaper, depending on the brand of disposables.

Plant a tree for a baby

Give a gift tree to mark the birth of a baby. When you buy a gift tree, you're effectively giving a donation to a tree-planting organization so that it can plant and care for a tree (or trees) on your behalf. American Forests' Global ReLeaf program plants native trees in rural and urban ecosystem restoration projects across the United States and around the world. TreeGivers, a New England–based memorial tree-planting business, allows you to select the US state or Canadian province where your gift tree is planted.

More info: www.american forests.org/planttrees and www.treegivers.com.

Plant a tree

The best thing you can do for the environment is to teach your child to care for and respect the planet. One way is to plant a tree for your newborn baby or get an older child to plant one with you. They can watch the tree grow, thinking of it as "my tree."

You can even choose trees to attract birds and butterflies. In fact, your own backyard can become an important piece of urban habitat for local native wildlife. Ask your local nursery or municipality about trees that are native to your local area.

If you don't have a garden but would still like to plant a tree with your child, your municipality will probably be able to give you contact details for local tree-planting groups or community garden co-ops.

Have some good green fun

Give your child positive associations with the planet. We're all more motivated by fun and encouragement than by guilt, so give your child (and yourself) the gift of good times spent in the natural environment.

Kids love a party, so celebrate Earth Day (April 22) or World Environment Day (June 5) each year with your child and his or her friends by organizing a litter cleanup day at a local park followed by a barbecue, or go on a fun nature hike.

Set an example

As with all aspects of parenting, practise what you preach. As your children grow, they learn from you what is normal and acceptable behaviour. When they are old enough, get them to help you with the recycling. If you can demonstrate respect for the environment, your children will adopt your example.

FOR A GREENER BABY:

ENADY a low-toxin pregnancy.

CONSIDER using cloth diapers.

FEED your child green food.

SET a good example.

3

Hot Topics >>

If we're going to save the planet, it helps to understand what's wrong with it in the first place. To follow is everything you need to know about the major environmental issues.

>> What's up with the planet?

Most of us are at least vaguely aware
that the planet has some serious health
problems that the human race has
caused. But you may be wondering
exactly what all the fuss is about.

We've come out of a century that has
seen unparalleled environmental
degradation. But there is a light at the
end of the tunnel, if we choose to head
in that direction. We've harmed the
planet, but hopefully we've learned
from our mistakes. Our planet is a
wonderful, resilient, living thing.
Let's help it to heal itself.

It's an advantage to understand what
the terms you hear all the time in the
media really mean, so you can put
all your efforts into perspective. And
if nothing else, you'll have some
interesting information, facts, figures
and trivia that will enable you to hold
your own if dinner-party conversation
turns to the environment.

Many issues such as acid rain,
deforestation, El Niño and biodiversity
have been brought to our attention
through the efforts and protests of
environment groups and activists, such

as Greenpeace. This has helped to raise
the public's awareness of environmental
issues and how human activities have
caused or contributed to them. They
also act to pressure businesses and
governments into addressing these
environmental problems.

Not everyone is comfortable with
confrontation, controversy or protest.
However, the work that these groups
do is important because it helps to
define and highlight environmental
problems that may have otherwise gone
on unnoticed. Now that businesses,
governments and individuals are
becoming aware of these problems and
how we influence them, we can also
start to become part of the solution.

Remember, though, that no matter
what legislation is introduced, it is the
way people live their lives that really
makes the biggest difference to the
state of our planet.

Acid rain

Imagine how your potted plants would grow if you watered them regularly with lemon juice or vinegar and you'll have some idea of how acid rain affects plant life.

Basically, acid rain is what you get when you mix rain clouds with air pollution, sulphur oxides and nitrous oxides. In the presence of sunlight and catalysts, these gases react with water vapour to form sulphuric and nitric acids. These acids can travel great distances, dissolved in cloud droplets. They precipitate as acid rain, snow and fog.

Acid rain poisons both aquatic and terrestrial life, making plants and animals susceptible to disease, temperature extremes, pests and other stresses, which in turn can kill them. On land, acid rain causes the release of aluminum and heavy metals in soil. These metals damage roots and soil cultures and are washed into waterways, where they also can kill fish and other marine life. The acidic rain also damages the leaves of plants, decimating forests, damaging crops and reducing soil fertility. In water ecosystems, acid rain is making lakes acidic and killing aquatic life.

In Canada, acid rain is more of a problem in the eastern provinces, where the soil and water systems lack the natural alkalinity (found in lime-based soils) that would neutralize the acidity. Weather patterns and the locations of industrial centres also result in the acid rain–causing pollution from the US midwestern and Canadian industrial heartlands being swept over Canada's eastern provinces. It has been estimated that around half of the sulphate deposited in Canada is derived from sources in the US.

The effects of acid rain aren't confined to the natural world. Acid rain also corrodes bronze and other metals, dissolves paintwork and eats into stone buildings and statues. Several of the world's most famous monuments are under threat from acid rain erosion, including the Sphinx in Egypt, the Taj Mahal in India, the Parthenon in Greece, and Gettysburg monuments and the Statue of Liberty in the US.

The good news is that tougher laws governing industrial pollution have made a difference, and by 1999 the total acid rain–causing sulphur dioxide emissions in eastern Canada had dropped by 40% from 1980 levels. However, many forests are still seeing declines in growth rates, so we still have some way to go.

What you can do

We can reduce our contribution to air pollution and acid rain by cutting down our use of fossil fuels. Choose energy from green electricity programs and take measures to cut down your car use.

Air pollution

It's easy to think of air as harmless, and in most cases it is. However, air is simply a mixture of gases. While it's easy to avoid drinking from bottles with skulls and crossbones on the label, it's very difficult to avoid breathing toxic fumes, particularly when they're colourless and odourless. If you're surrounded by polluted air, it is very hard not to breathe the pollution into your lungs and hard to keep it out of the sensitive tissues of your eyes. Our nasal passages, eyes and lungs provide an entry point for these gases to come into our bodies and potentially affect our health.

The harmful gases that contribute to air pollution, such as carbon monoxide in car exhaust, can cross the membranes in the lungs of humans and other animals and lead to health problems. Some gases are heavy and will tend to gather close to the earth's surface. Others are light and will gradually float to higher levels of the atmosphere. Gases also diffuse, which can lower the concentration of a particular gas in a given location. However, too many polluting industries rely too heavily on diffusion. Some gases need only tiny amounts to start interfering with the environment or wildlife.

The biggest single contributor to air pollution and the greenhouse effect is the burning of fossil fuels, such as coal and gasoline. These are used to drive internal combustion engines, power industrial furnaces and fuel electric power plants. Wildfires also add to air pollution, as does the disposal and decomposition of solid waste. Additives to fuels, such as lead added to gasoline, also add to the nasty chemical cocktail of air pollution.

What you can do
Careful selection and maintenance of your vehicle, using cleaner and greener heating systems and changing to green electricity will make a huge difference to the quality of the air you breathe.

Aquaculture

Recent trends in diet and nutrition have seen a global increase in demand for fish and seafood. Sushi handrolls look set to catch up with and perhaps overtake burgers as the fast food of choice, being the healthier and lower-calorie option. People are also interested in the nutritional value of omega-3 fatty acids, which are found in high levels in oily fish.

This increasing demand for fish has seen the development of the aquaculture sector, with fish farms becoming bigger and more common. Many are managed unsustainably, with serious effects on local aquatic ecosystems and native fish stocks. Salmon farming began on the Atlantic and Pacific coasts of Canada in the '70s. Salmon farms are floating netcages, raising salmon in densely packed conditions for commercial sales and profit. Like all intensive farming, they produce huge amounts of wastes, including drug-laden feces and excess food. Farmed salmon are given more antibiotics by weight than any other livestock. This is contributing to the development of antibiotic-resistant strains of disease-causing bacteria. Some farm fish escape from their netcages and compete with native fish for food and habitat. These fish farms also pass parasites and disease to wild populations.

What you can do
Avoid farmed salmon and choose fish and seafood from sustainable sources. Visit www.montereybayaquarium.org to view or download the Monterey Bay Aquarium Seafood WATCH program's guide to sustainable seafood choices.

Biodiversity

"Biodiversity" comes from the words "biological diversity." It refers to the number of different species in a particular habitat or area and reflects the rich variety of life forms that live on our planet.

There are three aspects to biodiversity. First, there's the variety that occurs within a single species through the differences in genetic makeup. For example, humans are a single species, but we come in myriad different sizes, shapes, hair and skin colours and other features, according to our genes. A large population helps to preserve biodiversity by avoiding the detrimental effects of inbreeding.

Second, there's the variety of different species that exist in different environments. Finally, there's the variety of different ecosystems, such as grasslands, estuaries and alpine forests. These all combine to make up the biodiversity of our unique planet.

Biologists have identified around 1.5 million different species so far, and every year more are discovered. Estimates of earth's total number of species range from 10 million to 100 million.

Biodiversity is important because no species or individuals can exist alone.

>>

Ecological footprint

The Earth Council, an environmental organization, calculated the ecological footprint per capita of a number of nations. Here are some of the results.

Australia	9.0 hectares per capita
Bangladesh	0.5
Belgium	5.0
Canada	7.7
China	1.2
Hong Kong	6.1
New Zealand	7.6
United Kingdom	5.2
USA	10.3

To calculate your own ecological footprint, go to the LINKS Redefining Progress website at www.lead.org/leadnet/footprint/intro.htm.

Instead, groups of species live together in mutually beneficial ecosystems, providing each other with food, water, air and dissolved gases. The unexplored biodiversity of South America's tropical rainforests may yet give us a cure for cancer or provide other medicinal plants. Human beings are part of this interdependence and, like all other species, rely on continuing biodiversity for their survival.

What you can do
Be aware of and respect all creatures and their environments.

Avoid products that result in a loss of habitat for threatened species.

Ecological footprint
The ecological footprint is a way of measuring the environmental impact of a person's lifestyle. It estimates the amount of land or space needed to provide the resources to support that standard of living.

Things like the size of your house, your energy use, the kinds of food you eat and the transportation you use all affect the size of your ecological footprint. The amount of space available per person on earth is 2.2 hectares, but it's shrinking because of overpopulation, land degradation and pollution.

The average Canadian ecological footprint is 7.7 hectares. This means that we would need at least two more Planet Earths for all of the world's population to have the same standard of living as that enjoyed in Canada.

What you can do
If you're disappointed in your own footprint, consider ten ways in which you might apply the information in this book, and do them for a month. Revisit the website and your score – you, and the planet, might be in for a pleasant surprise.

El Niño
El Niño, which means "boy child" in Spanish, is a change to the normal temperature, wind and weather patterns in the Pacific Ocean. Trade winds normally drag warm conditions along the equator from east to west, bringing rain to Australia and cool, nutrient-rich water to the South American coastline. In an El Niño event, this climatic pattern is reversed, which is part of the earth's normal climatic variation.

The result is warmer ocean temperatures and higher rainfall along the South American coastline. The warmer water has lower nutrient levels, leading to declines in marine life and disaster for local fisheries. El Niño causes floods in the southwest United States and western Latin America, and drought in eastern Australia, Southeast Asia and southern Africa.

For Canada, El Niño brings a range of effects, including unusually mild winters, thinner ice on lakes, strong winds and storms in BC, and sometimes flooding, landslides and avalanches. The lack of winter snow on the prairies in 2002–3 was bad news for drought-stricken farmers and ski-resort operators alike. This drought contributed to the severe wildfires experienced in the summer of 2003.

Recent years have seen dramatic El Niño events. Many, but not all, scientists believe that global warming is altering El Niño patterns, leading to more frequent and more intense El Niño events.

What you can do
Anything that we can do to prevent and combat global warming by reducing our contribution of greenhouse gases will lessen the chances of more frequent and severe El Niño events.

Energy: renewable
Renewable energy resources are those of which we have an unlimited supply, or that can be replaced quickly through the normal cycles of nature. Solar energy and wind power, for example, are inexhaustible. Crops that produce bio-fuels are also said to be renewable, as long as the rate at which they're grown isn't outstripped by the rate at which we use them.

Around the world, governments, corporations and consumers are dipping their toes into renewable energy, for both environmental and political reasons. Renewable energy brings a whole range of options to the table. For example, countries with large, powerful river systems are already harnessing the power of a river's current in hydroelectric plants.

Similarly, windy coastlines are becoming dotted with wind farms, and countries that lie on geothermal belts, such as New Zealand, are experimenting with geothermal energy. Perhaps the most hopeful option of all is the sun, which is able to provide an unlimited supply of solar energy to pretty much all of the world.

Countries can look at their landscape and choose the option that best suits their natural conditions and economy. For the first time in decades, some are able to imagine a future where they have energy security and independence. In the past, the domination of fossil fuels meant that many countries had to buy the fuel for their energy needs from other countries.

It's important to remember that renewable energy sources, while better than fossil fuels for the health of the planet, are not without their own environmental impacts. For example, hydroelectric schemes can upset the flow of river systems and the health of the related ecosystems. Alternative energy sources need to be well chosen and carefully developed so that the solution to our energy problem doesn't become a problem itself.

What you can do
Consumer selection of renewable energy supplies will allow these emerging energy options to become more and more widely available, as well as cheaper.

Energy: non-renewable

Non-renewable energy sources are those that will eventually run out or that will take millions of years and certain climate and geological conditions to replace. There is a limited amount of the nuclear fuel uranium in the earth's crust. Once it's used, there is no more, so nuclear energy from uranium is not renewable. Fossil fuels, such as natural gas, LPG, coal and oil, are also non-renewable.

What you can do

Think carefully about your options when choosing and using appliances, heating options or cars. These items and the way they use energy can greatly reduce the rate at which these limited resources are disappearing.

Extinction

It's been conservatively estimated that 27 000 species disappear each year. We're seeing earth's sixth period of mass extinction and this time it's our fault. Over the past 500 million years there have been five massive extinctions. It took 20 to 100 million years for biodiversity to recover after each one. This current period of mass extinction is seeing species lost at a faster rate than before.

There are great hopes that the tropical rainforests of the world will give us new species and substances that will cure diseases and ease suffering. If we continue to liquidate our planet's natural assets, we'll lose them long before we ever get a chance to discover their full value.

Many people hope that cloning will enable the human race to bring animals such as the Tasmanian tiger and even dinosaurs back from extinction. This idea is taking away some of the feeling of urgency to protect endangered species. However, experts say that there may not be enough samples of Tasmanian tiger DNA to provide the genetic variation needed to re-establish the species. Dolly, the famous sheep who was the world's first cloned mammal, suffered from arthritis before her early death, raising concerns that cloning may cause genetic defects. With extinction, like most problems, prevention is preferable to cure.

Governments are starting to impose international bans on the trade of

Canada's endangered species

did you know...

According to the Committee on the Status of Endangered Wildlife in Canada, there are currently over 400 plant and animal species at risk in Canada, including the whooping crane, swift fox, North Atlantic right whale, peregrine falcon, piping plover, karner blue butterfly and monarch butterfly. For more info, see www.speciesatrisk.gc.ca.

animal products from endangered species. Zoos are working on breeding programs to keep species on the verge of extinction from being lost. Some nations are scaling back land clearing and deforestation. Programs are also being developed to control feral animals and plants and to prevent more from being introduced. It is hoped that these measures will bring certain species back from the verge of extinction.

What you can do
You can contribute to the reversal of species loss by supporting causes and associations such as World Wildlife Fund, David Suzuki Foundation, Greenpeace and Planet Ark. Avoid products that result in a loss of habitat for endangered species.

Fossil fuels
Fossil fuels provide around 80% of the world's energy. They provide fuel to power motor vehicles and manufacturing plants and are burned to drive turbines in power stations for the generation of electricity.

Not only are fossil fuels environmental offenders, but supplies are slowly running out, with the remaining reserves becoming increasingly hard to extract. The extraction itself has an environmental impact, harming habitats and contributing to erosion and pollution. Burning fossil fuels also pollutes the air, causing respiratory problems in humans, harming wildlife and causing acid rain. The biggest problem is that

the fossil fuels we currently use produce greenhouse gases, which scientists believe are contributing to global warming and causing the climate to change.

Fossil fuels are on their way out, from both an environmental and a long-term economic point of view. Business and industry know that supplies will eventually run out, so some are looking at the alternatives now. Environmentally, we need to dramatically reduce our use of fossil fuels long before supplies dwindle. While we can see the bottom of the oil barrel approaching, there's still enough oil and coal left to seriously affect our planet's climate through the greenhouse effect.

What you can do
Consider your own use of fossil fuel, and how it can be reduced for a positive effect on the planet's supplies.

Genetically modified organisms
In the past, farmers and horticulturalists have cross-bred plants from the same family to produce plants with desired characteristics, such as a different flavour in fruit or varied flower colours. With the advent of gene technology, genetic engineers can now swap genes between unrelated species. Plants can be spliced with a fish gene to make them less sensitive to cold weather, for example. Crops can be engineered to be pest-resistant. They can even be engineered to be resistant to the herbicides used on crops to kill weed plants. Currently,

genetically modified (GM) crops have been developed largely to make farms more productive. The benefits are for the food producer, not the consumer. However, the supporters of gene technology ultimately wish to engineer crops to have better nutritional value or even to contain therapeutic properties.

The claimed benefits of GM technology are that more people can be fed with the same amount of land and that world hunger could potentially be solved. The need for pesticides is also, theoretically, decreased.

However, there are some major environmental concerns with GM crops. The drawbacks of GM food crops are:
• Pest-resistant crops engineered to kill a target pest insect can also kill other, sometimes beneficial, insects. For example, pollen from GM plants can kill monarch butterflies, which are already endangered.
• Crops engineered to be resistant to weedkillers will encourage overuse of herbicides, wiping out all other plant life except for the crop plant. This will remove food sources for local wildlife, such as birds and small mammals.
• GM crops are hard to contain. GM plants can contaminate non-GM crops and honey production and are a threat to the organic farming industry.
• Once released into the environment, they are difficult to "recall."
• GM crops have had very little testing. The long-term effects of consuming GM food are unknown.

When GM foods were first introduced in the US, authorities basically concluded that, for example, if a GM tomato looked the same, smelled the same and tasted the same as a normal tomato, then it effectively was the same food and didn't need any additional testing or labelling. Canada followed the lead of the US. However, in April 2004 Standards Canada announced the adoption of a national standard for voluntary declarations of GM content or the lack of GM content to ensure truth in claims made in advertising and labelling. Many scientists believe that GM foods should undergo the same rigorous testing as pharmaceuticals, with independent scientific reviews and extensive human trials. We may yet find out that they're safe.

What you can do
Look for foods labelled "GE-free," "not genetically modified" or "certified organic." Greenpeace Canada has produced the "How to Avoid Genetically Engineered Food" shoppers' guide to help consumers identify GM-free brands. For more information, go to <u>*www.greenpeace.ca/shoppersguide*</u>.

Global warming & climate change
We all know how uncomfortable it is to sleep in a bed with too many blankets. That's what global warming is like and it's making the planet too warm for comfort.

On the surface, a few more degrees of warmth would actually improve places like Melbourne, Seattle and most of

England and Canada. "So what's the big deal?" you may ask. Global warming and the consequent changes to climate patterns are among the nastier threats to the health of the planet.

Scientists predict that the global temperature could rise by up to 2°–3°C (4°–6°F) over the next 20 years. This would make the planet the warmest it's been for 2 million years. Water warms more slowly than land, so it's expected that the effects on the oceans won't be felt until the middle of this century.

To understand global warming, first consider that materials expand slightly when heated. This thermal expansion will cause sea levels to rise by around 0.6 m (2 ft.) for every 1°C increase in global temperature. Then add the extra water from melted glaciers and the polar ice caps. Coastlines around the world will be submerged. Coastal cities such as Sydney, Hong Kong, New York, Tokyo and Amsterdam will be under threat. Many low-lying Pacific islands will simply disappear. And that's looking just at the rise in ocean levels.

Global warming would also result in a shift in the world's weather patterns. Extremes in weather, such as drought, hurricanes and flooding, would become more common. Crop yields would be reduced in many of the planet's current food-producing nations. Food shortages, already felt in many poorer countries, would become a worldwide problem.

A warmer global temperature will further affect the balance of gases in our atmosphere. Sea-water plankton soak up carbon dioxide and release oxygen. If you look at net production of oxygen, oceans are more accurately the "lungs of the earth" than rainforests. However, plankton decline in warmer water, soaking up less carbon dioxide and producing less oxygen.

Then there are the effects on plants and animals. Flooding will cause an increase in water-borne disease, and areas prone to disease-carrying insects will also grow.

Already, the West Nile virus has reached Canada. Some animals are particularly sensitive to temperature changes. Warm water depletes the

Signs of global warming

>> The ten warmest years between 1880 and 2000 have all occurred since 1983.
>> Most of the ten warmest years on record have happened since 1990.
>> In the last century, the average global temperature has risen by about 0.5°C (1°F).
>> In the second millennium, the warmest century was the twentieth century, the warmest decade was the 1990s and the warmest year was 1998. The years 2002, 2001, and 2004 were the second, third, and fourth warmest years on record (between 1880 and 2004 inclusive).

Source: US EPA and the World Meteorological Organisation

energy reserves in migrating salmon, for example, which in turn would result in some fish not reaching their spawning grounds. This would put Canada's salmon populations and the fisheries they support at risk.

Polar bears are also suffering from shortened and milder winter seasons. Winter is their feeding season, the time when they hunt on the ice and build up a fat store to survive over the remainder of the year. With more open water, fewer seal pups – the food of choice for the polar bear – are surviving, making it harder for polar bears to find food. Scientists report that polar bears are skinnier than they were 30 years ago and consequently are having fewer pups. There is a risk that polar bears may disappear from the Hudson Bay area within 50 years if things get worse. Global warming generally places even more stress on animals already struggling with habitat loss.

What you can do
Reduce your contribution to global warming and the greenhouse effect by cutting down your energy and gasoline use and by choosing green electricity.

Greenhouse effect
The traditional greenhouse is a glass garden house that allows sunlight in to warm air and surfaces and stops that warmed air from escaping. Air inside the glass house is therefore maintained at a warmer temperature than that outdoors. In much the same way, a layer of "greenhouse" gases in the atmosphere insulates the earth. The gases allow sunlight in, which warms the earth. Some of this heat bounces off the earth as infrared radiation. The layer of greenhouse gases in the atmosphere acts like a blanket to stop heat escaping to space, keeping the temperature at the earth's surface relatively even and accommodating for life. In fact, the greenhouse effect is necessary to make life on earth possible. The big environmental problem is that we're seeing an enhanced greenhouse occurring.

Prior to last century, greenhouse gases (such as carbon dioxide and methane) came mainly from the gas exchange of plants, the excrement of animals and the rotting of dead plants and animals. Photosynthesis uses these gases to build carbohydrates in plant tissues. This is part of the "carbon cycle." Constant and inter-connected cycles of photosynthesis and respiration, along with consumption, growth and decay, move the carbon in its various forms through plants, animals, the earth, air and water. While a relatively small amount of carbon is in the atmosphere as greenhouse gases, much of the carbon is stored carbon, "locked" in complicated organic molecules in plants and in fossil fuels.

Since industrialization, humans have been logging forests and burning huge amounts of fossil fuels such as coal, oil and natural gas to provide power. The burning of fossil fuels unlocks the stored carbon, producing an oversupply of carbon dioxide and other greenhouse gases to the atmosphere. They are adding to the planet's blanket, and the blanket's getting too thick.

The sad truth is that the global emissions of greenhouse gases need to be drastically slashed to stop global warming.

What you can do

You can make a huge difference by reducing your energy use and getting your energy from renewable, cleaner sources. Make a commitment to use green power.

Hazardous waste

We produce around 400 million tonnes of hazardous waste worldwide. A lot of this waste comes from mining and manufacturing.

As well as displacing huge amounts of earth, mining operations use chemicals such as cyanide, mercury and sulphuric acid to extract the metal from the ore. The discarded tailings (the excavated rock left over once the ore is removed) are often highly toxic and can seriously pollute groundwater and surface waterways.

Manufacturers have also produced some nasty by-products and not known what to do with them. Drums of toxic chemicals, solvents, pesticides and tar have been dumped or buried. The problem with buried hazardous wastes is that they're often forgotten.

Many of these toxins are harmful to the health of the environment and that of humans. Of particular concern

are the chemicals such as dioxins that accumulate in the fatty tissues of animals and build up in the food chain. While it is hard to pinpoint the causes, there are increasing incidences of cancer, particularly in areas of high pollution.

What you can do

It often feels futile to try to fight multinational corporations that have irresponsible waste disposal procedures, but increased vigilance with your own waste at a local level is within everybody's power.

Health issues

Day after day, human activity dumps solid waste on the land, washes chemicals and contaminated liquids into the water and releases poisonous gases into the air. Slowly we are poisoning the food, water and air supplies of all living things, including ourselves. These poisons are accumulating in the food chain, with meat-eating humans at the top.

Industrial pollution is seeing plants and animals come into contact with highly dangerous chemicals that their tissues weren't designed to cope with. Exposure to chemicals such as DDT, dioxins and PCBs and to a range of other toxins and carcinogens is increasing. Many of them are entering our diets. There is growing evidence that exposure to these chemicals is increasing cancer risk and the incidences of other illnesses. We used to take safe drinking water for granted

– until May 2000, when water contaminated with a deadly strain of E. coli caused seven deaths and thousands of illnesses in Walkerton, Ontario. This highlighted the importance of monitoring and protecting water supplies to ensure our health.

Clean air is essential for quality of life. Harmful gases and fine airborne particles are posing a very serious danger to human health and the health of other animals. Air pollution causes respiratory diseases and is linked with lung cancer and asthma. In the last 30 years, developed countries have reduced the amount of airborne particulate pollution, so the air appears cleaner and less sooty or hazy. However, many toxic gases are odourless and colourless. Just because you can't see them doesn't mean that they can't hurt you.

What you can do
Consider the health of the people and animals around you. Start making changes in your home, and then encourage similar changes in the wider environment.

Kyoto
In 1992 at Earth Summit in Rio, governments agreed to develop measures to stabilize greenhouse gas emissions in an effort to avoid climate change. The Kyoto Protocol is the follow-up to these green intentions and is a legally binding agreement to cut greenhouse gases.

The Kyoto Protocol was agreed upon by 160 government participants at a 1997 UN climate change conference held in Kyoto, Japan. Governments agreed to reduce the amount of greenhouse gases produced by developed countries by 5.2% of 1990 levels during the five-year period of 2008–13.

The Kyoto Protocol became legally binding once ratified (approved at government or parliament level) by 55% of the signatories representing 55% of the carbon dioxide emissions of developed countries. Russia's December 2004 ratification of Kyoto Protocol saw this minimum level reached.

Many countries, including Canada, New Zealand, Japan and the countries of the European Union, have ratified Kyoto. Australia and the United States are the only two major industrialized nations that have not ratified the agreement. The withdrawal of the USA meant that for a number of years the Kyoto treaty was in danger of collapsing.

With February 2005 the date for the treaty to take effect, the signatory countries will now undertake legislation changes, energy reform, industrial reform and community education programs to meet their target greenhouse gas reduction.

What you can do
Ratify Kyoto in your own backyard! Since greenhouse gas emissions relate to energy use, set yourself your own

Kyoto target and cut down your energy consumption using the tips in this book. The savings on your energy bills will help you to keep score.

Land clearing & deforestation

Forests covered a third of the earth's land 10 000 years ago. Then came agriculture, forestry and industrialization. Now we've lost a quarter of our planet's forests, and only 12% are still in their natural state. Each year we're still losing at least 16.2 million more hectares (40 million acres) of our forests through logging and land clearing, placing around 10% of the world's tree species in danger of extinction.

Canada is home to one-tenth of the world's remaining forests. These forests are home to a diversity of plant and animal life, including the red fox, woodland caribou, wolf, beaver, black bear and a host of bird life. In Canada, over 116 species that depend on forest habitat are endangered. In addition, over 142 salmon runs in British Columbia alone have become extinct, with over 600 more vulnerable, at least in part, due to logging.

Canada's Boreal forests are also an integral part of the culture of our indigenous people. The First Nations and Métis people rely on the forest for sustenance, their livelihood and their spiritual well-being.

Land clearing and deforestation are contributing to air pollution and climate change. Bulldozed, rotting and burning forests unlock carbon and release massive amounts of greenhouse gases and other pollutants into the air. Deforestation, combined with erosion and high rainfall, can also cause landslides and river flooding.

Forests are logged to provide timber for construction and furniture making, and wood pulp for tissue and paper products. In Canada, over 90% of the area allocated or licensed by the government to logging companies is clearcut. Clearcut logging is a highly destructive way to harvest timber. It strips an area of forest bare, leaving behind too few trees to enable the forest to regenerate itself.

Tropical rainforests are also disappearing at an alarming rate. Rainforests help to stabilize the global climate and purify the air and water, and they contain more than half of all the world's plant and animal species. This biodiversity contributes billions of dollars to the world's economy through the production and sale of products that come from rainforests. The plants alone produce a range of hardwoods, rubber, essential oils, fruit, spices, coffee and medicines. Tropical rainforests still hold hundreds of undiscovered species and many more that haven't been fully investigated. Some species may have great medical potential. Rainforests are rapidly being destroyed. At the current rate of destruction they will be gone by 2050.

Wood can be harvested in an ecologically sustainable manner and the wood products made can be certified in line with the Forest Stewardship Council (FSC) standard.

Is Canada water-wealthy?

did you know...

Canada has around a fifth of the world's fresh water. However, much of this is non-renewable "fossil water" (the remains of the melting of continental ice sheets), frozen in glaciers or inaccessible groundwater. Our share of the planet's renewable water is more like 6 to 9%.

Other "good woods" include wood reclaimed from demolished buildings, wood from community and First Nation forest operations, wood from sustainably managed plantations and recycled plastic "lumber."

What you can do
Recycled and "ancient-forest-friendly" timbers are good woods for building and furniture making. Think about alternative fibres, such as bamboo for flooring. Wherever possible buy paper, cardboard and tissue products made from recycled materials.

Lethal litter
No one likes the look of litter. It makes our streets and landscapes look dirty and unattractive. When stormwater washes litter off the streets, it leads to water pollution. It can also be lethal for wildlife. Here are some examples:
• Plastic shopping bags can be blown into the sea, where they do a very good impersonation of jellyfish. Huge knots of this plastic have been found in the bellies of dead whales and other large marine mammals that have mistaken them for food.

• An estimated 100 000 marine mammals and turtles are killed each year around the world by plastic litter.
• Fishing line, netting, rope and other litter from sport and commercial fishing can trap and strangle animals.
• The honeycomb plastic that holds a six-pack of cans together is also lethal. The strong plastic rings can strangle and slit the throats of small marine animals.
• Cigarette butts are a common litter problem. These fibrous pellets of poison can kill birds, turtles and other marine animals that swallow them. Studies have also linked cigarette-butt pollution to tumours in marine animals. On land, flicked cigarette butts can cause wildfires, which can kill animals and burn their habitat.

What can you do
Prevention is better than cure. Think about what you buy and how it is packaged. Consider your own litter practices and start picking up litter in your neighbourhood. Someone has to.

Material resources
In July 2002, WWF International released the "Living Planet Report

2002." The report stated that humanity could face a sharp drop in living standards by the middle of the century unless it stopped its current depletion of the earth's natural resources. One WWF representative likened the current use of resources to making withdrawals from a bank account faster than it is being fed by deposits or interest payments.

Only a small percentage of our current resource use actually ends up as durable products. Materials and energy are lost through inefficiencies right through the processes that make them. If we are to make our economy sustainable, we'll have to cut our current resource use by a staggering 75%–90%. Improving resource efficiency is vital.

Using resources more productively involves changing both a product's design and the way it's manufactured. Already energy authorities are working with businesses and factories to see where they can improve their energy efficiency. Also, research organizations and universities, such as the RMIT in Australia and the Rocky Mountains Institute in the United States, are working with businesses to improve their use of resources.

What you can do
Each individual can help to do more with fewer resources by saving water and energy, by avoiding over-consumption and overpackaging and by reusing and recycling materials wherever possible.

Nuclear energy
Nuclear energy is not considered a renewable energy source because it relies on fuels such as uranium. Supply is limited by the amount that can be extracted from the earth's crust. The key benefit of nuclear fuels is that they are not fossil fuels and do not contribute to the greenhouse effect. Some people venture to call nuclear energy a "clean" source of energy.

There's a certain romance and excitement to the sound of the phrase "harness the energy of the atom." In an ideal scenario there would be no accidents and we would discover a way to make radioactive waste safe so we could all enjoy the benefits of clean, limitless energy. In reality, accidents do happen and have happened. When they do happen, the consequences are horrific, as seen with the Chernobyl disaster. Until nuclear power becomes safe, both in normal and worst-case scenarios, it will continue to be a gamble with incredibly high stakes.

There is always a small, generally safe amount of background radioactivity in nature. However, the advent of nuclear power has produced radioactivity in quantities that can kill. The radioactivity of both the mining waste and the spent reactor waste is a huge risk to environmental health. The waste must first be sealed in aluminum foil to block alpha and beta radiation from escaping, then sealed in lead to block X-ray radiation, and finally sealed in a thick layer of

Victims of the *Exxon Valdez* spill

Although it is hard to measure the direct and indirect damage caused by the *Exxon Valdez* oil spill in 1989, scientists estimate that:
>> around 20 killer whales died, probably through eating contaminated fish
>> up to 5000 sea otters died, with many more displaced by local food shortages
>> up to 300 harbour seals died
>> up to half a million seabirds died
Since 1970 there have been around 50 spills as big as the *Exxon Valdez* spill. The worst oil spill disaster was the Gulf War.

concrete to block the gamma radiation.

Exposure to uranium and other sources of radioactivity has been linked with cancer and other major health problems. Even if adequate solutions can be found to clean up uranium mining sites and take care of the problem of radioactive waste, the experience of Chernobyl should teach us that nuclear energy is not worth playing with. There's too much to lose if things go wrong.

What you can do
Nuclear power generation is one of the sources of electricity in Ontario, New Brunswick, Nova Scotia and Prince Edward Island. If nuclear energy becomes, or already is, an issue where you live, take every opportunity to voice your opposition.

Oil spills
Oil spills from oil tankers and pipelines wreak havoc on the marine environment. Oil smothers and poisons the animal and plant life that lives in and around the sea. The infamous 42 million litre (11 million gallon) *Exxon Valdez* spill of 1989 killed thousands of aquatic mammals and hundreds of thousands of seabirds and shut down the local fishing industry. Seabirds were coated in oil, which ruined the waterproofing effect of their feathers. They died from exposure to the cold.

Even low-level oil pollution can damage wildlife. The relatively minor 6800 litre (1800 gallon) diesel spill near the Galapagos Islands in January 2001 at first appeared to take no casualties. A recent study has found that 62% of the iguanas on one of the affected islands died within a year of the accident.

The oily road run-off from a city of 5 million could release as much oil into the ocean over a year as one large tanker spill. In fact, its been estimated that Canadians spill or dump the equivalent of seven *Exxon Valdez* tankers of used motor oil into our waterways every year.

What you can do
Remember that stormwater run-off is another killer of wildlife in the ocean, so think about what you put down the drain.

Ozone depletion
Think of the ozone layer as SPF 30+ sunscreen for the planet, blocking out the more harmful wavelengths of the sun's radiation. Too much UV radiation would increase the number of people with skin cancers and eye cataracts, natural vegetation and crops would all be damaged, and plankton, the basis of the marine food chain, would deplete. So we definitely want just the right amount of ozone in the atmosphere.

Ozone is a molecule containing three oxygen atoms. There's a relatively high concentration of ozone 14–45 kilometres above the earth's surface in a diffuse gaseous layer called the ozone layer. However, ozone-depleting gases, particularly chlorofluorocarbons (CFCs), are slowly eroding this protective layer. CFCs were commonly used to make certain types of plastics and foam packaging, in refrigerators and car air conditioners and as a propellant gas in aerosol cans.

When CFCs in the atmosphere are exposed to sunlight, they release highly reactive chlorine atoms. This chlorine reacts with ozone, converting it to oxygen. The chemical reaction destroys ozone but re-forms the reactive chlorine atom. One free chlorine atom can destroy thousands

of ozone molecules and itself remain intact. Our atmosphere still has a vast reserve of these ozone-destroying chlorine atoms that will remain there, wreaking havoc, for decades.

Scientists have discovered fluctuating holes in the ozone layer over the polar regions, along with areas of decreased ozone concentration. Holes over the inhospitable poles are one concern, but more alarming is the gradual thinning of the atmospheric ozone at middle and high latitudes. These are the areas where most of the world's agricultural productivity occurs and where the most people live.

In 1987 an international agreement to phase out CFCs in manufacture came into force. The aerosol industry was one of the first to respond and phased out CFCs and other halocarbons. However, we can't rest on our laurels. The production of CFCs needs to cease, and old CFC-containing products, such as unwanted fridges or the air conditioners in scrapped cars, must be carefully disposed of so that the remaining CFCs are contained. Remember that we still have the problem of the active ozone-destroying chlorine atoms that are already in the ozone layer. Let's not exacerbate the problem by adding more.

What you can do
When your car or old refrigerator comes to the end of its life, make sure you dispose of it appropriately instead of dumping it.

Saving the animals

The green movement has often focused on saving dolphins, whales, koalas, pandas and other cuddly, intelligent or beautiful creatures. It's harder to motivate people to save the less photogenic species, such as lobsters, prawns, krill, shrimp and crabs. They're not exactly the kind of creatures you want to hug, yet they're vital to the marine environment. Crustaceans are the vacuum cleaners of the ocean, removing pollutants from the sea to give the other marine life a healthy environment. Krill are also the main food source for a number of species of whale. It's all well and good to talk about saving the whale or the dolphin, but we also have to save all of the other species, plant and animal, that together provide a supporting environment that whales and dolphins can thrive in.

Whales, dolphins and koalas are the supermodels of the natural world. Saving them without looking after the plants and animals that support them is sentimental pseudo-environmentalism. In other words, it's being a fake greenie. True environmentalists seek to conserve all of nature's biodiversity and respect the complexity of the environment. They understand that sometimes the beautiful plants and animals rely on ugly species to survive.

What you can do

Look after all creatures great and small by reducing the pollution that you contribute to this world that we share. Respect their habitat while you're exploring the natural environment and avoid products that destroy animal habitat in their production.

Sustainability

In the eighties business climate, greed was good. Then in the nineties we tightened our belts and the customer was always right. In the new millennium, everyone is talking about the triple bottom line and making their business sustainable. In fact, "sustainability" is almost becoming a buzzword.

There's nothing new or complicated about the concept of environmental sustainability. It's based on themes that we learned in kindergarten. Instructions like "you made the mess; you clean it up" and "don't take more than your fair share" sit just as well in the grown-up rat race as they do in the schoolroom.

Anything that can go on indefinitely is said to be sustainable. A sustainable situation is one in which the current needs of the population are met without compromising the ability of future generations to meet their own needs.

In business, people often talk about sustainability in terms of three aspects: economic, environmental and social sustainability. These elements are commonly referred to as the triple bottom line for companies. Companies that adhere to the triple bottom line principles are financially viable, can be sustained by the natural environment and are socially responsible. They are the good corporate citizens.

What you can do

Supporting such companies, via your product purchase or share investment decisions (ethical investing), is the best way to encourage even more companies to behave in an environmentally and socially responsible manner.

Trash

Very few of us in our First World suburban backyards set about deliberately poisoning the earth. We're not exactly burying used plutonium under our maple trees. However, our consumer-based lifestyles produce a huge amount of waste. Part of this is the waste we actually see, the things we put into our own garbage bin that are taken away to landfill by the local garbage collection service.

Organic waste such as food and garden scraps will eventually decompose, whether in a compost bin in your backyard or in a landfill. Bacteria and earthworms know what to do with this organic matter. However, humans have invented a range of new substances, such as plastics and metal alloys. These are new to nature and rely on chemical decomposition to break down. They can't rely on biological decomposition; the bacteria don't know what to do with them and the worms don't want to eat them. As a result, we've got this mounting pile of rubbish that won't go away.

Recycling is providing a way for us to reduce the amount of waste we dump and to get further use from our planet's limited resources. Materials such as steel, aluminum and glass need huge amounts of energy to be mined and/or manufactured from raw materials. When you recycle, you're making these materials available for use again. In many cases it takes less energy and water to make a new product from recycled materials than it does from raw materials. There are many industries that view waste as secondary raw material, valuable manufacturing feedstock that they can make new products out of. So don't bury useful materials in landfill.

Garbage dumps have their own environmental problems. When it rains, the rainwater leaches harmful substances from the garbage into the soil, where they can pollute groundwater. Many governments have set up hazardous waste collection programs so that people can dispose of any hazardous items they have in a safe, controlled collection program. Garbage dumps also give off gas. This gas includes greenhouse gases and occasionally some poisonous chemical gases. Many dumps collect the gas, which contains a lot of methane, and burn it to produce electricity.

Ultimately, landfill is not a long-term solution to our waste problems. Landfills can go on producing polluting gases and liquid run-off for 20–30 years after they're closed. Landfill leaves the proper solving of the waste problem to future generations.

What you can do
Avoid producing the waste in the first place. Appropriate recycling, composting and sorting of your household waste can have an immediate, positive impact. Educating family and friends to do the same will have a multiplier effect.

Water pollution
Water is relatively cheap in Canada, the US and the UK. However, in countries where safe drinking water is in short supply, it's a precious and expensive resource.
• In parts of Sudan, up to half of the average household income is spent on water.
• In Bogota, Colombia, pirates steal water by drilling into water mains.

While we're creating a demand for water, human activities are also polluting our supplies of it and interfering with the natural mechanisms that help to purify it. Vast tracts of land are being sealed with suburban sprawl. Stormwater run-off from the concrete jungle washes litter and chemicals into rivers and lakes. We're chopping down the trees whose root systems help to filter the water. Agricultural run-off and effluent overflows from animal farms also pollute our waterways. The industrial sector contributes a cocktail of chemical nasties to the mix. Unfortunately, water systems have long been used to take waste away from factories in the hope that they'll be sufficiently diluted downstream to become harmless. The waterways and oceans have also provided a convenient mode of transportation through shipping, but not without environmental consequences, such as oil spills and other water pollution.

As governments and businesses in developed countries have become more aware of the consequences of water pollution, outflows from industry have become more tightly regulated. Now industries have to closely monitor and control their factories' contribution to water and air pollution, though even "acceptable" levels of some pollutants can be harmful to the environment. Regulations cover only licensed operators going about their day-to-day business. Often the more dramatic and harmful cases of water pollution come from accidents or illegal dumping.

What you can do
At a local level, careful monitoring of what you put down the drain will lead to a cleaner run-off.

Water: supply and demand
All living things, including humans, plants, animals, crops and livestock, need water to survive. The UN World

Summit on Sustainable Development 2002 in Johannesburg, also known as Earth Summit 2, highlighted adequate supplies of safe drinking water as one of the biggest issues facing our world. Ideally, there has to be enough fresh water readily available in places where it is needed. Agriculture is by far the largest user of water, representing over 60% of the world's total water consumption. Together with the water we use in our homes, this creates a need for fresh water that will keep increasing as the world's population grows.

We tend to take water for granted. We turn the tap on and water comes out. However, there is not an endless supply of water. Although Canada is one of the world's fresh water–rich countries, we're starting to face problems in meeting demand. Whether or not water restrictions are in force, we're going to have to start using less water in our homes.

Part of the problem is that water in Canada tends to flow to the north, eventually emptying into Hudson Bay and the Arctic Ocean. This means that it is flowing away from where the bulk of Canada's population lives in the south of the country. Water supplies are less plentiful on the prairies and in parts of British Columbia. The water in the Great Lakes is already spoken for by existing uses and is also suffering from pollution. In addition, our cities are supplied with tap water and sewage services through an extensive infrastructure system of pipes, reservoirs and treatment facilities. The more water we use and the more wastewater we produce, the more demand and strain we place on this infrastructure. We also need to remember that the more water we extract from lakes and rivers, the less there is to play its important role in the natural environment.

Sooner or later we're going to be paying a lot more for the water we use. A number of water policy and consumption studies have been done around the world. Many of them recommend that water authorities increase the price per kilolitre of water to give the public the financial incentive to reduce their water use. It's also likely that manufacturing standards and building codes will change in the future to ensure that all new products and homes are more water-efficient.

What you can do

Following the water-saving tips in this book will ensure that you save precious drops, as well as dollars, in your home and office.

>> Epilogue: a step further

Next time you go to the beach, go hiking or camping or take a trip to the zoo, look around you. Our planet is a beautiful, unique place that is well worth saving. The power to do so rests in your hands. Apart from the things you can easily change on a daily basis, there are other things you can do to make a difference.

Get informed

If you care about the state of the environment, it's important to be informed about what's happening around the globe, what the problems are and what's being done about them. Without awareness and information, the green movement would not exist.

An easy way to stay up to date is to read news extracts from the Planet Ark Daily World Environment News Service. Sponsored by Reuters, Planet Ark publishes up to 40 environmental news stories, written by Reuters journalists worldwide, each weekday on the Planet Ark Internet site. The service covers over 100 different green topics, from A (air pollution) to Z (zoo news). You can also subscribe to the service for free and receive a daily newsletter containing the day's news headlines and links to the full stories. Visit www.planetark.org/news.

Get active

Get involved in practical conservation efforts, planting trees and restoring natural vegetation. You can call your municipality to find out about local conservation groups. Alternatively, join the national NatureWatch (www.naturewatch.ca) series of volunteer-based ecological monitoring programs, which help to identify changes occurring in our environment. Similarly, the Space for Species (www.spaceforspecies.ca) program involves young Canadians in tracking the migration movements of certain animals.

Get political

Don't be afraid to speak out about the issues that concern you. Write letters or e-mails to the relevant politicians and government departments and let them know how you feel. However, don't just protest – offer your thoughts on solutions too.

Pass the message on

Help your friends and family to green up their lives. Share you favourite eco-tips with them. The more people we can enlist to help the environment from the comfort of their own homes, the bigger difference we can make to the health of the planet.

>> Notes on the text

Keys to a greener house

General information on energy sources, green energy sources and marginal energy sources by province: Planet Ark, *Do Something!* video; Australian Greenhouse Office (AGO), *Your Home – Good Residential Design Guide* (2001); *Philip's Nature Encyclopedia* (George Philip Limited, 1998); David Suzuki Foundation, *The Green Guide to David Suzuki's Nature Challenge 2002;* Statistics Canada, *Electric Power Generation, Transmission and Distribution 1999;* Friends of the Earth Green Energy campaign.

Source of personal greenhouse gas emissions in Canada diagram: Government of Canada, *Climate Change Plan for Canada,* November 2002, ISBN: En56-183/2002E, catalogue 0-662-33172-9. Reproduced with permission of the Minister of Public Works and Government Services, 2004.

Comparison of standby power with energy use of a refrigerator: Office of Energy Efficiency, *Energy Efficiency Trends in Canada,* 1990 to 2001.

EnerGuide labels: © Reproduced with permission of the Minister of Natural Resources, Canada 2005.

ENERGY STAR® symbol: The ENERGY STAR® mark is administered and promoted in Canada by Natural Resources Canada and is registered in Canada by the United States Environmental Protection Agency.

Use of water in the average Canadian household graph: Environment Canada's Freshwater Website (www.ec.gc.ca/water), 2004. Reproduced with the permission of the Minister of Public Works and Government Services, 2005.

Per capita carbon dioxide greenhouse gas contribution: 16.8 tonnes figure from David R. Boyd, *Canada vs. the OECD: An Environmental Comparison* (University of Victoria, 2001).

Renewable energy: Western Power website (www.westernpower.com.au); Australian Greenhouse Office; Marion A. Brisk, *1001 Ideas for Science Projects on the Environment* (Arco/Macmillan, 1997); various brochures from the Sustainable Energy Authority Victoria (SEAV) and the Sustainable Energy Development Authority (SEDA); David Elliott, *Energy, Society and Environment* (Routledge, 1997); numerous stories from the Planet Ark/Reuters Daily World Environment News (WEN) Service (www.planetark.org/news).

Amount and types of water in the world: Marion A. Brisk, *1001 Ideas for Science Projects on the Environment* (Arco/Macmillan, 1997); City West Water, *Making Waves*, no. 11 (Oct.–Dec. 2001).

Water use diagram and statistics: Environment Canada Freshwater website – daily water use estimate of 343 litres per person based on 1998 figures.

Per capita water use statistics for Canada and other nations: David R. Boyd, *Canada vs. the OECD: An Environmental Comparison* (2001).

Water situation analysis information: David R. Boyd, *Unnatural Law: Rethinking Canadian Environmental Law and Policy* (UBC Press, 2003).

The green kitchen

Buffalo meat reference: Planet Ark/Reuters WEN story, "US mad-cow scare may prompt taste for buffalo meat" (January 8, 2004).

Electricity sources: *SBS World Guide,* 11th edition. (Hardie Grant Books, 2003).

Salmon farming information: Monterey Bay Aquarium and the David Suzuki Foundation Sustainable Oceans program.

Figure for number of households: Statistics Canada, 2001 census.

Food production: Greg Pahl, *The Complete Idiot's Guide to Saving the Environment* (Alpha Books, 2001).

Grain equivalents: The Worldwatch Institute.

Food additives and their codes: Bill Stratham, *The Chemical Maze* (POSSIBILITY.COM, 2001); Maurice Hanssen, *Additive Code Breaker* (Lothian, 1986); Calgary Allergy Network; Federation of European Food Additives and Food Enzymes Industries.

Food irradiation: Australian Food and Grocery Council's Food Science Bureau food technology factsheet "The Facts

About Irradiation"; Donna Welsh, "Food Irradiation," *Wellbeing,* vol. 79 (2000).

Organic food: Sheridan Rogers, Australian Food and Grocery Council, "All About Organics," *The Age, SundayLife!* magazine; brochures and articles from the Canadian Organic Growers website.

Genetically modified organisms: "Seeds of Doubt," *Four Corners* (ABC), first broadcast September 13, 1999, produced by Lisa McGregor (Australian Broadcast Commission); numerous stories from the Planet Ark/Reuters Daily WEN Service; Greenpeace, *True Food Guide.*

Food labelling laws: Health Canada.

Gas and electric stove: *Organic Style* (March/April 2002); Asthma Victoria. Some **microwave safety information** from Rebecca Ephraim, "To Microwave or Not," *Conscious Choice* (Nov. 2001).

Dollar estimates of energy bill savings when comparing appliances with varying EnerGuide ratings: NRCan EnerGuide booklet "Consumer's Guide to Buying and Using Energy Efficient Appliances." This booklet listed dollar savings for comparison purposes only, based on the national average price of electricity of $0.0814 per kWh.

Energy-smart cooking and kitchen appliances: SEDA; SEAV (particularly the brochure "Energy Smart Cooking"); AGO, *Global Warming, Cool It!*

Figure for heat loss from oven: EnerGuide, *Range Tips.*

Reference to energy to heat water in dishwasher: EnerGuide, *Dishwasher Tips.*

Packaging and recycling: Recycling Council of Ontario; Dofasco Steel; 1996 National Packaging Survey commissioned by the Canadian Council of Ministers of the Environment; Paper & Paperboard Packaging Environmental Council; virtualrecycling.com; Manitoba Product Stewardship Council; Environment and Plastics Industry Council (EPIC); Saskatchewan Waste Reduction; *Planet Ark Recycling Report* (1997 and 2000); ACI Glass Packaging; Steel Can Recycling Council; Publishers National Environment Bureau; Aluminium Can Group; Australian Liquidpaper Cartonboard Manufacturers Association (ALC); VISY Recycling; Plastics and Chemicals Industry Association (PACIA); EcoRecycle Victoria; Amcor Recycling; Beverage Industry Environment Council.

Endocrine disruptors: EPA Endocrine Disrupter Screening and Testing Advisory Committee's reports and factsheets; Natural Resources Defence Council's "Endocrine Disruptors" factsheets; Greenpeace International "Toxic Toys" campaign. Some **health information:** Dr. Andrew Weil, *Natural Health, Natural Medicine* (Warner Books, 1995).

"Down the drain": Advice from Melbourne Water and the New South Wales and Victoria EPAs.

The green living room

Heat loss percentages: various OEE publications, including *Keeping the Heat In.*

Energy loss comparison with nuclear plant output: EnerGuide *Energy Saving* list of tips.

Geothermal energy figures: Geothermal Education Office (GEO).

Heater and air conditioner prices: Based on estimates from EnerGuide and BC Hydro and the average portable heater prices of range available at Sears and Canadian Tire retail.

Estimates of lighting costs and the proportion of energy converted to light in incandescent bulbs: NRCan OEE lighting tips.

Energy saving figure for changing one bulb per house: ENERGY STAR.

Lightbulb recycling information: "A Bright Idea for Recycling," *Canadian Geographic,* http://www.canadian geographic.ca/Magazine/MJ03/ Etcetera/brightidea.asp; Ikea; various municipal waste information articles.

Controlling heat loss and gain: Planet Ark, *Do Something!* video; EnerGuide booklet *Keeping the Heat In;* AGO, *Global Warming, Cool It!;* SEDA's "Live Energy Smart" brochures; SEAV's brochures "Home Cooling Hints, Home Heating Hints" and "Sealing Out Draughts"; "Sustainable Building, Sustainable Lives" tipsheets 1 and 2 from GreenHome – Washington, DC; Paul Hawkins, Amory Lovins and L. Hunter Lovins, *Natural Capitalism* (Little, Brown and Company, 1999).

Heating and cooling product guides: BC Hydro's series *Guides to Energy Management;* various EnerGuide brochures and information sheets; Geothermal Education Office; Canadian Solar Industries

Association; SEAV's brochures "Choosing a Heating System" and "Choosing a Cooling System"; Reach for the Stars' "Guide to Energy Smart Air Conditioners"; AGO, *Your Home – Good Residential Design Guide;* Australian Consumers' Association, "Electrical Personal and Room Heaters," *Choice* (Feb. 2001); indoor air quality aspects from Asthma Victoria.

Wood fire: Government of Canada's "Burn It Smart" program; Environment Australia Air Quality factsheet "Woodsmoke"; Asthma Victoria; SEAV's brochure "Operating Hints for Wood Heaters."

Lighting: Planet Ark, *Do Something!* video and Earth Disk educational software; "Sustainable Building, Sustainable Lives" tipsheet 3 from GreenHome – Washington, DC; SEAV's brochure "Energy Smart Lighting."

Standby wattage: International Energy Association brochure "Things That Go Blip in the Night"; ENERGY STAR initiative; Australian Consumers' Association *Choice* report on standby wattage (April 2001).

Signs of standby power: Maritime Electric website article, a condensed version of a CADDET Energy Efficiency newsletter article

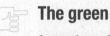

The green bathroom

Comparison with old-fashioned bathrooms: *The 1900 House* (PBS). Some **green bathroom tips:** Sarah Callard and Diane Millis, *Green Living* (Carlton, 2001).

Water-saving tips: Planet Ark, *Do Something!* video and website; savewater.com.au; Sydney Water and Yarra Valley Water.

Hot water cost estimate for a family of four: Environment Canada – Freshwater website.

Dripping tap figures: Planet Ark, Earth Disk.

Water heater information: BC Hydro brochure "Guide to Energy Management: Domestic Water Heating"; EnerGuide website information on choosing a water heater; "Living Green" tips from Environmental Action Barrie.

"What not to flush": advice from Melbourne Water.

Composting toilet: Alternative Technology Association, particularly *The Green Technology House & Garden Book* (ATA Publications, 1993).

The green laundry

54 kilotonnes of cleaners figure: from the Environmental Choice Program

Spider information: Health Canada

Reduced emissions resulting from using cold water estimate: District of North Vancouver website.

Washing machine: based on figures from water-consumption rating label figures, other information from the savewater.com.au site and the Water Services Association of Australia, and energy-consumption comparisons from the Energy Rating label program.

Dollar estimates of energy bill savings when comparing washers with varying EnerGuide ratings: NRCan EnerGuide booklet "Consumer's Guide to Buying and Using Energy Efficient Appliances."

Whitegoods recycling: "Planet Ark Recycling Report" (2000); RMIT University Centre for Design.

Dry cleaning: Sarah Callard and Diane Millis, *Green Living* (Carlton, 2001); dry cleaning and general laundry information from Stephen P. Ashkin, "Organic Style," *The Delicate Cycle* (Jan./Feb. 2002).

Laundry product guide and ingredients: Based on articles written by Planet Ark's Director of Research, Paul Klymenko; John Elkington and Julia Hailes, *The Green Consumer Guide* (Choice Magazine, Australian Conservation Foundation and Penguin Books, 1989); *Margaret Gee's Green Buyer's Guide* (S & W Information Guides, 1989); Total Environment Centre factsheet "Toxic Chemicals in Your Home"; P.W. Atkins, *General Chemistry* (Scientific American Books, 1989).

Green-cleaning: John Elkington and Julia Hailes, *The Green Consumer Guide* (*Choice* Magazine, Australian Conservation Foundation and Penguin Books, 1989); Julia Richardson, "The Healthy House," *Our House* (May 2001); Total Environment Centre factsheet "Household Cleaning Agents: Alternatives"; Northern Sydney Waste Board, *The Easy Guide to Natural Cleaning; Domestic Bliss: Molly Dye's Recipes for Good Living,* edited by Christine Whiston (Nationwide News, 2001); *Barbara Lord's Green Cleaning Guide* (Schwartz and Wilkinson, 1989); and

years of my own household experimentation.

Pest control: Based on Planet Ark's Earth Disk; the Sydney Water Pesticides Project; various factsheets on pest control from the Total Environment Centre and Government of Yukon, Department of Environment.

The green bedroom

Furniture and bedding: Sarah Callard and Diane Millis, *Green Living* (Carlton, 2001); Helen Lewis and John Gertsakis, *Design + Environment: A Global Guide to Designing Greener Goods* (GreenLeaf, 2001).

Conventional cotton in jeans figure: Cleaner Cotton Campaign (www.sustainablecotton.org).

Estimate of time spent indoors: Canadian Mortgage and Housing Corporation (CMHC).

Recycled PET fiberfill statistics: EPIC.

Ventilation information and advice: CMHC; Home Ventilation Institute (www.hvi.org); OEE.

EMF information: Hydro Quebec brochure "Electric and Magnetic Fields and Human Health"; Sarah Callard and Diane Millis, *Green Living* (Carlton, 2001); Health Canada.

Indoor air quality: Asthma Victoria; Marion A. Brisk, *1001 Ideas for Science Projects on the Environment* (Arco/Macmillan, 1997).

Fabric comparisons: "Design + Environment," *Greenhouse Living* (Spring 2000); Planet Ark/Reuters

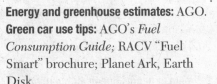

WEN story, Oliver Bullough, "British hemp industry sees bright future" (March 7, 2002); interview with Giorgio Armani in *Organic Style* (March/April 2002); John Elkington and Julia Hailes, *The Green Consumer Guide* (Choice Magazine, Australian Conservation Foundation and Penguin Books, 1989). **Dust mite advice:** Asthma Victoria, Asthma Australia and the National Asthma Campaign; Calgary Allergy Network.

The green office

Household computer and Internet use statistics: Statistics Canada, *Selected dwelling characteristics and household equipment* (2002 figures).
Figure for the growth in OECD paper consumption: Markets Initiative.
Amount of recyclable paper waste estimate: 80% figure from Recycling Council of Ontario; 50% figure from Environment Canada Atlantic Region, *Working Your Way to a Green Office*.
Electricity use of computers and monitors figure: Government of Canada, *Climate Change Plan for Canada*, November 2002, ISBN En56-183/2002E, catalogue 0-662-33172-9.
Estimate of the amount of e-waste by weight: National Office of Pollution Prevention, I*nformation Technology (IT) and Telecommunications (Telecom) Waste in Canada* (2001).
Starbucks paper-saving figure: estimate of 586 800 pounds from www.starbucks.com.

The green garage

Energy and greenhouse estimates: AGO.
Green car use tips: AGO's *Fuel Consumption Guide;* RACV "Fuel Smart" brochure; Planet Ark, Earth Disk.
Fuel: GreenFleet; Natural Gas Vehicle Alliance brochure "Natural Gas Vehicles"; OEE Personal Vehicle Initiative.
Estimates of fossil fuel reserves: Australian Institute of Petroleum website.
Tips for buying a car: Environmental Defence "Green Cars" campaign; OEE EnerGuide, *Fuel Consumption Guide;* Auto$mart program.
Sustainable car: Toyota Prius and Honda Insight press kits and product brochures; "Fuelling the 21st Century," *Nova: Science in the News* (Australian Academy of Science, 1998); GreenFleet.
Alternatives to cars: Planet Ark, Earth Disk; GreenFleet; Smogbusters "Way to Work" project.
Road salt figure: Environment Canada.
Tire pressure statistics: Canadian Automobile Association.
Estimates of cruising-speed fuel economy and winter fuel consumption increases: OEE Auto$mart program.
Information about the effects of Iraq war on car sales and oil prices: Planet Ark/Reuters WEN story, "Gas prices mute America's love for big SUVs" (May 14, 2004).
Oil recycling information: Environment Canada; www.UsedOilRecycling.com; Waste Diversion Ontario.

Estimate of time saved by jackrabbit driving: Quoted by Auto$mart guide from G. Lenaers and I. De Vlieger, "Moderate Driving Behaviour Cuts Fuel Consumption" *CADDET Newsletter,* no. 4 (Dec. 1995).

Estimate of deaths due to air pollution: Environmental Defence.

The green garden

General information on the importance of plants to the environment: Planet Ark National Tree Day information; Marion A. Brisk, *1001 Ideas for Science Projects on the Environment* (Arco/Macmillan, 1997).

General green gardening: Planet Ark, *Do Something!* video and Earth Disk.

"Living Soil" figures: Marion A. Brisk, *1001 Ideas for Science Projects on the Environment* (Arco/Macmillan, 1997).

Gardens in fire-prone zones information: Institute for Catastrophic Loss Reduction.

Canadian waste statistic: Waste Reduction Week materials.

Estimate of average toad's earwig consumption: Canadian Wildlife Federation.

Rooftop garden insulation figure: Environment Canada, *Science and the Environment Bulletin* (July 1999).

Invasive species information and estimate of alien species in Ontario: Environment Canada, *Invasive Species of Natural Habitats in Canada,* quoting Kaiser, J. 1983. *Native and exotic plant species in Ontario: a numerical synopsis.* The Plant Press 1(2): 25–26.

Organic weed control: Soil Association of South Australia.

Garden water conservation and rainwater tank: "Water Saving Ideas," *Greenhouse Living* (Summer 2001); Environment Canada's Freshwater website; Gina Lazenby, *The Healthy Home* (Conran Octopus, 2000); "Planet Ark Mulch Report."

Composting and worm farming: "Planet Ark Recycling Report"; "Planet Ark Mulch Report"; campaign information from Planet Ark's National Worm Week initiative; garden recycling factsheets from the Recycling Council of Ontario and Clean Calgary Association.

Organic gardening and pest control: "Go For Green" Active Living and Environment Program; Brenda Little, *Companion Planting in Australia* (New Holland, 2000); various factsheets on pest control from the Total Environment Centre's Toxic Chemicals in Your Home initiative.

Green building and renovation

General sustainable building: Numerous interviews with Graham Treloar PhD, MArch, lecturer at the School of Architecture & Building, Deakin University, and with Paul Klymenko, Director of Research, Planet Ark. General sustainable building information from the Australian Greenhouse Office publications *Global Warming, Cool It!* and *Your Home – Good Residential Design Guide;*

Western Power, *Smart Home;* Michael Mobbs, *Sustainable House* (Choice Books, 1998); Alternative Technology Association, *The GreenTechnology House & Garden Book* (1993).

Material resources: RMIT Centre for Design (particularly its publication *EcoSpecifier*).

Floor covering: Cork information from Amorim Group and Cork Masters; other material information from the RMIT *EcoSpecifier* and Sarah Callard and Diane Millis, *Green Living* (Carlton, 2001).

Dichloromethane (used in some paint strippers): listed as a suspected carcinogen by the EPA.

EnerGuide retrofit and grant example: Home.Performance.com

Proportion of waste stream from construction: Government of Canada sector profile document *Sustainable Development: Sustainable Development: Canadian Solutions for Global Need – The Construction Sector* (2002).

EnerGuide for Houses and R-2000 information: NRCan.

Dwelling-type statistics: Statistics Canada, *Selected dwelling characteristics and household equipment 2002.*

Green shopping

General information: Planet Ark's "Buy Green" and "Products" web pages and its Green Consumer campaigns; Government of Canada Environmental Choice (EcoLogo) program; John Elkington and Julia Hailes, *The Green Consumer Guide* (*Choice* Magazine, Australian Conservation Foundation and Penguin Books, 1989); *Margaret Gee's Green Buyer's Guide* (S & W Information Guides, 1989).

Plastic bags: Planet Ark's plastic bag environmental campaign; Government of Ireland; Clean Up Australia. The figure of 55 million per week is commonly quoted for Canadian plastic bag usage, including in the Whistler "It's Our Nature" Household Tool Kit.

Environmental Choice EcoLogo: Reproduced by permission of TerraChoice Environmental Services Inc.

Labelling: International Standards Organisation; John Lawrence, "Verifying 'Green' Claims," *ISO Bulletin* (August 1999); Australian Consumers' Association, "Eco-ads: Are We Being Duped?" *Choice* (2000).

Green grooming

General information: See notes for "Green Shopping" chapter; Aubrey Hampton, *What's in Your Cosmetics* (Odonian Press, 1995).

Rose oil chemical name: John C. Leffingwell, *Chirality & Odour Perception: 1,6-Dihydrodamascones* (Leffingwell & Associates, 2001).

Cosmetic ingredient explanations: Altruis Biomedical Network (www.cosmetics-information.com); Wendy Block, "Beauty with a Conscience: The Chemistry of Natural Cosmetics," *Delicious! Living*

(Aug. 1997); John McMurray, *Organic Chemistry* (Brooks/Cole, 1988); Aubrey Hampton, *What's in Your Cosmetics* (Odonian Press, 1995).

Sunscreen ingredient: Marc Reisch, "What's That Stuff? Sunscreens," *Chemical & Engineering News*, vol. 80, no. 25 (June 24, 2002); Therapeutic Goods Administration, "Sunscreens – Potential Oestrogenic Activity" (Dec. 2001), a response to Schlumpf et al., "In-vitro and In-vivo Estrogenicity of UV Sunscreens," *Environmental Health Perspectives*, vol. 109, no. 3 (Mar. 2001); website information prepared by Dr. John R. Sullivan (Australian College of Dermatologists, 2001).

Sun protection: Health Canada.

Successful boycotts: www.ethicalconsumer.org

Animal welfare and testing: Coalition for Consumer Information on Cosmetics (CCIC); Choose Cruelty Free; People for the Ethical Treatment of Animals (PETA); The Body Shop, "Environmental Performance Statement 2000" and "Against Animal Testing."

Leaping Bunny Logo: Reprinted by permission of the Coalition for Consumer Information on Cosmetics, www.leapingbunny.org.

Packaging: RMIT Centre for Design; Helen Lewis and John Gertsakis, *Design + Environment: A Global Guide to Designing Greener Goods* (GreenLeaf, 2001).

Homemade cosmetics recipes: From my hippie mother and experiments with friends during my teen years.

How to have a green baby

Preparing for pregnancy: Francesca Naish, *Natural Fertility* (Sally Milner Publishing, 1993).

Dioxins: Greenpeace; New South Wales EPA; John Elkington and Julia Hailes, *The Green Consumer Guide* (*Choice* Magazine, Australian Conservation Foundation and Penguin Books, 1989).

Laundry and bathing: See notes for "Laundry" and "Bathroom" chapters.

PVC toys: Greenpeace "Toxic Toys" campaign.

Diaper figures: Environmental Choice program and diaper manufacturer Kimberley-Clark.

Diapers: Women's Environment Network diaper campaign; "Nappies and the Environment," *Choice*; Cuddly-Bub Baby Products, "Cloth vs. Disposables: Facts & Figures"; link to male infertility from ABC News in Science (abc.net.au/science/news) story "Disposable nappies linked to male infertility (September 26, 2000); "Diaper Debate,"*Families Magazine's Online*.

Hot Topics

Estimate of sulphate from US sources deposited in Canada: Environment Canada Atlantic Region acid rain web pages; drop in SO_2 levels from Environment Canada national acid rain information.

Polar bear information: Government of Canada's Climate Change website.

Global water use in agriculture estimate: AAA Atlas of the Environment website.

Aquaculture and sustainable seafood information: David Suzuki Foundation and Monteray Bay Aquarium.

Genetically modified organisms: "Seeds of Doubt," *Four Corners* (ABC), first broadcast September 13, 1999, produced by Lisa McGregor; numerous stories from the Planet Ark/Reuters Daily World Environment News Service; Greenpeace, *True Food Guide*.

Global warming and climate change, the greenhouse effect, ozone depletion, acid rain, air pollution and El Niño: *Philip's Nature Encyclopedia* (George Philip Limited, 1998); Marion A. Brisk, *1001 Ideas for Science Projects on the Environment* (Arco/Macmillan, 1997); David Elliott, *Energy, Society and Environment* (Routledge, 1997); numerous stories from the Planet Ark/Reuters Daily WEN Service.

Water – supply and demand, water pollution and oil spills: *Philip's Nature Encyclopedia* (George Philip Limited, 1998); Marion A. Brisk, *1001 Ideas for Science Projects on the Environment* (Arco/Macmillan, 1997); RMIT/savewater.com.au Water Sensitive Design Seminar; additional oil spill information from stories from the Planet Ark/Reuters Daily WEN Service.

Extinction, biodiversity, land clearing and deforestation: The Wilderness Society's Forests campaign; Environment Australia's factsheet "Broadscale Vegetation Clearing" (February 2002); Marion A. Brisk, *1001 Ideas for Science Projects on the Environment* (Arco/Macmillan, 1997).

Crustaceans: From an interview with marine biologist Vicki Barmby.

Health issues: The Natural Resources Defence Council, "Breath-taking Report" (1996); Marion A. Brisk, *1001 Ideas for Science Projects on the Environment* (Arco/Macmillan, 1997); Dr. Andrew Weil, *Natural Health, Natural Medicine* (Warner Books, 1995).

Trash and hazardous waste: "Planet Ark Recycling Report" (1997 and 2000); Greg Pahl, *The Complete Idiot's Guide to Saving the Environment* (Alpha Books, 2001).

Lethal litter: Clean Up Australia Day annual Rubbish Reports; "Planet Ark Butt Report" (1997); Queensland EPA, Protecting the Environment – Beach and Ocean Litter initiative.

Material resources: WWF International, "Living Planet Report 2002"; Rocky Mountains Institute website (www.rmi.org); "Planet Ark Recycling Report" (1997 and 2000); Paul Hawkins, Amory Lovins and L. Hunter Lovins, *Natural Capitalism* (Little, Brown and Company, 1999).

Ecological footprint: The Earth Council website; LINKS Redefining Progress website (www.lead.org/leadnet/footprint/intro.htm); Claire Miller, "How My Life Helps Kill Earth," *The Age* (2000).

Renewable energy, non-renewable energy, fossil fuels and nuclear energy: *Philip's Nature Encyclopedia* (George Philip Limited, 1998); Australian Greenhouse Office (AGO); Australian Conservation Foundation's Nuclear Energy campaign; numerous stories from the Planet Ark/Reuters Daily WEN Service.

>> Further Information

Keys to a greener house

Energy product rating initiatives

EnerGuide
http://oee.nrcan.gc.ca/energuide

Energy Publications
http://energy-publications.nrcan.gc.ca

ENERGY STAR® initiative
For information on Canada's ENERGY STAR initiative, call the toll-free publications line of Natural Resources Canada's Office of Energy Efficiency at 1-800-387-2000, or visit the website at energystar.gc.ca.

Energy authorities

Office of Energy Efficiency (federal government)
The Government of Canada's centre of excellence for energy efficiency and alternative fuels information and programs. It operates as part of NRCan.
Office of Energy Efficiency
Natural Resources Canada
580 Booth St., 18th Floor
Ottawa, ON K1A 0E4
http://oee.nrcan.gc.ca

Office of Energy Efficiency – rebates and incentives
The Government of Canada also offers rebates and other incentives for industry, businesses and homeowners who take certain measures to improve their energy efficiency. More information is online.
http://oee.nrcan.gc.ca/corporate/incentives.cfm

BC Hydro Power Smart (British Columbia)
This site has extensive information relating to energy efficiency both at home and at work.
www.bchydro.com/powersmart

Green Power information, products, providers and generators

National
Friends of the Earth (FOE) Canada's Green Energy Campaign
FOE Canada is running a Green Energy Campaign to raise the awareness of the environmental and health implications of electricity generation, to research and compare the green electricity products on offer and to find ways to reduce the costs of green energy and encourage the Canadian government and business sectors to support the development and uptake of renewable, clean energy.
www.foecanada.org

Vision Quest Windelectric Inc.
Vision Quest Windelectric Inc. is a wholesale wind energy producer with a number of business and utility customers across Canada.
www.visionquestwind.com

Provincial – Ontario

Citisource Green Energy from Toronto Hydro

Toronto Hydro Energy services offers an EcoLogo-certified green electricity product, sourced from wind, solar, biomass, biogas and run-of-the-river sources. Also visit its website for information on the Green$aver home energy audit program.
www.torontohydro.com/greenpower

Ontario Power Generation (OPG) Evergreen

OPG offers a range of green power products to business customers as well as to energy retailers, who resell it to residential customers.
www.opg.com

Green Tags from Grey-Bruce Renewable Energy Co-op

By buying Green Tags you pay the additional costs involved in developing and producing green energy.
Phone: 1-866-546-8414
www.greentagsontario.com

Windshare from Toronto Renewable Energy Co-op

In addition to paying directly for green power, you can invest in green electricity generation. You can become a member of the Windshare co-op by investing in it and so become a producer of green electricity.
www.windshare.ca

Provincial – Alberta

Greenmax from Enmax

Enmax is an energy retailer that sells power to both commercial and residential customers. The Greenmax program offers wind-generated green electricity to residents for a small additional premium on their monthly energy bill.
Phone: 310-2010 (toll-free in Alberta)
Fax: 1-866-993-6629
www.enmax.com/greenmax

Green Power ECO-PACK from EPCOR

EPCOR Utilities Inc. sells green power to home, farm and small business customers in the form of ECO-PACKs – blocks of green power generated from a range of sources, including small hydro, wind, biomass and solar.
E-mail: CustServ@epcor.ca
Phone:
Edmonton: 412-4000
Toll-free in Alberta: 310-4300
North America: 1-800-667-2345
Ontario (residential customers):
1-866-490-4111

Provincial – British Columbia

Green Rate option from West Kootenay Power

West Kootenay Power is a municipal utility offering a green energy option to its customers.
E-mail: powersense@utilicorp.com

Green Power Certificates from BC Hydro (business customers only)

BC Hydro is offering Green Power Certificates to its business customers as a Power Smart product.
www.bchydro.com/greenpower

Provincial – Prince Edward Island

Green Energy from Maritime Electric

Maritime Electric offers wind-generated Green Power purchased from the PEI Energy Corporation to its residential customers when they pay a small monthly premium.
Phone: 902-629-3799 or
1-800-670-1012

Water

Environment Canada's Green Lane – Freshwater website

The Freshwater website has information about water and its role in the environment, information about water management, pollution prevention and water conservation, and interesting facts and figures.
www.ec.gc.ca/water/e_main.html

Canadian Water and Wastewater Association

www.cwwa.ca

US Environmental Protection Agency (EPA)

Visit the EPA's water efficiency website for updates on the development of a rating system for products that help to conserve water.
www.epa.gov/water/water_efficiency.
html

The green kitchen

Food – organic

Canadian Organic Growers

Canadian Organic Growers Inc. is a national education and networking organization representing Canada's organic farmers, gardeners and consumers. Visit its website for information on organic products, its Directory of Organics in Canada, information on where to by organic products and the latest information on organic standards and regulation.
Canadian Organic Growers National Office
Phone: 506-375-7383, or toll-free at
1-888-375-7383
www.cog.ca

Common Organic Certification Labels found in Canada

Demeter
Farm Verified Organic (FVO)
Garanite Bio
Columbia certified Organic
OCIA Cartified Organic
Canadian Organic Certification Co-op
Organic Producers association of
   Manitoba
Quebec Vrai Certified Organic
SOCA certified Organic
Maritime Certified Organic
NSOGA Organically Grown Soil
   Association
USDA Organic
California Certified Organic Farmers

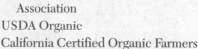

Food – genetic modification issues

Greenpeace "True Food" Campaign

Visit Greenpeace Canada's website for more information about its campaign against genetically modified food products. At this site you can use the online version of the guide booklet "How to Avoid Genetically Engineered Foods" or download a copy.
www.greenpeace.ca/shoppersguide

Planet Ark Environmental News Stories

The Planet Ark Reuters Daily World Environment News (WEN) Service has an archive of over 28 000 environmental news stories from around the world. This online archive is fully searchable. Enter "genetically modified food" or "GM food" (or a similar phrase) as a search query to see stories from the last few years on movements in this global debate.
www.planetark.org/news

Recycling

Waste Reduction Week

Waste Reduction Week in Canada is an environmental education program and awareness initiative. The initiative aims to encourage households, communities, schools and businesses to have better habits with waste and resource use. The program's website has activities, education resources, information about events and useful contacts to help you to reduce waste and recycle more.
www.wrwcanada.com

Provincial recycling contacts

Recycling Council of British Columbia (RCBC)

Phone the RCBC Recycling Hotline: 604-732-9253 in the Lower Mainland, or 1-800-667-4321 throughout BC.
www.rcbc.bc.ca

Recycling Council of Alberta

Phone: 403-843-6563
www.recycle.ab.ca

Resource Conservation Manitoba

Phone the Waste Reduction Week information line: 204-925-3777, or toll-free at 1-866-394-8880
www.resourceconservation.mb.ca

Saskatchewan Waste Reduction Council

Phone: 306-931-3242
www.saskwastereduction.ca

Recycling Council of Ontario

Phone: 416-657-2797
www.rco.on.ca

Réseau des ressourceries du Québec

Phone: 514-875-5869
www.reseauressourceries.org

More provincial contacts and links are listed on the home page of the Waste Reduction Week website at
www.wrwcanada.com/index.html

The green living room

Heating and cooling

General

"Keeping the Heat In"
A publication produced by Natural Resources Canada's Office of Energy Efficiency that is both available online or through Natural Resources Canada offices. The Office of Energy Efficiency has a range of energy conservation brochures and booklets. This publication can be viewed online at http://oee.nrcan.gc.ca/keep_heat_in or downloaded from the energy publications section at http://energy-publications.nrcan.gc.ca
Phone: 613-995-2943 or
1-800-387-2000
Fax: 819-779-2833

BC Hydro, "Guides to Energy Management"
BC Hydro has produced a series of information-packed factsheets called "Guides to Energy Management." This series covers a wide range of topics, including draftproofing, thermostats and the many different methods of heating and cooling.
www.bchydro.com

The Heating, Refrigeration and Air Conditioning Institute of Canada (HRAI)
HRAI is an industry group for heating, ventilation, air conditioning and refrigeration manufacturers, wholesalers, retailers and contractors. Contact HRAI to find a qualified specialist in your area should you need advice on your whole home systems.
Phone: 905-602-4700 or 1-800-267-2231
www.hrai.ca

Heating with wood

"Burn It Smart!"
This is the Government of Canada's wood-heating education program.
Phone: 1-866-838-5661 (toll-free)
www.burnitsmart.org

The green laundry room

Green cleaning

Nature Clean
Environmentally preferred cleaning and personal care products.
www.franktross.com/nature

Pest information

Health Canada – West Nile Virus information
Health Canada has a website with information about the West Nile virus, which is transmitted by mosquitoes. The West Nile Monitor part of the site has information on where outbreaks have occurred so that people can be aware of whether or not their local region is at risk. The site also contains more detailed information on how people can better protect themselves and their families.
www.hc-sc.gc.ca/english/westnile

Health Canada – spider information

Health Canada has a website with useful information about spiders commonly found in Canada.
www.house-spider.ca

The green bedroom

Bedding and towels

Willow Natural Home

Willow Natural Home is a natural and organic bedding company with an extensive product range, including mattresses, sheets, pillows, comforters, blankets, towels and infant bedding.
Phone: 1-877-4WILLOW (toll-free)
www.willownaturalhome.com

Nature's Bedding & Bath

Nature's Bedding and Bath manufactures a range of natural and organic bedding, including mattresses, sheets, pillows, comforters, futons, towels and infant bedding.
Phone: 905-773-9787, or toll-free at 1-866-266-2266
www.naturesbedding.com

Three Herons Organic Cotton

A range of organic cotton towels and washcloths. The cotton growing and manufacturing all happens in North America.
www.threeheronsorganiccotton.com

Alternative fibre clothing and textiles

Infiknit

A Toronto-based textile and yarn wholesaler that supplies retailers and manufacturers. Its range includes organically grown and vegetable-dyed textiles and yarns, including Ecoknit organic cotton knitting yarn and Foxfibre naturally coloured cotton. Its main focus is supplying business customers. However, its website has a list of retailers in each province that its sell its yarns to.
Phone: 1-800-408-1522
Fax: 416-487-3296
E-mail: info@infiknit.com
www.infiknit.com

Organic Trade Association

The Organic Trade Association (OTA) is the membership-based business association for the organic industry in North America.
www.ota.com

Saskatchewan Hemp Association (SHA)

The SHA is a membership driven, provincially registered non-profit association dedicated to the development of the industrial hemp sector in Saskatchewan and Western Canada.
www.saskhemp.com

EMF and allergy information

**World Health Organization –
EMF Information**
www.who.int/peh-emf/en

Calgary Allergy Network
The Calgary Allergy Network is a
community-based network of
concerned people who aim to share
information about and the experience
of living with allergies and asthma.
The Network's website offers practical
information and resources. It also has
a marketplace page that is a great
resource for allergy suffers who want
help finding low-allergy products.
www.calgaryallergy.ca

Allergy/Asthma Information Association
AAIA National Office:
Phone: 416-679-9521 or 1-800-611-
7011
Fax: 416-679-9524
E-mail: national@aaia.ca
www.aaia.ca

Regional Offices:

AAIA BC/Yukon
Phone: 250-764-7507, or toll-free at
1-877-500-2242
E-mail: bc@aaia.ca

AAIA Prairies/NWT/Nunavut
Phone/Fax: 780-456-6651
E-mail: prairies@aaia.ca

AAIA Ontario
Phone: 519-284-4222, or toll-free at
1-888-250-2298
E-mail: ontario@aaia.ca

AAIA Quebec
Phone: 514-694-0679
E-mail: quebec@aaia.ca

AAIA Atlantic
Phone/Fax: 506-459-4475

The green office

General

**Environment Canada – "What You Can Do
- At Work"**
Environment Canada's collection of
environmental tips and advice for the
workplace.
www.ec.gc.ca/eco/wycd/work_e.html

Natural Capitalism
The Rocky Mountains Institute has
developed a new business model
called "natural capitalism," in which
businesses are environmentally
sustainable and profitable. See Paul
Hawkins, Amory Lovins and L.
Hunter Lovins, Natural Capitalism
(Little, Brown and Company, 1999).
www.naturalcapitalism.org and
www.rmi.org

Green procurement

Buy Recycled Business Alliance (BRBA)

The BRBA is a national non-profit organization with a broad-based business membership. Corporate members aim to lead by example, by using their purchasing power to create a demand for products made from recycled materials.
www.nrc-recycle.org/brba

Buy Green

This Canadian NGO website provides information on "green" products and services, as well as tips on how you can set up a green procurement program.
www.buygreen.com

Computer recycling contacts

Computers for Schools

This is an Industry Canada program that takes donations of computer equipment and provides it to public libraries and schools "classroom ready." Computers for Schools welcomes donated equipment in good working order, including desktop computers and laptops, colour monitors, keyboards, mice, printers, modems, scanners, digital cameras, CD-ROM drives and servers.
http://cfs-ope.ic.gc.ca

HP Planet Partners recycling service

HP's Planet Partners program recycles HP-brand printing supplies (such as toner and inkjet cartridges) as well as any brand of computer equipment.
Phone: 1-800-387-3867
www.hp.ca/recycle

IBM Certified Used PCs

IBMs PC-buyback and recycling program pays money for some used computer items. IBM also sells certified refurbished secondhand PCs at a fraction of the cost of new models, including IBM Certified Used Equipment.
E-mail: dispose@ca.ibm.com
Phone:1-888-SHOPIBM (toll-free), select option 1 and then enter extension 27615
http://ibm.com/financing/ca/en/dispose
or www.ibm.ca

reBOOT Canada

ReBOOT Canada is a non-profit organization providing computer hardware, training and technical support to charities, non-profits and people with limited access to technology. Drop off your computer, or have it picked up for a fee.
www.rebootcanada.ca

reBOOT Canada Provincial office addresses:

British Columbia: 876 Cordova Diversion, Vancouver, BC
Ontario:
139 Duro St., Peterborough, ON
201 King St. E., Hamilton, ON
201, 145 Spruce St., Ottawa, ON
Quebec: 5060 Des Sources, Pierrefonds, QC

New Brunswick: 65 Brunswick St., Fredericton, NB
PEI: 41 Wood Islands Hill, Montague, PEI
Newfoundland and Labrador: Suite 201, Virginia Park Plaza, St. John's, NL

Electronic Product Stewardship Canada

A not-for-profit corporation formed to find a solution to Canada's growing e-waste problem. Its website has news, reports and information about computer and electronic waste.
www.epsc.ca/

The green garage

General

Environment Canada – "What You Can Do – On the Road"

Environment Canada's collection of environmental tips and advice for greener transportation.
www.ec.gc.ca/eco/wycd/road_e.html

NRCan Personal Vehicle Program

Visit the website of the NRCan Office of Energy Efficiency Personal Vehicle Program for detailed information on a range of transportation energy issues, including practical tips, advice and information on fuel efficiency.
http://oee.nrcan.gc.ca/vehicles

Vehicle comparisons

American Council for an Energy Efficient Economy (ACEEE)

Visit this site for the ACEEE's annual Green Book: The Environmental Guide to Cars & Trucks – a buyers' guide for new vehicles on the market in the US.
www.greenercars.com

Environmental Defence Green Cars campaign

Environmental Defence adapts ACEEE information for the Canadian market as part of its Green Cars campaign. Each year it releases its 10 greenest and 10 meanest vehicles lists for Canada as well as providing information on greener vehicle choices and the top-rated models within each class of vehicle.
www.environmentaldefence.ca

Oil Recycling

UsedOilRecycling.com

This website is a joint initiative between five provincial Used Oil Management Associations. At time of printing, there are 1000 EcoCentres or oil collection points across BC, Alberta, Manitoba and Saskatchewan. Visit the website to find a local oil-recycling drop-off point. Alternatively, contact your municipality for advice.
www.usedoilrecycling.com

Waste Diversion Ontario (WDO)
WDO is an NGO created under the
Waste Diversion Act. WDO was
established to develop, implement
and operate waste diversion programs
for a wide range of materials that
include blue-box waste, used tires,
used oil material, household special
waste, electronic waste, organic
materials, pharmaceuticals and
fluorescent tubes.
www.wdo.ca

The green garden

General gardening information

**Go For Green – The Active Living and
Environment Program**
Go For Green is a national non-profit,
charitable organization encouraging
Canadians to pursue healthy outdoor
physical activities while being good
environmental citizens. The
"Gardening for Life" program pages
on its website has great articles and
factsheets on greener and organic
gardening, native gardens,
alternatives to chemical pesticides
and water-efficient gardening.
Phone: 613-748-1800, or toll free at
1-888-822-2848
www.goforgreen.ca

Organic gardening info

World Wildlife Fund (WWF) Canada
WWF Canada's booklet "Your Guide
to Natural Pesticide-free Gardening"
is available for a $2.00 donation to
WWF Canada at Loblaw Companies
Ltd. Garden Centres in Ontario,
Quebec and the Atlantic provinces,
including, Loblaws, Zehrs, Fortinos,
Valumart and Atlantic Superstores.
WWF members living elsewhere in
Canada can request a copy from the
WWF.
www.wwf.ca

Habitat-friendly garden information

Canadian Wildlife Federation
Phone: 613-599-9594 or
1-800-563-WILD
E-mail: info@cwf-fcf.org
www.cwf-fcf.org,
www.wildeducation.org,
www.wildaboutgardening.org or
www.spaceforspecies.ca

Composting contacts
You local municipality is worth
contacting, as it may offer subsidized
compost bins or worm farms.

Clean Calgary Association
The Clean Calgary Association has a
fantastic composting website with
information on the principles of
composting, different methods of
composting, worm farming and
troubleshooting.
www.cleancalgary.com/info/composting

Recycling Council of Ontario

The Recycling Council of Ontario's website has a series of useful factsheets on composting and worm farming, as well as on household recycling.

www.rco.on.ca

Natural pet products

Natural Pet Market

This US-based mail-order and online shopping company offers all-natural and environmentally preferred pet products and delivers to Canada. Products available include dog and cat food, grooming products, toys, flea- and tick-control products, other pet health products and more.

Phone: 630-534-6682
Fax: 630-534-6683
www.naturalpetmarket.com

Green building and renovating

General

EnerGuide for Houses

For information about the EnerGuide for Houses program, home energy-efficiency evaluation services, details of certified organizations and EnerGuide advisers and information on retrofit grants.

http://oee.nrcan.gc.ca/energuide/houses

R-2000

R-2000 is a standard for home building. The program is a joint initiative between NRCan and Canada's home construction industry. Awarded homes meet or exceed certain requirements for energy efficiency, reduced environmental impact and the provision of a healthy indoor living environment.

http://oee.nrcan.gc.ca/r-2000

Home inspection and evaluation contacts

EnerGuide for Houses evaluation services

http://oee.nrcan.gc.ca/energuide/houses

Canadian Association of Home Inspectors

For information about home inspections and details of member inspectors. The website also has contacts for the various provincial association branches.

www.cahpi.ca

Building and interior materials

Environmental Choice (EcoLogo) program

There is a wide range of building and renovating materials and products certified under the EcoLogo program.

www.environmentalchoice.ca

The Eco-Lumber co-op
A Vancouver-based supplier of
certified timber and timber products
for building and furniture-making.
Warehouse/showroom: #150–14480
Knox Way, Richmond, BC V6V 2Z5
Phone: 604-278-4300, or toll-free at
866-827-4352
www.ecolumber.ca or
www.ecolumber.ca/furniture.htm

Flooring and floor coverings

Bamboo Direct Flooring Ltd.
Suppliers of bamboo flooring
products.
Phone: 604-926-4257
www.bamboodirect.ca

K&M Bamboo Products Inc.
Suppliers of bamboo and other flooring
products, including Silkroad bamboo
flooring, which is an EcoLogo-certified
hardwood floor covering. Its range
includes bamboo flooring, bamboo
plywood and veneer, cork flooring, and
FSC-certified maple flooring.
Phone: 905-947-1688
www.silkroadflooring.com

Floorworks
Supplier of flooring materials,
including EcoLogo-certified products.
Products include stained and unstained
northern hardwoods, sustainably
harvested and/or plantation-grown
tropical woods and bamboo.

Address: 365 Dupont St., Toronto,
Ontario M5R 1W2
Phone: 416-961-6891
www.floorworks.ca

Jelinek Cork Group
Suppliers of cork flooring and a host of
other cork products. Its showroom –
The Cork House – has a huge range of
cork products, including wall tiles,
wallpaper, cork furniture, custom-
printed coasters, gift items, cork shoes
and fabrics.
Phone: 905-827-4666 or 1-800-959-0995
www.corkstore.com

The Cork House (showroom)
Address: 2441 Neyagawa Blvd.,
Oakville, Ontario L6H 6Y3
Phone: 905-257-5588

NFP Imports Inc.
Suppliers of cork flooring products
Phone: 250-491-3991, or toll-free at
1-888-321-CORK (1-888-321-2675)
www.nfpimports.com

Plant-based paints, sealants and finishes

Livos Natural Paints
Natural pigments, stains and
varnishes from Germany.
Distributor: Sensitive Design
Phone: 604-925-4602

Green shopping

Information

The Environmental Choice (EcoLogo) Program

The Environmental Choice Program is Environment Canada's eco-labelling initiative, which helps consumers identify products and services that are less harmful to the environment. Visit the program's website for lists of EcoLogo-certified products and services across a broad range of catagories.
www.environmentalchoice.ca

Green outlets and online shopping

WWF Canada Panda Store

Shop online for eco-themed gifts and other items, with profits supporting WWF's conservation programs.
www.wwf.ca/pandastore

P'lovers – The Environmental Store

The founders of P'lovers describe it as "an environmental department store," with five retail store locations, an online catalogue and a mail-order facility. P'lovers has a huge range that includes recycled paper and stationery, homewares, personal care products, organic cotton towels, hemp products, baby clothes, gardening and outdoors products, books and green-cleaning aids.

Head office and main store:
5657 Spring Garden Rd., Box 224, Halifax, NS B3J 3R4
Phone: 902-422-6060 or 1-800-565-2998

Other locations:
229 Queen St., Port Perry, Ontario L9L 1B9 (Phone: 905-982-0660)
3 Edgewater St., Mahone Bay, NS (Phone: 902-624-1421)
13 York St., Stratford, Ontario (Phone: 519-271-3883)
11 Main St., Bayfield, Ontario (Phone: 519-565-5161)

FOUR the Love of Dirt

FOUR the Love of Dirt offers a range of natural garden supplies, including organic fertilizers, natural soil amendments and chemical-free pest control. It also has a range of natural home products, including alternative-fibre (organic cotton, hemp, hemp/cotton and linen) bedding, towels and clothing, candles, toiletries and baby products. Its resources section includes books, magazines, government information and material from related gardening, organic, biodynamic and environmental organizations.
Address: 504 Dominion Ave., Midland, Ontario L4R 1P8
Phone: 705-528-0550
Fax: 705-528-7447
E-mail: gooddirt@csolve.net
www.fourtheloveofdirt.ca

Granola Groovy

A natural-lifestyle store offering natural products and gifts, including organic cotton towels, hemp accessories and natural soaps.
Address: 1005 Broad St., Victoria BC V8W 2A1
Phone: 250-477-0146
E-mail: info@granolagroovy.com

Grassroots Store

A community-based retailer of environmentally preferred products. Products are available through its website or at two retail stores. Phone orders can be made through either of the stores.
Phone: 1-888-633-5833 (toll-free)
www.grassrootsstore.com

Grassroots Riverdale

Address: 372 Danforth Ave., Toronto, Ontario M4K 1N8
Phone: 416-466-2841
Fax: 416-466-2798

Grassroots Annex

Address: 408 Bloor St. W., Toronto, Ontario M5S 1X5
Phone: 416-944-1993
Fax: 416-944-9180

Green grooming

Cosmetics industry regulation and information

Health Canada Cosmetics Programme

www.hc-sc.gc.ca/hecs-sesc/cosmetics/index.htm

Canadian Cosmetic, Toiletry and Fragrance Association (CCTFA)

The Canadian Cosmetic, Toiletry and Fragrance Association is a trade association for the personal care products industry.
Phone: 905-890-5161
Fax: 905-890-2607
www.cctfa.ca

Animal testing and issues

Coalition for Consumer Information on Cosmetics (CCIC) – Leaping Bunny logo

The CCIC promotes a single comprehensive standard and an internationally recognized "leaping bunny" logo to help make shopping for animal-friendly products easier and more trustworthy.
Phone: 1-888-546-CCIC (toll-free)
www.leapingbunny.org

Animal Alliance of Canada

Phone: 416-462-9541
www.AnimalAlliance.ca

Group for the Education of Animal-Related Issues (GEARI)
The GEARI website has a list of animal ingredients and the alternatives.
www.geari.org/ingredients.html

Shopping for organic beauty products online

Saffron Rouge
Saffron Rouge is a Canadian-based online retailer for organic skin care, cosmetics and body care.
www.saffronrouge.ca

Beauty brands with an environmental slant

Aesop
www.aesop.net.au

Avalon Organic Botanicals
www.avalonnaturalproducts.com

Aveda
www.aveda.com

Caqti
www.caqti.com

Deserving Thyme
www.deservingthyme.com

Lush
www.lushcanada.com

Mountain Sky
www.mountainskysoap.com

The Body Shop
www.thebodyshop.com

How to have a green baby

Go Smokefree
Health Canada's program to help people quit cigarette smoking. The "Go Smokefree" website is a fantastic resource for people wanting to quit smoking.
Phone: 1-866-318-1116 (toll-free)
www.gosmokefree.ca

BabyOrganic.com
A home delivery service for Baby's Only Organic products
Phone (Canadian orders): 740-927-2207
www.babyorganic.com

Greenpeace – "Toxic Toys" Campaign
The Greenpeace campaign to reduce toxic materials, including PVC, is currently on hold, but you can visit the Greenpeace International website and search its archives using the search term "toys."
www.greenpeace.org

Hot Topics and Conservation Action

David Suzuki Foundation's "Sustainability Within a Generation"

Greeniology focuses on how individuals can lessen their impact on the environment, aiming for sustainability at home. However, it's important to remember the bigger picture of sustainability at a national and global level. The David Suzuki Foundation has come up with a green blueprint for our country. You can read about the David Suzuki Foundation's new vision for Canada – "Sustainability Within a Generation" – online at the foundation's website.
www.davidsuzuki.org/WOL/Sustainability

Nature Conservancy Canada (NCC)

NCC is Canada's only national charity dedicated to preserving ecologically significant areas through outright purchase, donations and conservation easements.
www.natureconservancy.ca

Evergreen

Evergreen is a registered national charity with a mandate to bring nature to cities through naturalization projects. Visit its website to see details of conservation events and volunteering opportunities around Canada.
Phone: 416-596-1495, or toll-free at 1-888-426-3138
Fax: 416-596-1443
www.evergreen.ca

Skyfish Project

The Skyfish Project is an online forum for sharing thoughts, ideas, information and inspiration about the world we live in and the influence we have on it. This Internet-based think-tank was started by environmentalist Severn Cullis-Suzuki and a group of her friends. Visit the site to state your sustainable intentions through the Recognition of Responsibility, or to read *Soup* magazine.
www.skyfishproject.org

>> Acknowledgements

Thank you to my husband, Andrew, daughter Jasmin and son Archer for their love, support and patience (in other words, for putting up with me while I was writing this book) and to my family and friends for similar reasons – Mum, Daryl, Jill, Graham, Tanya, Marina, David, Dad, Auntie Grace, Nick, Sandra, Brian, Nicole, Chris and Vanessa. I'd especially like to thank my brother-in-law, Dr. Graham Treloar, who has shared with me his expertise as an architect and research scientist and who has spent many hours letting me bounce ideas off him and has given me his valued thoughts and feedback.

Thanks to the team at Planet Ark for their support and ongoing work – Anne-Marie, Daniela, Lucy, Wayne, Annie, Dominique, Stephen, Vanessa, Rebecca and Pat Cash – and to my boss, Jon Dee (Planet Ark's founder and managing director), for his support and for giving me an opportunity to work in the environmental movement. A special thank you to Planet Ark's other two directors, Paul Klymenko and Peter Shenstone, the quiet achievers behind Planet Ark's work. Thanks also to the many sponsors, supporters, media organizations and individuals who have supported Planet Ark, our campaigns and our efforts to involve ordinary people in helping the environment.

Thanks to Kylie Minogue, Olivia Newton-John, and Severn Cullis-Suzuki for their support of this book and for their ongoing work for the environment.

A huge thank you to my precious piece of Canada Down Under, Nina Tuason – your help and encouragement has been invaluable.

It takes a huge amount of work to turn a manuscript into a book – a lot of which I didn't have to do! Thank you to the Australian team at Allen & Unwin – Sue Hines, Marie Baird, Andrea McNamara and Briony Cameron; the Australian design team – Andrew Treloar and Nick Mau for their illustrations and everyone at MAU Design; and finally the Canadian team at Penguin Canada – in particular Helen Reeves, Tracy Bordian, Catherine Dorton and Stephanie Fysh.

A very special extra thank you to *Greeniology*'s two guardian angels (one for each edition): the in-house editors Andrea McNamara (at Allen & Unwin) and Helen Reeves (at Penguin Canada). Such people are the unsung heroes of book publishing. They keep us difficult authors on track with their day-to-day gentle guidance and encouragement.

Finally, a heart-felt thank you to the past, present and future readers of *Greeniology* – in particular those who heed the advice and put these words into action. You are our hope for the future.

>> Index

>> About Planet Ark

Tanya Ha, the author of *Greeniology*, is campaign development manager for the environmental group Planet Ark. Planet Ark shows people and business the many ways that they can reduce their day-to-day impact on the environment.

Heavily supported by the media, Planet Ark is an Australian organization that was set up by tennis player Pat Cash and international charity campaigner Jon Dee in June 1991.

Planet Ark is an unashamedly populist organization. We try to keep our environmental campaigns as positive as possible. This approach has struck a strong chord with the Australian public, millions of whom have joined in our environmental campaigns. We're now taking this approach to North America and the United Kingdom.

Planet Ark initiatives include the following:

• In July 2004, over 225 000 volunteers on 3000 sites across Australia planted over a million trees in two days as part of Planet Ark's National Tree Day. The event was fronted by Planet Ark supporter Olivia Newton-John and many other well-known celebrities, all of whom donated their time to the event.

• Over half a billion greeting cards have been recycled for our "Cards 4 Planet Ark" greeting card recycling campaign.

• Over 10 million individuals visit the Planet Ark website every year. Our website is sponsored by Reuters and hosts hundreds of pages of environmental news and information. It is the world's biggest online environmental news service.

• In partnership with resource recovery specialists and major product brands, Planet Ark has pioneered extensive public recycling programs for mobile phones, printer cartridges and other forms of "ewaste." These programs, such as "Cartridges 4 Planet Ark" ensure that valuable materials are recovered and pollution prevented, with virtually nothing going to landfill.

• Our "Do Something!" environmental education kit is currently being used in thousands of primary schools Australia-wide.

• Planet Ark runs a wide range of other campaign and initiatives including National Recycling Week and the Plastic Bag-Free Towns program.

Planet Ark is bringing about real and measurable environmental change. For further information, check out www.planetark.org.